WALT DISNEY WORLD®
with Kids
2013

D0752586

**KIM WRIGHT WILEY and
LEIGH WILEY JENKINS**

Twenty-Third Edition

Fodor's

Authors: Kim Wright Wiley and Leigh Wiley Jenkins
Editor: Douglas Stallings
Editorial Production: Carrie Parker
Production/Manufacturing: Angela L. McLean
Cover Photo: © Disney

To all the families who have shared
their Disney stories
with me throughout the years.

Published by Fodor's Travel, a division of Random House, Inc.

Fodor's is a registered trademark of Random House, Inc.

www.fodors.com

Every effort has been made to make this book complete and accurate as of the date of publication. In a time of rapid change, however, it is difficult to ensure that all information is entirely up to date. Although the publisher and authors cannot be liable for any inaccuracies or omissions in this book, they are always grateful for corrections and suggestions for improvement.

All products mentioned in this book are trademarks of their respective companies.

This book is available for special discounts for bulk purchases for sales promotions or premiums. Special editions, including personalized covers, excerpts of existing books, and corporate imprints, can be created in large quantities for special needs. For more information, write to Special Markets/Premium Sales, 1745 Broadway, MD 3-1, New York, NY 10019, or email specialmarkets@randomhouse.com.

Twenty-Third Edition

ISBN: 978-0-307-92922-8

ISSN: 1945-9238

PRINTED IN THE UNITED STATES OF AMERICA

10 9 8 7 6 5 4 3 2 1

Contents

Chapter 3   Once You Get There   99

Chapter 4   Touring Tips and Plans   117

Chapter 5   The Magic Kingdom   147

Chapter 6 Epcot   189

Chapter 7 Disney's Hollywood Studios   219

Chapter 12 Disney After Dark 351

Chapter 13 The Disney Cruise Line 361

HELPFUL PHONE NUMBERS

All Orlando numbers have a 407 area code. Be sure to make all Disney hotel reservations by calling 934–7639 (W–DISNEY), and use the resorts' direct lines only to report a delayed check-in, to call Guest Services (aka Guest Relations), or to reach a registered guest.

General Walt Disney World Information Phone Numbers

General Information	824–4321
WDW Resort Information	934–7639 (W–DISNEY)
WDW Dining Information and Advance Reservations	939–3463 (WDW–DINE)
WDW Recreational Information	939–7529 (WDW–PLAY)
WDW Golf Information	939–4653 (WDW–GOLF)
WDW Tour Information	939–8687 (WDW–TOUR)
Disney Cruise Line	800/951–3532
Disney Travel Company	828–8101

Walt Disney World Resort Phone Numbers

All-Star Movies	939–7000
All-Star Music	939–6000
All-Star Sports	939–5000
Animal Kingdom Lodge	938–3000
Art of Animation Resort	934–7639 (W–DISNEY)
Beach Club Resort	934–8000
Best Friends Pet Care	877/493–9738 (877/4–WDW–PETS)
BoardWalk Inn and Villas	939–5100
Caribbean Beach Resort	934–3400
Contemporary Resort	824–1000
Coronado Springs Resort	939–1000
Dolphin Resort	934–4000
Fort Wilderness Campground	824–2900
Grand Floridian Resort	824–3000
Old Key West Resort	827–7700

Polynesian Resort	824–2000
Pop Century Resort	938–4000
Port Orleans Resort	934–5000
Saratoga Springs Resort and Spa	827–1100
Swan Resort	934–3000
Wilderness Lodge and Villas	824–3200
Yacht Club Resort	934–7000

Universal Orlando Phone Numbers

| General Information | 363–8000 |
| Universal Orlando Resort Information | 888/273–1311 |

SeaWorld, Discovery Cove, and Aquatica Phone Numbers

SeaWorld	351–3600
Discovery Cove	877/434–7268
Aquatica	800/327–2420

Other Helpful Phone Numbers

Alamo Car Rental	800/462–5266
American Airlines	800/433–7300
Avis Car Rental	800/331–1212
Budget Car Rental	800/527–0700
Delta Airlines	800/221–1212
Dollar Car Rental	800/800–4000
Hertz Car Rental	800/654–3131
Mears Shuttle Service	423–5566
National Car Rental	800/227–7368
Orlando Visitors Bureau	800/255–5786
US Airways	800/428–4322

HELPFUL WEBSITES

LIST OF MAPS

LIST OF QUICK-GUIDE REFERENCE TABLES

ABBREVIATIONS, TERMS, AND ICONS

Abbreviations and Terms

Downtown Disney	A shopping, dining, and entertainment complex
Hollywood	The Disney's Hollywood Studios Theme Park
Water parks	Typhoon Lagoon and Blizzard Beach
Major parks	The Magic Kingdom, Epcot, Disney's Hollywood Studios, and Disney's Animal Kingdom
Off-season	The less crowded times of the year—specifically those weeks between September and May that do not flank major holidays
On-season	The most crowded times of the year—specifically summers, holidays, and spring break
Off-site	Any resort or hotel not owned by Disney
On-site	A Disney-owned resort
TTC	Ticket and Transportation Center: The monorail version of a train station, where you can transfer to monorails bound for Epcot, the Magic Kingdom, or monorail-line hotels. You can also catch buses at the TTC bound for the parks and Downtown Disney.

Icons

 Helpful Hint

 Hidden Mickey

 Insider's Secret

 Money-Saving Tip

 The Scare Factor

 Time Saving Tip

PREFACE

How Has Walt Disney World Changed?

The simple answer is, it's gotten bigger. And they're still building.

In the 24 years since I first began researching this guide, Disney has added one major park, three minor ones, eight hotels, a cruise line, and more attractions and restaurants than I can count. It was once possible for a fleet-footed and well-prepared family to see most of Walt Disney World during a four-day stay. But that's no longer true. As the Disney complex expands, it's more vital than ever that you target what you want to see, work these priorities into your schedule, and then relax. Anything beyond that is pure gravy.

Sometimes I'm asked whether the prevalence of travel guides makes them less useful to their readers. After all, if everyone knows about a "secret tip," is it still a secret?

Good question, but even with all those books on the market, a relatively small number of WDW visitors actually make advance preparations. Most people still show up late and wander around aimlessly, so anyone with any sort of touring plan at all is automatically a step ahead of the crowd.

It's tempting to treat Orlando as if it were a kiddie version of Las Vegas—you go there to play the numbers, and a family that hits 24 attractions in a day must, by definition, be having twice as much fun as a family that sees 12. Not so.

You'll find a lot of crying kids and exasperated parents by mid-afternoon, largely because everyone is frantic with the idea that this trip is so expensive they darn well better squeeze the most out of every minute. Actually, the most successful touring plans boil down to a few simple guidelines:

1. Plan your trip for those times of year when the parks are less crowded. When people write to me about having had bad experiences at Disney World, it seems that about 90% of the disasters happen either over spring break or in July.

2. Buy tickets and arrange all hotel and dining reservations well in advance. Every phone call you make from home is a line you won't have to stand in later.

3. Read up on attractions and let each family member choose three or four must-see attractions per park. An amazing number of parents plan this trip for their kids without really consulting them about what they'd most like to do.

4. Accept your differences and be willing to split up occasionally. Forcing a sullen 13-year-old onto it's a small world or strapping a terrified 5-year-old into Rock 'n' Roller Coaster in the interest of family togetherness will guarantee at least one tantrum per hour.

5. Arrive at the parks early, rest in the afternoon, and return to the parks at night. Walt Disney World can be very tiring, and regular rest stops are key.

Those fiv1e tips are always in fashion, but in the past three years there have been a few other changes worth noting:

1. The popularity of the Disney Dining Plan has changed the face of Disney restaurants—even for families who don't opt to purchase the plan. The reason? Families who once would never have considered herding the kids into top on-site

restaurants are now deciding it's cost-effective to give fine dining a try. So suddenly you're seeing even toddlers in restaurants like the Brown Derby, Citricos, Flying Fish, or California Grill. Although they're still great places to eat, the Dining Plan is indirectly taking a little of the adult feel and glamour out of these top restaurants. And the fact that so many more visitors are vying for seats inside the restaurants means that making reservations before you leave home is more important than ever. I've gotten tons of mail from families who waited until they got to Orlando to make dining reservations and found themselves closed out of the restaurants they most wanted to visit.

2. Spring and fall are becoming slightly more crowded, especially during the two weeks flanking Easter and the fall weekends in which the Mickey's Not-So-Scary Halloween parties are offered. The off-season is still a better choice than visiting in summer or at Christmas, but be aware that it's not quite as "off" as it used to be.

3. Princess power reigns supreme. The character breakfasts have always been popular, but those featuring the princess characters are so hot that they require more planning than a NASA launch. Little girls can also get styled like their favorite princess at the Bibbidi Bobbidi Boutiques, and you see more little girls than ever walking around the parks in full princess regalia. There's some effort to counterbalance this girl-power invasion with activities that boys will enjoy, such as the Jedi Training Academy at Hollywood, the Pirates and Pals Fireworks Cruise that leaves from the Contemporary Resort, the Pirates League, and Captain Jack's Pirate Tutorial at Adventureland in the Magic Kingdom. But for now, at least, the prevalence of the princesses is undeniable, and most little girls come under its spell. Bring

costumes from home if you have them. If not, prepare to purchase.

What hasn't changed in 24 years is my belief that Walt Disney World is the best family travel destination on the planet. There's truly something for everyone within these gates, and the spectacular, awe-inspiring rides are juxtaposed with sweet, small moments of joy. As one father shared: "My best-of-all moment was my 23-month-old daughter standing on the seat of Disney's Magical Express as we entered the gates of Walt Disney World yelling 'Mickey . . . don't worry . . . I coming!' That made it worth all the trouble and expense before we'd even arrived."

Throughout this book I've included such comments as the one above from Disney visitors who've written to me to share their best tales, tips, and "never again" stories. I'd love to hear how your trip went and any feedback you have about this book. If you'd like to share your travel experiences with me, please take a few minutes to respond to my survey online at www.fodors.com/disneysurvey, email me at kwwiley@fodors.com, or write to me at Fodor's, 1745 Broadway, New York, NY 10019. Thanks for your time, and have a great trip!

—Kim

1

Before You Leave Home

What Time of Year Should We Visit?

Crowd levels at Walt Disney World vary seasonally, so one of the most important decisions you'll make is deciding when to go.

Spring

Spring is a great time to visit. Except around spring break and Easter, crowds are manageable—not as sparse as in fall, but smaller than in summer. While park hours don't run as late as they do in summer, they're generally longer than in either fall or winter. And the weather is sublime, with highs in the 70s, lows in the 60s, and less rainfall than in any other season.

Summer

The good news about summer is that everything is open and operational and the parks run very long hours. The bad news is that it's hot and crowded—so crowded that the wait for many rides can be as long as 90 minutes.

If you have preschoolers, babies, or seniors in the party, avoid summers like the plague. But if the schedules of school-aged kids dictate that you must visit in the summer, the first

Insider's Secret
To check projected hours of operation during the weeks you're considering, visit www.disneyworld. com. Park hours generally remain as projected but can change; to be safe, revisit the site a couple of weeks before you leave home to reconfirm theme-park hours.

two weeks of June and the last two weeks of August are your best bets.

Fall

Fall has lighter crowds than summer and the weather is often great. There are, however, disadvantages to a fall visit. You have to work around the fact that older children are in school. The parks run shorter hours in fall; the Magic Kingdom, Animal Kingdom, and Hollywood may close as early as 5 pm, although Epcot always remains open later. Earlier closings mean that some of the special evening presentations, such as the evening parade in the Magic Kingdom, are scheduled only on the weekends.

Fall is the season for two of Walt Disney World's most popular events: Mickey's Not-So-Scary Halloween Party at the Magic Kingdom (with selected dates beginning just after Labor Day) and the Epcot International Food & Wine Festival. These

Helpful Hint
The size of the crowds corresponds with the school schedule. Any time the kids are out of school (i.e., summers, spring break, and major holidays) is the "on-season." Any time children are traditionally in school is the "off-season."

events are doing exactly what Disney designed them to do—drawing people in during slower times. Consult www.disneyworld.com to buy tickets early, or to note the party dates if you want to avoid them.

Late summer and early fall make up hurricane season in Florida, so there is some risk that you'll schedule your trip for

Insider's Secret

One of the major changes since we began doing this book 24 years ago is that the number of fall visitors has steadily grown. It's still less crowded than summers and holidays, but the special events (especially the über-popular Halloween parties) have influenced crowd flow. If you want to go to the Halloween parties, great. The fun is worth the extra effort. But even if you don't, be aware of the dates. The Magic Kingdom closes early on evenings the parties are scheduled to run, so you can't go there, but with so much of the crowd clustered at the Magic Kingdom, it's the perfect time to visit the other parks.

the exact week that Hurricane Laluna pounds the coast. Fortunately, Orlando is an hour inland, meaning that coastal storms usually yield only rain and, should worse come to worst, Disney has "ride out" plans (i.e., a hurricane policy) to ensure your safety. Furthermore, there are more rainy days in summer than there are in the fall, so, in general, the advantages of autumn touring far outweigh the disadvantages.

Winter

Winter is a mixed bag. The absolute worst times are holidays. Christmas and New Year's can pull in as many as 90,000 visitors per day and even extended hours can't compensate for crowds of this size. But if you avoid the holiday weeks, winter can be an ideal time to visit. With the exception of the week-ends around Martin Luther King Jr. Day and Presidents' Day, January and February aren't crowded—and they're pleasantly cool. The first two weeks of December, when the Christmas decorations are already up but the crowds have not yet arrived, are wonderful options. The parks run the same shortened hours in winter that they run in fall, but since the crowds are so much lighter, you'll still have time to see everything you want.

Insider's Secret

Mickey's Very Merry Christmas Party, held each year on several evenings throughout December, is madly popular. If you want to attend the party, get tickets early—they sell out months in advance. Dates for each year's parties are listed on www.disneyworld.com.

Off-Season Touring Caveat

Some parents have written in to say that they like taking the kids to Orlando during the off-season, but that they've heard this is when Disney is most apt to close attractions for refur-bishing. It's a valid point. On a recent trip in January, I found five attractions closed for refurbishing, including Space Moun-tain in the Magic Kingdom and Star Tours at Hollywood. But I still believe it's better to tour during the off-season. Here's why: during that same January week, the most popular Magic Kingdom attractions, such as the Many Adventures of Winnie the Pooh and Splash Mountain, were posting wait times as short as 20 minutes, about a third of what they normally are, so even taking closings into account, you'll still ride more and wait less during the off-season. If your kids have their hearts set on a certain attraction, you can avoid last-minute disappointments

Insider's Secret
Water babies take note: pools may be closed for re-furbishing in January and February. Generally, only one water park is open at a time in winter and both may shut down if the temperature dips below 55 degrees.

by checking www.disneyworld.com to see what's scheduled to be closed during your trip.

How Long Should We Stay?

It will take at least four days for a family to tour the major parks. If you also want to visit the water parks and Downtown Disney, make that five days. Six days are best for families who'd like to work in sporting options like boating or golf, or those who would like to tour at a more leisurely pace.

If you plan on visiting other area attractions, such as Sea-World or Universal Orlando, allow a week.

Insider's Secret
Certain annual events—most notably the marathon in January, College Week in April, Gay Day in June, and various press events throughout the year—bring large groups into the parks. Ask about events or groups before you book so you'll know what to expect.

Should We Take the Kids out of School?

Even if you're sold on the advantages of off-season touring, you may be reluctant to take your children out of school. However, there are ways to highlight the educational aspects of a trip to Disney World. Work together with your child's teacher to cre-

Epcot Projects

- The Behind the Seeds greenhouse tour in the Land is full of information on space-age farming.
- Marine biology is the theme of the Living Seas pavilion.
- The World Showcase demonstrates the culture—including music, architecture, food, and history—of several foreign countries.
- Innoventions offers a hands-on preview of technological advances.

ate a plan that keeps him from falling behind. Ideally, half of the makeup work should be done before you leave: the post-trip blues are bad enough without facing three hours of homework each night. Also, timing is everything. Don't plan your trip for the week the school is administering exams or standardized testing.

In addition, help your child create a project that's related to the trip—perhaps something like a scrapbook. The mother of one first-grader helped him design an "ABC" book before he left home, and he spent his week at Disney World collecting souvenirs for each page—Goofy's autograph on the "G" page, a postcard of a Japanese pagoda on the "P" page, and so on. An older child might gather leaves from the various trees and shrubs that were imported to landscape the countries in the World Showcase. Or a young photographer could demonstrate her proficiency with various lighting techniques by photographing Cinderella Castle in early morning, high noon, sunset, and after dark.

You can even work on math. If a car containing six people departs from the Test Track loading area every 20 seconds, how many riders go through in an hour? A day? If the monorail av-

Animal Kingdom Projects

- The Cretaceous Trail—a path filled with plants that have survived from the Cretaceous period—is an excellent introduction to botanical evolution.

- Rafiki's Planet Watch is the park's research-and-education hub, where kids can observe veterinary labs and watch interactive videos about endangered animals.

- It's always fun to do a report on one of the animals you see on Kilimanjaro Safaris or along one of the exploration trails. Animal-crazy kids who are 8 or older will get a lot out of the Wild Animal Trek, a three-hour tour that takes you behind the scenes of the Animal Kingdom.

erages 32 mph, how long does it take it to travel the 7 miles from the Magic Kingdom to Epcot? Once you get going on these sorts of questions, they're addictive. Or give your kids a set amount of mythical money to spend, such as $1,000. Then let them keep track of expenses, deducting purchases from their starting total and making decisions about what they can and cannot afford on their budget.

Other Orlando Educational Programs

Disney World isn't the only place in Orlando that can be educational. Consider the following:

SeaWorld

SeaWorld offers daily tours as well as weeklong classes and overnight programs in summer and during holidays. Visit www.seaworld.org for information on the extended Adventure Camps. If your kids aren't up for a full program or you're visiting at a time when they're not offered, it's easy to work in one of SeaWorld's behind-the-scenes tours, which run throughout the year.

Orlando Science Center

This impressive facility has oodles of hands-on exhibits and programs for kids of all ages. Something is happening all the time—especially in spring and summer when most of the camps are held—and the prices are reasonable.

Admission to the center is $17 for adults, $16 for students and seniors, and $12 for kids ages 3 to 11. Classes are individually priced. To see what's happening during your visit, call 888/OSC-4FUN (4386) or 407/514–2000 or visit www.osc.org.

Kennedy Space Center

Orlando is only about an hour's drive from the Kennedy Space Center, so it's an easy day trip. Kids will enjoy seeing the rockets and the IMAX films about space exploration. The Shuttle Launch Experience takes place in a looming, six-story structure that looks like "the real thing." It requires riders be 44" tall and is included in your general admission ticket.

Insider's Secret

The Kennedy Space Center's Astronaut Training Experience (ATX) is ideal for kids 7 and up. This is a full-immersion experience—you ride in flight simulators, build and launch rockets, and play crew in a mock-up of a shuttle mission. The half-day experience is $145 per person. Make reservations in advance at www.kennedyspacecenter.com.

Crew passes, which include a bus tour of the space center as well as the IMAX film, are $45 for adults and $35 for kids ages 3 to 11. Visit www.kennedyspacecenter.com for details on launch dates and tours.

Should We Buy a Package?

This is a toughie. There are advantages to package trips, most notably that if you play your cards right, you can, indeed, save money. It's also helpful to know up front exactly what your vacation will cost. However, packages often require hefty prepayments, which are painful at the time, but at least you don't return home with your credit card utterly maxed out. And with the mega-popular Disney Dining Plan package, there's the convenience of having one card serve as your room key, theme-park ticket, and dining ticket. It eliminates the hassles of carrying cash and tracking how much you're spending.

Package trips can have drawbacks. Like buying a fully loaded car off a dealer's lot, you may find yourself paying for options you don't want and don't need. Unless you're certain you'll use most of the features contained in the package, you'll probably end up losing money on the deal. At the other end of the spectrum are deeply discounted packages that place you in run-down or out-of-the-way hotels.

Money-Saving Tips

- AAA and travel agents can provide genuine bargains, especially if you don't need to stay on Disney property.
- For deals online, check out www.expedia.com, www.hotels.com, www.smallworldvacations.com, or www.vacationoutlet.com.
- If you're calling to book your room, whether onsite or off-site, always ask, "Are there any discounts or special offers available?" Sometimes you'll learn about deals over the phone that aren't listed on the resort website.

Airline Packages

If you're flying, check out the airline's own packages, which include airfare, theme-park tickets for Disney and other Orlando attractions, and lodging at either on-site or off-site hotels. Again there's a huge range of amenities—you can have valet parking and bottles of champagne if you're willing to pay for them. And again the packages can be fine-tuned to meet your needs.

Cruise Packages

Some of the most popular Disney packages are those that combine a cruise with a vacation in the parks. Check out www. disneycruise.com, call 800/951–3532, or contact your travel agent. See Chapter 13 for more information.

Money-Saving Tip

Don't automatically assume that a package will save you big bucks. Unless you're sure you'll use every feature—or almost every feature—that the package includes, you may end up losing money on the deal. Run the numbers.

Disney Package Vacations

By far the most popular packages are those offered by Disney itself. The basic Magic Your Way package includes a hotel room on Disney property and theme-park tickets. You can choose any resort in any price range as well as the ticket options that suit your family's needs. Magic Your Way allows you to customize your package to the nth degree, fine-tuning the time of year, length of stay, resort, type of ticket, and type of dining. The good news is, it gives you lots of options. The bad news is . . . it gives you lots of options.

So how do you know what to choose? Let's start with tickets. The rule of thumb is, if your kids are young or this is your first trip to Disney World, you'll probably be spending most of your time in the four major theme parks, so choose a package with base tickets. If your kids are 8 and up, consider upgrading to the Park Hopper Pass, since it gives you the flexibility to move from one park to another in the course of the day. The more expensive premium and platinum options are really only helpful for families who've been to Disney World before and want to explore beyond the basic parks and those whose kids are old enough to enjoy the water parks, sporting options, tours, and Cirque du Soleil. For most families, either the base ticket or the base ticket with the Park Hopper Pass works fine.

How does the ticket type affect the cost of the trip? Let's take a mythical family of four and walk them through the process. If they're traveling during the off-season, let's say in October, a five-night package at a value resort with base tickets will cost them approximately $1,600. Pretty reasonable, huh? If they add the Park Hopper option to their tickets, the price will rise to $1,800.

The resort category—from value to moderate to deluxe to deluxe villa—and the season also affect the price of a package. (Chapter 2 outlines the pluses and minuses of each on-site resort; for now, you just need to consider how much this choice affects costs.) So, let's go back to our mythical family of four who can get five nights at a value resort for $1,600. In peak season that same package will cost them approximately $1,900. Still pretty reasonable. But what if they upgrade their hotel? A stay at a deluxe hotel for five days during the off-season will cost them approximately $3,300. The same five-night package in the same deluxe hotel during peak season is closer to $4,200. So by making two changes—the type of resort and the time of year—our family has literally tripled its vacation price.

Going through the exercise above has probably done two things: given you sticker shock and overwhelmed you. Still, it's a good introduction to the Disney vacation experience, which involves an almost staggering number of choices. Your best bet is to go to www.disneyworld.com, click on the pricing bar, then start tweaking, eliminating, or downgrading options, changing the dates of your visit, etc., until you arrive at a price you can live with.

Before you go to the site, however, you also need to decide whether or not to add a dining plan, which ups the package price by about $130 a day for a family of four.

Should You Add a Dining Plan?

The standard dining plan includes, for each day of your trip, one full-service meal, one counter-service meal, and a snack from a list of the 100-plus participating Disney restaurants that are scattered throughout the four theme parks and on-site hotels. Note: You need to decide yes or no on the dining plan before you leave home—unlike ticket upgrades, you can't add it once you get to Orlando.

Is it worth it? If you have big eaters in the party, since the standard plan can save you about 30% over the individual cost of meals. But, if 6-year-old Katie eats nothing but cereal and 3-year-old Danny grows so restless that sit-down dinners are a nightmare, it's unlikely they'll eat enough food to justify the cost of the standard dining plan.

Certain experiences, like dinner shows, some character meals, and the "signature" (i.e., most upscale) restaurants, are worth more than your daily full-service meal allowance. For one of these exceptional dining experiences, you must swap out two of your regular full-service meals. But the swap can still save you a bundle on what would otherwise be a very expensive dinner. One mother wrote, "By eating at counter-service places for a couple of days beforehand we saved enough credits for dinner at California Grill and it was superb."

Another mom wrote that "the Disney Dining Plan makes a lot of sense if you want to take in multiple character meals. We were able to attend three: at Crystal Palace, Chef Mickey's, and 1900 Park Fare, and we could not have afforded all this without the plan."

A father from Texas added, "I'm a little compulsive, at least according to my wife, and I ran a tally of what we would have paid if we'd ordered menu items on our own versus going with the dining plan. Trust me, the dining plan is a great value."

One family of foodies from New York opted to upgrade to the Deluxe Dining Plan, which allows sit-down dining at every meal and further added the "Wine and Dine" option. "For us, it was worth it," said the mother. "We had some terrific meals which were, thanks to the plan, reasonably priced. And our kids are old enough to enjoy the ambience of the restaurants, which are actually as full of Disney atmosphere as the resorts and parks."

On the other hand, a couple from Georgia with three children under age 10 said that the standard meal plan wasn't for them: "In our opinion," said the father, "adding meals to your package only makes sense if you're prepared to eat 6,000 calories a day and spend three hours a day in restaurants." A mom from New York added, "We considered it a hassle to have to plan all our full-service meals in advance and make reservations. Normally we're pretty flexible on vacations—but not this time."

To make sure you get your money's worth on the dining plan, follow these steps.

1. Start at www.disneyworld.disney.go.com/dining. There are four options, but most people traveling with kids can safely eliminate the premium and deluxe plans, which include so much food you'll spend your entire vacation in restaurants. The vast majority of families go with the Quick Service Dining Plan

(two quick-service meals and two snacks per person each day) or Standard Plan (one table-service meal, one quick-service meal, and one snack per person each day).

2. If you've gone with the standard plan, lock in your dining reservations at table-service restaurants at least 90 days in advance, either by booking them online or calling 407/WDW–DINE. This is especially key if you're traveling during the on-season.

3. If you want to try one of Disney's swank signature restaurants or if your kids have their hearts set on a certain character breakfast, combine two table-service credits for these special experiences and book them well in advance.

4. When you arrive at your Disney hotel, your dining plan information is programmed into your Key to the World card,

Money-Saving Tip

If your kids are too young to sit still for table service and you're not planning to splurge on a character meal, consider the Quick Service Plan. It allows you to eat small amounts four times a day—perfect for kids who get hungry frequently but who don't eat a lot at one sitting—and will increase the package price for a family of four by roughly $100 a day. If $100 a day sounds like a lot for fast food and snacks, welcome to Disney. Most of the families who've written to me report they believe the Quick Service Plan is still a good deal. One mom did the math and reported a 30% savings over ordering the same meals à la carte, and if you're worried about facing a whole vacation eating nothing but burgers and fries, relax. Disney has done a good job of expanding their quick-service options, especially at Epcot. With a little preplanning, you should be able to find a wide variety of food options.

which is also your theme-park ticket and room key. Handy, huh? Present it to your server or cashier before ordering, and the card automatically monitors your allotted meals. Your receipt will show your balance so you can easily keep track of how many meals are left on the plan.

5. For families on the standard plan, it usually shakes out like this: an in-hotel muffin or bagel breakfast as the "snack," a quick-service lunch, and a full-service dinner. But you don't have to have your big meal at night; some families sit down at lunch to rest up, regroup, and escape from the parks during the hottest and most crowded times of the day.

6. Another thing to consider: The number and categories of meals you've purchased is loaded onto your ticket, but you can redeem them in any order. So if you want to use two of your full-service credits on your day at Epcot, which has lots of swell restaurants, and use two quick-service credits on your day at the Magic Kingdom, which isn't exactly a dining mecca, that's fine.

7. To get the most use out of your dining plan, study up in advance. The menus on www.disneyworld.com/dining will help you decide which, if any, signature restaurants are worth a multicredit splurge. You can also find out which character meals require two credits and which don't. And, perhaps most important with kids, you can find restaurants that serve foods your whole family will enjoy.

What Kind of Tickets Do We Need?

Under Disney's flexible Magic Your Way ticketing system, you can customize your tickets to reflect your family's priorities and length of stay.

Let's say you have a long weekend to visit and want a three-day ticket. The base price is $242 for ages 10 and up, which comes to $80 a day, a savings over the one-day ticket price of $89. However, this base price lets you into only one

Money-Saving Tip

If you know for sure that you'll be returning to Orlando in the future, it could make real sense to buy a ticket with multiple days and the No Expiration option. For example, a seven-day adult ticket with a No Expiration option is $478, which breaks down to $68 a day, a significant savings over the present one-day ticket price of $89 and an even more significant savings if (and when) Disney raises the prices again. Just make sure to hang on to your tickets. I've received letters from several families who paid for the No Expiration option and then lost their pricey tickets sometime during that relocation to Omaha. At least take a picture of the back of your tickets with your camera phone when you get them; if Guest Relations (aka Guest Services) has the ticket numbers, they can reissue them.

park per day. From there, you can add the Park Hopper Pass, which allows you to move from park to park within a day. This will bring the price of your three-day ticket to $299. If you add on Blizzard Beach, Typhoon Lagoon, and DisneyQuest—called the Water Park Fun & More option—your ticket price once again rises to $299. If you want both the Park Hopper Pass and the Water Fun option, the price rises to $321.

Confused yet? Hang on, it gets even more complicated. Although your tickets won't expire if you don't go to the parks, say, every day (indeed, most families like to space out their park visits), there's the matter of the No Expiration option. Without it, Magic Your Way tickets expire 14 days after their first use. Adding it to a three-day adult ticket will cost an additional $35.

Theme-Park Ticket-Price Chart

TICKET OPTIONS								
TICKET	**10-DAY**	**7-DAY**	**6-DAY**	**5-DAY**	**4-DAY**	**3-DAY**	**2-DAY**	**1-DAY**
BASE TICKET Ages 10–up	$318	$288	$278	$268	$256	$242	$176	$89
Ages 3–9	$300	$270	$260	$250	$239	$226	$164	$83

Base Ticket admits guest to one of the four major theme parks per day's use.
Park choices are: Magic Kingdom, Epcot, Disney Hollywood Studios, Disney's Animal Kingdom.
8-day and **9-day** tickets are also available.

ADD: Park Hopper	$57	$57	$57	$57	$57	$57	$57	$35

Park Hopper option entitles guest to visit more than one theme park per day's use. Park choices are any combination of: Magic Kingdom, Epcot, Disney Hollywood Studios, Disney's Animal Kingdom.

ADD: Water Park Fun	$57 10 visits	$57 7 visits	$57 6 visits	$57 5 visits	$57 4 visits	$57 3 visits	$57 2 visits	$57 1 visit

Water Park Fun option entitles guest to a specified number of visits (between 2 and 10) to a choice of entertainment and recreation venues. Choices are: Blizzard Beach, Typhoon Lagoon, DisneyQuest, and Wide World of Sports.

ADD: Both	$79	$79	$79	$79	$79	$79	$79	$79

Adding both the *Park Hopper* and *Water Park* option entitles guest to all the privileges under both specific options above.

ADD: No Expiration	$275	$190	$165	$130	$85	$40	$30	n/a

No Expiration means that unused admissions on a ticket may be used any time in the future. Without this option, tickets expire 14 days after first use.

MINOR PARKS AND ATTRACTIONS		
TICKET	**AGES 10-UP**	**AGES 3-9**
TYPHOON LAGOON OR BLIZZARD BEACH 1-Day 1-Park	$55	$47
DISNEYQUEST 1-Day	$47	$40
CIRQUE DU SOLEIL'S *LA NOUBA*	$78–$136	$62–$109

*All prices are subject to Florida sales tax.

If you want the Park Hopper Pass and the Water Park Fun & More option and the No Expiration option—in other words, the whole ticketing enchilada—the cost of your three-day ticket leaps all the way to $377.

So, how do you know what ticketing options to buy? If this is your first trip to Disney World, keep it simple. If you have young kids, you'll likely spend most of your time in the four major parks, so a base ticket is fine. As a mom with three preschoolers said, "We bought the Park Hopper option but the logistics of moving around with that many strollers and backpacks was just overwhelming. After one day of trying to park hop we decided it would be less stressful to stay in a single park every day. So we basically paid extra for nothing."

Money-Saving Tip

The more days you buy, the less your per-day cost. If you're staying for a week, your ticket price per day drops significantly. An adult buying a seven-day basic ticket ends up paying around $41 per day, a downright huge savings over the one-day ticket price of $89.

Not sure about upgrades? Buy the basic. If you get down to Orlando and decide that you'd like to park hop or go to the water parks, you can always upgrade your ticket there . . . which is much better than paying for options that you end up not using. "We paid for the water-parks option," says one mom from Massachusetts, "only to arrive on a week full of thunderstorms when the water parks were closed at least half the time."

Disney "adjusts"—that is, raises—prices regularly, so you should always confirm these numbers by calling 407/824–4321 or visiting www.disneyworld.com. Also note that children under age 3 are admitted free.

But if your kids are older and able to withstand a long day, the Park Hopper Pass is worthwhile. The Park Hopper also comes in handy if you're traveling during the off-season when the Magic Kingdom and Hollywood Studios close earlier; without it you may find yourself with little to do after 6 pm. And it's also good for people who've been to Disney World before and know exactly what attractions they want to see or who know they like to move around swiftly, revisiting these favorites. (Many of the touring tips in this book assume that you

Helpful Hint

There are a couple things to keep in mind about theme-park tickets, which are also your room keys if you're staying on-site. They demagnetize easily, so keep them in a separate pocket away from your credit cards and cell phone. If your ticket does become demagnetized and won't swipe at the entrance turnstiles, Disney will gladly replace it. But this involves a trip to Guest Relations and it's exasperating to have to make this detour when you're itching to get to the rides or exhausted after a day in the parks.

Disney uses a biometric identification system to keep track of exactly who is using those multiday tickets. The first time you enter a Disney park, you'll be asked to do a finger scan and the minute measurements will be recorded. You'll be re-scanned each time you use a ticket to enter a Disney park; this is to make sure that the finger measurements match. It's a high-tech way to cut down on ticket swapping and the black-market sales of multiday tickets.

Fear ticket loss? Either write down the numbers on the back of your tickets and keep that info in a separate place, or use your camera phone to take a picture of the backs. If Guest Relations has the ticket numbers, replacing them will be a lot easier.

have the ability to move from one park to another in the course of the day.) If any of these conditions applies to you, the vote on the Park Hopper Pass should be "yes."

Finally, the Water Park Fun option makes sense if you have older kids who would enjoy the water parks and DisneyQuest, or if you've been to Disney World before and are looking to venture outside the four major parks. On the other hand, if this is your first trip to Disney World, you'll have all you can handle just visiting the four major parks. And if your kids are very young, you may find that your hotel pool is a far more practical way to cool off than trekking to a water park. So, it's a "yes" on Water Park Fun & More only for families with kids over 8 or who are visiting Disney World for the second time. For first-time visitors or families with kids under 8, the answer is usually "no." And remember that if you get to Orlando and change your mind, not to worry. You can add the options at any time during your vacation.

Transportation

If you're flying to Orlando, another major decision is whether or not you need to rent a car. For families staying on-site and focusing primarily on Disney attractions, the answer is probably "no," especially since Disney offers free bus transportation between the airport and your Disney hotel. Quite a few families have reported that they used their rental car less than they anticipated. "We paid $350 for the privilege of driving from the airport to our hotel and back," wrote one father.

But for families staying off-site or anyone planning to visit both Disney and non-Disney attractions, renting a car often makes sense. "We got a great hotel rate, but it was about 15 miles from Disney World," one mother reported. "We also spent a day at Universal and a day at SeaWorld, so we would have been sunk if we hadn't had our own transportation."

Another mother added, "Our kids get so excited at Disney that they go full-out the whole time, running around in a frenzy.

Insider's Secret

At times it may make more sense to use a taxi than a rental car or Disney's transportation. Taxi rides around Disney property average $15, and parking (at least for guests not staying at a Disney resort) is $14—virtually equal. If you plan to drive around a lot it makes sense to have your own car, but if you need direct transportation only occasionally, a cab is a perfectly fine option. Consider taking a cab if:

- You'd like quick direct transportation from the airport to your hotel.
- You'd like quick direct transportation from one resort to another.
- You're headed to a minor park like Downtown Disney or the water parks and don't want a lengthy shuttle commute.
- You're staying at a Disney hotel but heading to Universal Orlando or SeaWorld for the day.
- Everyone's absolutely exhausted. If you've pushed too far and the kids are in a meltdown, cabs are the fastest way to get back to your room. They're always waiting near the theme-park exits and, at times, this is $15 well worth spending.

But when they collapse, they really collapse. There were a couple of times when even having to wait 15 minutes for a bus would have been a disaster. Every time we left a theme park, they'd be asleep in the car before we were even out of the parking lot."

Transportation with a Rental Car

An average weekly rental fee for a midsize car is around $350. Don't be fooled by the quoted rate of $30 a day; by the time you add on taxes and insurance it's closer to $50.

Time-Saving Tip

OK, you're staying on-site, and you have a car—either a rental or your own. Is it faster to drive to the theme parks or to take Disney transportation? If your resort offers monorail or boat access to a certain park, take it. It will always be your fastest way there. If your resort only offers bus service to a certain park, the decision is a little trickier. The buses can be slow, especially if you're staying at a big sprawling resort like Port Orleans/Riverside or Caribbean Beach, where it can take 15 minutes for the buses to simply circle the resort property. If you're planning to park hop, having your own car will save you some time, and, as long as your hotel car pass is visible on your dash, theme-park parking is free to on-site guests.

The time difference is unlikely to be more than 15 minutes between the bus ride and the car ride, so it pretty much boils down to your preference. Do you want to be in complete control of your destiny, able to change plans on a whim? Take your car. Do you want to bliss out and forget all about maps, traffic, parking-row numbers, and dead batteries? Leave the driving to Disney.

Transportation Without a Rental Car

If you're not staying at a Disney resort and not renting a car, you have two options for airport transfers. The fastest and easiest is a cab; prices average about $50 to the Universal-SeaWorld area and $60 to the Disney area, plus tip. Alternatively, you can take the Mears Shuttle Service, which costs $30 round-trip for adults and $24 for kids. You can reserve your shuttle before leaving home by calling 407/423–5566. Shuttles may seem like a

Insider's Secret

The Magical Express airport buses usually stop at several hotels, and this can add up to a long commute time. If you're really eager to get your vacation going fast, take a cab. Also, some families have reported significant wait times for their luggage, so do pack essentials in a carry-on. "It took seven hours for our luggage to be delivered to our room," said one mother from Wisconsin. "We couldn't take the kids swimming, we didn't have our camera, and we ended up spending the whole first day walking around in 90-degree weather in long sleeves and jeans."

money-saving option, but note that if there are more than two people in your party, it's cheaper to take a cab.

If you're staying at a Disney resort, the Magical Express Service makes transport from the airport to your hotel room less costly, and, if all goes according to plan, more convenient. Here's how it works:

Check your bags at your hometown airport. This is the last time you'll see them until you're in your Orlando hotel room, so be sure to put anything you may need in the meantime, such as medication or summer-weather clothing, into your carry-on.

Insider's Secret

You just got to Orlando, so of course you're not thinking about going home yet. But, as a sadder-but-wiser mother from Ohio advises, "If you use the Magical Express for your return service to the airport, don't book your return flight before noon. They require you to be on the bus three hours before your flight time, which for us basically involved getting up and checking out in the middle of the night."

When your plane arrives, you don't have to go to baggage claim to pick up your bags—instead, follow the directions of the Disney representative waiting on the baggage-claim level. You'll board a motor coach and head for your resort, and—if all goes smoothly—your bags will arrive in your room about three hours after you do. You don't have to be on-site to sign for your luggage; if you want to go straight to the theme parks, the bags will be waiting for you when you get back.

The Magical Express Service not only saves you the hassle of tracking and dragging your bags every step of the way but it also means free airport-to-resort transport for all Disney hotel guests. This single perk will save a family of four somewhere between $120 and $350 when you consider that they would otherwise be taking a shuttle, a cab, or even renting a car.

Countdown to Disney World

Okay, let's summarize. Here's what needs to be done—and when.

As Soon as Possible

- Choose your resort. To help find the best on-site hotel for you, consult Chapter 2, and once you've narrowed your options, make reservations via www.disneyworld.com or 407/934–7639 (407/W–DISNEY).

- Book your room. Even if you're staying off-site, booking early is smart. A great way to get discounts on off-site lodging is to go to the Orlando Travel Bureau website at www.orlandoinfo.com to request an Orlando Vacation Planning Kit Magicard. It takes three to four weeks to get the package, but the card qualifies you for significant discounts at many off-site hotels.

- Buy your theme-park tickets. You can either buy online at www.disneyworld.com or call 407/934–7639 (407/ W–DISNEY).

Money-Saving Tip

The Magicard, offered through the Orlando Travel Bureau, is a great source of savings for families staying at off-site hotels, and you can download the card, as well as get lots of general Orlando information, by visiting www.orlandoinfo.com. Another way to cut your costs is to buy an entertainment discount-coupon book for your hometown. The books are best known for their local restaurant coupons, but few people realize that a nationwide directory of hotels offering discounts can be found in the back. Several off-site Orlando hotels are listed, and a discount can make an upscale resort as inexpensive as an interstate cheapie. But only a few rooms per hotel are earmarked for the discount, so your chances of cashing in improve if you're willing to book early.

Six Months in Advance

@ Flying? Book now.

@ If you need a rental car, reserve it now.

@ You can arrange for dining reservations, including character meals and dinner shows, 180 days in advance (90 days in advance during special promotions) by calling 407/939–3463 (407/WDW–DINE) or booking online at www.disneyworld.com. Online is faster if you know exactly what you want, but if you need advice, make the telephone call and talk to a real Disney cast member.

@ Does your little princess want to be styled at the Bibbidi Bobbidi Boutique? Sign her up 180 days in advance by dialing 407/939–7895 (407/WDW–STYLE).

@ Families who would like to take a behind-the-scenes tour or enroll their kids in one of the Grand Floridian programs—

such as the pirate-theme scavenger hunt or tea with Alice and the other Wonderland characters—should book at this stage. Call 407/939–8687 (407/WDW–TOUR) for the tours and 407/939–3463 (407/WDW–DINE) for the Grand Floridian programs. Kid-friendly tours and programs are explained in Chapter 10.

Four Months in Advance

@ To book a fireworks cruise, call 407/939–7529 (407/WDW–PLAY). See Chapter 10 for more information.

@ Interested in golf, parasailing, surfing, or some other sport? Book your time by calling 407/939–7529 (407/WDW–PLAY). See Chapter 10 for details.

@ Want a spa treatment? Call Saratoga Springs Resort & Spa at 407/827–4455 or the Grand Floridian Resort at 407/824–2332 for a reservation.

@ For Cirque du Soleil tickets, call 407/939–7600 or visit www.cirquedusoleil.com.

Two Weeks in Advance

@ You should be good to go. Just reconfirm theme-park hours at www.disneyworld.com and check over reservations, so when you get to Orlando all you'll have to focus on is having fun.

Helpful Hint

Numerous websites provide information and advice on Walt Disney World. Disney's official site, www.disneyworld.com, is definitely the place to start. But needless to say the Disney website will present every ride and restaurant as downright wonderful. For no-holds-barred reviews, check out www.mousesavers.com, www.disboards.com, and www.fodors.com/forums.

Things to Discuss with Your Kids Before You Leave Home

It's important to include the kids in the vacation planning, so discuss the following topics before you leave home.

The Trip Itself

There are two schools of thought on just how far in advance you should tell the kids you're headed to Disney World. Because many families make reservations as much as a year in advance, it's easy to fall into a "waiting for Christmas" syndrome, with the kids nearly in a lather of anticipation weeks before you leave. To avoid the agony of a long countdown, one couple packed in secret and then woke the kids up at 5 am and announced, "Get in the car, we're going to Disney World." The best method is probably somewhere between these two extremes. Tell your kids at the time you make the reservations and solicit their opinions about what activities to book in advance, but don't begin poring over the brochures in earnest until about a month before the trip.

The Layout of the Parks

Testimonies from the more than 1,300 families surveyed or interviewed for this book have shown that the amount of advance research you do directly correlates with how much you enjoy your trip. Don't get me wrong—visitors who show up at Disney World without any preparation can still have fun, but their comment sheets are peppered with "Next time I'll know . . ." and "If only we had . . ."

If you're letting preteens and teens roam around on their own, brief them on the locations of major attractions. But the pleasures of being prepared can extend even to preschoolers. If you purchase a few Disney World coloring books or a kids'

touring guide, even the youngest child will arrive able to identify Spaceship Earth and Splash Mountain. A little knowledge
before entering the gates is essential to helping you spend your
time in the parks wisely.

The Classic Stories of Disney

If your kids are under 8, another good pretrip purchase is a set
of Disney books with CDs or tapes. Even though parental eyes
may glaze over when Dumbo starts over for the 34th time,
these recordings and books help to familiarize kids with the
characters and rides they'll be seeing once they arrive. "I made
sure my 1-year-old was familiar with the Disney characters, but
what really helped was buying the Disney Classics CD before
the trip," wrote one mom. "We listened to it in the car every
day and when we were at Disney, we would get so excited when
he heard a song; we knew that he would jump around and try
to sing along."

Some families rent Disney movies before the trip. For example, viewing *Honey, I Shrunk the Kids* before you leave will
vastly improve your children's appreciation of the Honey, I
Shrunk the Kids Movie Set Adventure at Hollywood. Even
watching an old favorite like *The Little Mermaid* or *Aladdin* can
refresh your child's memory and make it doubly exciting when,
a few weeks later, he comes face-to-face with the characters in
the park.

Special Academic Projects

See the section "Should We Take the Kids Out of School?" earlier in this chapter for ideas. Whatever project you decide upon,
it's essential you get the kids on board before you arrive in Orlando. Once there, they'll be too distracted for your lectures on
academic responsibility.

Souvenirs and Money

Will you save all souvenir purchases for the last day? Buy one small souvenir every day? Are the children expected to spend their own money, or will you spring for the T-shirts? Whatever you decide, set the rules before you're in the park. Otherwise the selection of goodies will lure you into spending far more than you anticipated.

One excellent technique for limiting impulse buys is to purchase Disney Dollars the first day you're in WDW. (You can get them at any on-site hotel or at Guest Relations in any park.) Disney Dollars come in denominations of $1, $5, and $10 (with pictures of Disney characters where presidents would be) and are accepted throughout Disney World. You can give your kids an age-appropriate number of Disney Dollars at the beginning of the trip, explaining that this money alone is for souvenirs. You can accomplish the same thing with a gift card pre-loaded with a certain amount of spending money.

The Scare Factor

Finally, give some thought to the scare factor. A disappointing meal or boring show can ruin an hour, but if misjudging a ride leaves you with a terrified or nauseated child, that can ruin the whole day.

How frightening a ride is can be tough to gauge, because Disney World scariness comes in two forms—the atmospheric or creepy kind as in the cobwebbed old hotel in the Tower of Terror, or the motion-related kind. And note that while Space Mountain and Expedition Everest are obviously risky, some guests can lose their lunch on sweet little charmers like the Mad Tea Party.

Disney's guidance comes in the form of height requirements, but saying that a 40-inch-tall 5-year-old can ride Big Thunder Mountain is no indication that he should ride Big Thunder Mountain. As we all know, some 6-year-olds are fearless and some 11-year-olds easily unnerved. Read the ride descriptions and scare-factor ratings in this book to find out what you're dealing with.

Height Requirements

The Magic Kingdom

Barnstormer	35 inches
Big Thunder Mountain	40 inches
Splash Mountain	40 inches
Space Mountain	44 inches
Stitch's Great Escape	40 inches
Tomorrowland Speedway	32 inches

Epcot

Mission: SPACE	44 inches
Soarin'	40 inches
Test Track	40 inches

Hollywood Studios

Rock 'n' Roller Coaster	48 inches
Star Tours	40 inches
Tower of Terror	40 inches

The Animal Kingdom

Dinosaur	40 inches
Expedition Everest	44 inches
Kali River Rapids	38 inches
Primeval Whirl	48 inches

If you're still unsure, employ these strategies:

- *Do a Baby Swap.* (No, this does not mean you can trade your shrieking toddler for that angelic napping infant behind you!) If you have doubts about whether a ride is appropriate for your child, inform the attendant that you may need to do a Baby Swap. As you approach the attraction, one parent rides and returns with the verdict. If the first parent thinks the child will do okay, the second parent immediately boards and rides with the child. If the first parent thinks the ride is too wild, the second (yet-to-ride) parent passes the child through to the first parent and then rides him- or herself. It sounds confusing, but the attendants help you and it actually works smoothly.

@ *Slowly increase ride intensity throughout the day.* This advice runs counter to the touring tips you'll find later in this book that recommend you ride the big-deal attractions first thing in the morning, but if you're not sure your 7-year-old is up for a roller coaster, start her off slowly. Kids who begin with something relatively mild like Pirates of the Caribbean often build up their nerve throughout the day and close out the night on Space Mountain.

@ *Avoid motion sickness.* Obviously, steer clear of bumpy rides after eating. If you feel queasy on a motion-simulation ride like Star Tours, stare at something inside the cabin, like the seat in front of you, instead of the screen.

Don't Leave Home Without...

✔ *Comfortable shoes.* Forget about wearing sandals or slides in the parks—stick to sneakers. And this is no time to be breaking in new shoes.

✔ *Minimal clothing.* Many hotels have laundry facilities, and you can always wash out clothes in the sink. Most families over-pack, not figuring on all the souvenirs they'll bring back. Disney T-shirts are not only great for touring but can serve as swimsuit cover-ups and pajamas as well. And unless you're planning a special evening out at Victoria & Albert's, casual clothing is acceptable everywhere.

✔ *Lightweight jackets.* It rains in Orlando year-round, so jackets should be water-resistant.

✔ *Basic necessities.* These include disposable diapers, baby formula, camera, memory cards or film, and blank camcorder tapes. All these are available within Disney World, but at premium prices.

✔ *Sunscreen.* Keep a tube with you and reapply it often. Sunburn is the number-one complaint at the first-aid clinic in the Magic Kingdom. You need sun protection all through the year in Orlando, not just in summer.

✔ *A waist pack.* Unlike a purse, a waist pack frees up your hands for boarding rides, pushing strollers, and holding on to your kids. A backpack is another option and good for carrying snacks and water, but even a light one can start to hurt your shoulders after a while. Plus, some rides don't allow backpacks, so you may have to keep putting yours in a locker.

✔ *Resealable plastic bags.* Disney serves such large dining portions, even on kiddie meals, that some parents report they save some of the fruit or chips for a later snack.

Helpful Hint

One thing you probably don't want to bring with you is the family pet. If you do, board it at the kennel on Disney property, which is called Best Friends Pet Care (877/493–9738, www.wdw.bestfriendspetcare. com). They take excellent care of the animals there, with multiple walks per day; and our readers have been impressed with the cleanliness of the facility and professionalism of the staff. Prices vary according to the breed, time of year, and length of stay. Never—repeat, never—leave an animal locked in a car, no matter what time of year you're visiting. The Florida heat and humidity are far too dangerous.

✓ *Sunglasses.* The Florida sun is so blinding that more than once I've reached into my bag for my sunglasses only to realize I already had them on. Kids too young for sunglasses need wide-billed caps to cut down the glare.

✓ *Strollers.* Most Orlando hotels are huge, so if you have an infant or toddler, you'll need your own stroller just to get around your hotel.

✓ *Your iPhone.* This can have many in-park uses other than the obvious advantage of relocating each other when someone gets lost. In the MK you can download a wait-time app, Mobile Magic, that gives you real-time info on the length of lines at key attractions. And one enterprising father from Montreal reported that he used his iPhone every morning to take a picture of the family's parking spot du jour. "Otherwise," he said, "by day four we couldn't have possibly remembered where we'd left the car."

The Frantic Factor

Although I rate rides throughout this book according to their "scare factor," I've often thought that I should include ratings on the "frantic factor" as well, measuring how hysterical the average parent is apt to become in any given situation.

I'm often asked to speak to parent groups on the topic of family travel. Almost inevitably, someone wants tips on how to make a Disney vacation relaxing. These people are very earnest, but they might as well be asking me to recommend a nice ski lodge for their upcoming trip to Hawaii. The only honest response is, "If you want to relax, you're going to the wrong place." Disney World is a high-stimulation environment, a total assault on all five senses mixed in with a constant and mind-boggling array of choices. This is not the week to take your kids off Ritalin or discuss marital issues with your spouse. It helps to keep a sense of humor and to go in with a full understanding that, vacation or not, this is unlikely to be the most relaxing week of your life. As one French mother of three sagely points out, "You can sleep later, when Mickey is done with you."

Actually, high stimulation and a lively pace may be the reason most people go to Disney World in the first place. Families who slip over the line from happily stimulated to unhappily frantic often do so because:

1. They forget to build in adequate rest breaks

2. They've planned their trips for the busiest times of the year

3. They're confused about the logistics of touring

4. They're hell-bent on taking it all in because "We're paying through the nose for this!" and "Who knows when we'll get back?"

This book is full of tips to help you avoid the first three mistakes, but your attitude is pretty much up to you. Just remember that doing it all is not synonymous with having the most fun, and if time is tight, limit your touring to those attractions that have the most appeal for your particular group. As for when you'll get back, who knows? But using this as a rationale for pushing everyone in the family past his personal exhaustion limit only guarantees that you'll never want to come back. The way for parents to really relax at Disney (besides spending time in hotel hot tubs with adjacent bars) is to do a little less, and enjoy it a little more.

One wise-beyond-his-years 14-year-old admits, "I was really obsessive-compulsive about getting everything done, seeing every ride, parade, and show. This led to a couple of breakdowns halfway through the trip, but we pulled it together and the last few days focused more on having fun in the moment than planning what we would do next."

2

Choosing a Hotel

KEY

1 On-site hotel
20 Off-site hotel

MAGIC KINGDOM

Lake Sharp

Cast Dr.

Seven Seas Lagoon

Bay Lake

West Wilderness Rd.

Fort Wilderness Tr.

Monorail

Transportation and Ticket Center

Floridian Way

World Dr.

Monorail

Vista Blvd.

Magic Kingdom Entrance Toll Plaza

Epcot Center Entrance Toll Plaza

Epcot Ce

World Dr.

Epcot Resorts Blvd.

E

Reedy Creek

DISNEY'S ANIMAL KINGDOM

Reedy Creek

Buena Vista Dr. extension

DISNEY'S HOLLYWOOD STUDIOS

BLIZZARD BEACH

Sherberth Road

World Dr.

0 ___ 1 mile
0 ___ 1 km

On-Site & Off-Site Hotels

Lake Sheen

South Lake

Lake Pocket

535

Winter Garden - Vineland Rd.

435

Bonnet

Creek

Vista Blvd.

Bonnet Creek Rd.

Buena Vista Dr.

535

Cyprus Creek

TO LOEWS UNIVERSAL RESORTS

TO PALM PKWAY AND ORLANDO AND THE INTERNATIONAL AIRPORT

4

Lake Ruby

Lake Ave.

Lake St.

27

26

Center Dr.

19

25

24

Lake Buena Vista

Vineland Ave.

Little Lake Bryan

Disney Vacation Club way

18

Hotel Plaza Blvd.

EXIT 68

17

EPCOT

Buena Vista Dr.

DOWNTOWN DISNEY

16

TYPHOON LAGOON

Apopka - Vineland Rd.

Lake Bryan

22

23

EXIT 67B

Epcot Center Dr.

EXIT 67A

International Dr.

21

15

14

4

EXIT 65B

Osceola Parkway

Central Florida Greeneway

EXIT 65A

435

ESPN's Wide World of Sports Complex

EXIT 64B

Osceola Parkway

TO CELEBRATION

EXIT 64A

192

20

he ratings for the hotels discussed in this chapter are based on three factors: the responses of families surveyed; the percentage of repeat business a resort experiences, which is a reliable indicator of guest satisfaction; and the quality of the resort in relation to the price. Obviously, you'd expect more amenities and a higher employee-to-guest ratio at a $300-a-night resort than at a $100-a-night resort, so it's unfair to hold them both to the same standard.

With that in mind, I've rated the hotels on the basis of value for cost; that is, are you getting what you paid for? Do the advantages of this resort make it worth the price? And would you recommend this resort to families with the same amount of money to spend?

General Information About the On-Site Disney Hotels

- Disney hotels operate under the family plan, meaning that kids under 18 stay free with parents.

@ Check-in time is 3 pm at most Disney hotels. If you arrive before your room is ready, you can check in, store your bags, pick up your tickets and resort IDs, and go ahead to the parks.

@ Checkout time is 11 am, but, once again, you need not let this interfere with your touring. Check out early in the morning, store your bags, then go on to enjoy your last day in the parks.

@ When you check in, you'll be issued a room key/resort ID that allows you to charge meals, drinks, tickets, and souvenirs to your room and also gives you access to all Disney World transportation. Theme-park admission can also be added. If you've chosen the dining plan, your resort ID also serves as your meal pass. In short, one card does it all.

@ If you pay with a credit card, you can arrange for automatic checkout—a definite time-saver. An itemized statement is emailed to you on the day of your departure. If it's correct, you can keep it as your receipt and leave immediately.

Is It Worth the Expense to Stay On-Site?

Staying at one of the Disney-owned hotels is very convenient, and with rates as low as $82 a night at the All-Star resorts and Pop Century Resort, it's more affordable than you might think.

Off-site hotels fight back with special promotions and perks of their own, arguing that the Disney hotels still cost more and bring you only slightly closer to the action. On-site or off-site? Ask yourself the following questions to help you decide:

@ *What time of year are you going?*

If you're visiting Disney World in summer or during a major holiday, you'll need every extra minute, so it's worth the cost to stay on-site.

@ *How old are your kids?*

In the Florida heat and humidity it's nearly a medical necessity to keep young kids out of the sun in the middle of the afternoon, and an on-site hotel room makes it easier to return for a nap. If your kids are preteens or teens who can handle a whole day in the parks, commute time is less of a factor.

@ *Are you flying or driving?*

If you're flying and doing only Disney World, it may make more economic sense to stay on-site and use Disney World's transportation system in lieu of a rental car. But if you're driving to Orlando, it's just as easy to stay off-site. You'll be able to drive into the parks at hours that suit you without having to rely on shuttles.

@ *What's your budget?*

If money isn't a major issue, stay on-site. If money is a primary consideration, you'll find your best deals at the budget hotels along Interstate 4. Exits 62 and 68, the exits that flank Disney World, are chock-full of chain hotels and restaurants.

@ *How much do your kids eat?*

Food is expensive at Disney World, both in the parks and at the on-site hotels. If you're staying off-site, you can always eat in the numerous fast-food and family-style restaurants along Interstate 4, Route 192, and International Drive. Many off-site hotels have complimentary

Money-Saving Tip

Disney isn't exactly known for deep discounts, but when times are slow they're as eager to fill their rooms as any other hotel chain. The trouble is they don't always announce these discounts to people who seem ready and willing to pay the full price. When you call in to make your resort reservations, always ask, "Are there any special offers available during the times I'll be visiting?"

breakfast buffets, while the all-suites properties have in-room kitchenettes where you can fix your own meals.

Do you plan to visit other attractions?

If you'll be spending half your time at SeaWorld, Universal Orlando, or the other non-Disney World attractions, stay off-site—at least during those days. There's no need to pay top dollar for proximity to Disney if you're headed for Islands of Adventure.

Will your party be splitting up at times?

Does Dad want to golf one afternoon? Do you have teenagers who can spend a day at Blizzard Beach on their own? Will there be times when it would make sense for Dad to take the younger kids back to the hotel while Mom stays in the park with the older ones? Is your 5-year-old raring to go at dawn, whereas your 15-year-old sleeps until noon? If so stay on-site, where the use of the Disney World transportation system makes it easy for all of you to go your own way.

What's your tolerance level for hassles?

If you don't want to deal with interstate traffic, big parking lots, toting luggage, and carrying cash, stay on-site.

The Advantages of Staying On-Site

Extra Magic Hours

Extra Magic Hours work like this: Each day year-round, one of the four major theme parks opens for Disney resort guests an hour early or stays open an extra hour or two after the regular closing time. Mondo perk! This gives resort guests the chance to ride some featured attractions and greet the characters in a relatively uncrowded park. (Note the word "relatively." There are so many Disney resort guests that there are still plenty of people around, just not as many as usual.)

Generally only a few attractions per park are open for the Extra Magic Hour, but this is your chance to ride them easily. Just as important—in the morning you'll be deep inside the theme park when it officially opens so you can dash to other big-deal attractions before the rest of the crowd gets there.

For morning Extra Magic Hours your resort ID gets you into the park to ride anything that's up and running. For evening Extra Magic Hours you'll need to show your resort ID/room key card to board the rides.

When you check into your hotel you'll receive a brochure printed with the Extra Magic Hours schedule for the week; if you'd like this information in advance to help with your planning, visit www.disneyworld.com, where you'll find "Park Hours" under "Plan."

Magical Express Service

The Magical Express Service allows you to check your bags at your hometown airport and not see them again until you walk into your hotel room in Walt Disney World. You also get free shuttle service from the Orlando airport to your resort.

When it's time to go home, the system works in reverse. You check your bags and receive your boarding passes before departing from your Disney resort. Take another complimen-

Insider's Secret

The Magical Express Service is supposed to save you time and money, but in reality it doesn't always work seamlessly. Quite a few readers have complained of long delays, and one dad dubbed the system "Magical Distress." Comments range from: "We stopped at three hotels, and it took over an hour to get to ours from the airport" to "Thanks to this so-called benefit we began the whole trip with confusion and irritation."

Other families praise the perk, agreeing with the Chicago mom who wrote, "It's like Disney starts taking care of you the minute your plane wheels touch down in Orlando." The consensus seems to be that the system works well at times when it's not too crowded, but during peak travel times slow service is common. If you're traveling at such a time, consider handling your own bags and arranging for your own transportation between the airport and your hotel.

tary shuttle back to the airport and go directly to your flight. Your luggage will be waiting for you at baggage claim in your hometown. This also saves you the inconvenience of having to store your bags on the last day of your trip.

Transportation

On-site guests have unlimited use of the monorails, buses, and boats of the WDW transportation system. Between this and Magical Express Service, many on-site guests find they are able to forgo the cost of a rental car.

Free Parking at the Theme Parks

You don't have to pay the $14 daily fee to park. The attendant will wave you through when she sees the resort parking ID on your dashboard.

Package Delivery

Don't lug your souvenirs around while touring. When you make a purchase, you can fill out a form and Disney will deliver the package to your hotel gift shop for free. It's generally the next day before your purchases show up, so don't use the package delivery service on the last day of your visit.

Key to the World Card and Charging Privileges

Talk about hassle-free. This all-in-one card you receive upon check-in is your room key, theme-park ticket, and dining plan credit card. It also allows adults (and kids, if you opt to give them privileges) to charge tickets, food, and souvenirs back to their hotel room. It's certainly easier not to have to carry huge amounts of cash around, especially at the pool, water parks, and marinas.

It's up to you whether older kids have charging privileges. Giving them this privilege makes it easier to send Johnny to the snack bar for a round of Cokes, but be sure to impress upon kids that these IDs work like credit cards. They're not an open invitation to order pizza for all their new friends at the arcade, purchase all seven dwarfs from the hotel gift shop, or, heaven forbid, obtain cash advances.

Dining Plans

Many families swear by the Disney Dining Plan, which can be added to any on-site package. The plan saves you from having to carry around cash and—at least on the surface—masks the sting of coughing up nine bucks for a cheeseburger.

Helpful Hint

If a room card with charging privileges is lost, it should be reported to the front desk immediately to avoid unauthorized charges.

Family Atmosphere

All the on-site hotels are designed with families in mind. The ambience is casual, security is tight, and there are always other children around to play with. The on-site hotels have laundry facilities, generally near the pools and arcades, so that you can run a quick load while the youngsters play; there's late-night pizza delivery to your room; and if there's not a child-care facility at your particular hotel, Guest Relations (a.k.a. Guest Services) can help you arrange for an in-room sitter. The emphasis at the Disney hotels is on making life more convenient for parents.

Cool Themes

All the on-site hotels have themes that are carried out in mega-detail. At the Polynesian the staff greets you with "Aloha"; at the Port Orleans, jazz music plays all day; and at the All-Star Sports the dressers in the rooms look like gym lockers. This makes staying at an on-site hotel almost as exciting for kids as being inside the parks.

> **Insider's Secret**
> The on-site resorts often have fun little activities for kids such as scavenger hunts, pool races, or "unbirthday" parties. Activity schedules are usually posted around the pool areas or child-care centers.

In fact, because the on-site hotels are all so different from each other, it's fun to visit other hotels. Many families surveyed told us they enjoyed eating dinner at a different resort from their own.

Location, Location, Location

It doesn't take a Baby Einstein to figure out that the Disney hotels are closer to the theme parks than off-site hotels. Proximity makes it easier to return to your room after lunch for a nap, dip in the pool, change of clothes, etc.

Rating the On-Site Disney Hotels

The Orlando area has more than 140,000 hotel rooms, and a fair percentage of these are Disney owned. In other words, a family that has decided to stay on-site faces a bewildering number of choices. Does the convenience of being on the monorail line justify the increase in price? Do you want to stay amid Victorian splendor, or is a fort more your style? At which park do you plan to spend most of your time? As with all of WDW, making the best choice hinges on your awareness of what your family really needs.

On-Site Luxury Hotels

Luxury hotels are full-scale resorts with fine dining, health clubs and spas, valet parking, on-site child-care facilities, full room service, and lots of sporting options. There's a price attached—the Disney luxury hotels cost, on average, twice as much a night as the mid-price hotels. Luxury hotels include the BoardWalk, Yacht & Beach Clubs, Contemporary, Grand Floridian, Polynesian, Swan, Dolphin, Wilderness Lodge, and Animal Kingdom Lodge. (Note: The Wilderness Lodge and Animal Kingdom Lodge are at the lowest price point in the luxury category.)

On-Site Mid-Price Hotels

"Mid-price" is something of a misnomer, because both the price and the quality are higher than what you'd find in an off-site chain hotel in Orlando. You may pay a little more, but the hotels are beautifully maintained and landscaped, with their themes carried out to the nth degree. Resorts that fall into this category include the Caribbean Beach, Port Orleans, and Coronado Springs.

Helpful Hint

Disneyworld.com is a great planning tool, allowing you to compare the prices of different on-site hotels during the week you'll be visiting. You can comparison shop at leisure without a travel agent or phone reservation agent nudging you into a quick decision.

On-Site Value Hotels

The on-site value hotels include the All-Star Resorts, the Pop Century Resort, and the Art of Animation Resort.

Again, the resorts are well maintained and have eye-popping catchy graphics that dazzle the kids. You can find a food court but no sit-down dining; a swimming pool but no other sporting options; a lengthier check-in line and smaller staff, but rates that more than compensate for the minor inconveniences. The most important on-site benefits—transportation to the parks, help with tickets and priority-seating reservations, Extra Magic Hours, and charging privileges—are just as available to those paying $82 a night at All-Star Sports as to those paying $382 a night at the BoardWalk. And, hey, the housekeepers still leave your kids' stuffed animals in the window to greet them in the evening, so who can complain?

Villa-Style Accommodations

Larger families or those who like to prepare their own meals may want to rent a villa. Resorts included in this category are the Bay Lake Towers at the Contemporary Resort, Wilderness Lodge Villas, Saratoga Springs Resort, BoardWalk Villas, Beach Club Villas, Animal Kingdom Lodge Villas, and Old Key West Resort. Although these properties are part of the Disney Vaca-

Quick Guide to

Hotel	Description
All-Star Resorts	Very popular, great price
Animal Kingdom Lodge	An exotic African theme
Animal Kingdom Lodge Villas	Beautifully themed details, great views of animals
Art of Animation Resort	Elaborate theming and valued-priced suites
Bay Lake Towers	Sophisticated, high-tech villas adjacent to Contemporary resort
Beach Club Resort	Homey, lovely, and fantastic pool area
Beach Club Villas	Big suites in a great location
BoardWalk Inn	Rooms are spacious, modern, and attractive
BoardWalk Villas	Great location for both Epcot and Hollywood Studios
Caribbean Beach Resort	Tropical theme and the price is right
Contemporary Resort	Convenient and lively
Coronado Springs Resort	Elaborate pool with pyramid slide
Dolphin Resort	Adult atmosphere, great restaurant selection
Fort Wilderness Campground	Great for families who like to camp
Grand Floridian	Expensive and luxurious
Old Key West Resort	Lots of room, quiet
Polynesian Resort	Relaxed and casual with a loyal, repeat clientele
Pop Century Resort	5,760 budget rooms, lively theme
Port Orleans Resort	With French Quarter or Riverside options

NOTE: *The central reservations number for on-site hotels is 407/W–DISNEY.*

On-Site Hotels

Location	Rating	Price Range
Animal Kingdom	★★	$82–$141
Animal Kingdom	★★★	$290–$835
Animal Kingdom	★★★	$325–$1,780
ESPN Wide World of Sports Complex	N/A	$250–$400 (suite) $82–$141 (standard room)
Magic Kingdom	★★★	$450–$1,490
Epcot	★★★	$340–$845
Epcot	★★★	$390–$1,510
Epcot	★★★	$390–$845
Epcot	★★★	$390–$1,825
Epcot	★★	$149–$245
Magic Kingdom	★★	$300–$845
Animal Kingdom	★★	$159–$245
Epcot	★	$219–$459
Magic Kingdom	★★	$54–$82 (sites), $325 (cabins)
Magic Kingdom	★★	$465–$1,090
Downtown Disney	★★	$330–$1,370
Magic Kingdom	★★★	$425–$970
ESPN Wide World of Sports Complex	★★	$82–$141
Downtown Disney	★★★	$149–$245

(continued)

Quick Guide to

Hotel	Description
Saratoga Springs Resort and Spa	Amazing grotto pool, spacious
Swan Resort	Adult-oriented, great water areas
Wilderness Lodge	Rustic-looking, with an intimate feel
Wilderness Lodge Villas	Great setting, a bit more space
Yacht Club Resort	At the door of the World Showcase

NOTE: *The central reservations number for on-site hotels is 407/W–DISNEY.*

tion Club, they can be rented by any family seeking villa-style accommodations. Upon completion, the Art of Animation resort will add 1,120 value-priced family suites to the mix.

On-Site Camping

The Fort Wilderness Campground is a great choice for families who love to camp, and is by far the cheapest way to stay on-site and get on-site privileges.

Definition of Star Ratings for Hotels

★★★ This resort was a favorite among families surveyed and offers solid value for the money.

★★ Surveyed families were satisfied with this resort and felt they got what they paid for.

★ This resort is either more adult-oriented, with fewer amenities designed to appeal to families, or is more expensive than you'd expect considering the location or level of service.

On-Site Hotels

Location	Rating	Price Range
Downtown Disney	★★	$330–$1,390
Epcot	★	$219–$459
Magic Kingdom	★★★	$290–$625
Magic Kingdom	★★★	$395–$845
Epcot	★★★	$340–$1,510

Magic Kingdom Hotels

If the Magic Kingdom is your focus and you're willing to pay up, consider these resorts.

Contemporary Resort
★★
407/824–1000

You'll either love or hate Disney's original, always-hopping resort, which has 1,050 rooms surrounding a mammoth, high-tech lobby full of shops and restaurants. The glamorous Bay Lake Tower Villas are sleek and user friendly, and the location of the more expensive rooms is among the best on property. Where else can you sit in your own bathtub and watch the Magic Kingdom fireworks?

Proximity to the Magic Kingdom:	Excellent, via monorail
Proximity to Epcot:	Good, via monorail with a change at the TTC
Proximity to Hollywood:	Fair, via bus
Proximity to the Animal Kingdom:	Fair, via bus

Best On-Site Choices at a Glance

BEST MAGIC KINGDOM RESORT: POLYNESIAN

Always a favorite with readers, the lovely Polynesian
combines a casual, family-friendly feel with
great amenities and unbeatable access to the
Magic Kingdom.

BEST EPCOT RESORT: THE YACHT AND BEACH CLUBS

You like Epcot and Hollywood Studios? They're both
easy to get to from this prime location—and the pool
is to die for.

BEST MID-PRICE RESORT: PORT ORLEANS

Relaxed and homey, the Port Orleans resorts have the
charm of the luxury resorts for less. The French Quarter,
smaller and quieter than its sister, Riverside, is
easier for families with young kids.

BEST VALUE RESORTS: THE ALL-STAR RESORTS

Kids love the wacky themes at the simple but totally
adequate All-Star hotels. The Art of Animation Resort,
which has both rooms and value-priced suites, will likely
also be a contender in this category when complete.

BEST VILLAS: BAY LAKE TOWERS AT THE CONTEMPORARY

The trendy Bay Lake Towers have a major wow factor,
and the location is unparalleled.

Pluses

+ On the monorail line.

+ The easiest Magic Kingdom resort to book; discounts are
sometimes available.

+ Exceptional sporting options, including WDW's largest
tennis center and a full marina, with parasailing and waterskiing options.

+ Outstanding dining choices, including the California Grill, one of Disney's premiere restaurants; The Wave, which is excellent for breakfast; and Chef Mickey's, a great place to meet the characters for breakfast and dinner.

Minuses

— It's loud with a big-city feel, which is exactly what some families come to Florida to escape. "Like sleeping in the middle of Space Mountain," wrote one mother. Note that the rooms in the Garden Wings are quieter, cheaper, and more spacious than those in the main building.

— The futuristic ambience strikes some guests as sterile and ugly. "The pool area reminded me of a scene from a 1970s B movie that would depict future decay," wrote one disgruntled Canadian dad. "I expected Charlton Heston to come around the corner any minute, being chased by apes."

— Like all the other hotels on the monorail line, the Contemporary is expensive, with prices starting at $300 a night. Bay Lake Tower starts at $450, but can quickly climb higher.

Overall Grade: ★★ Convenient and lively. Perhaps a little too lively.

Fort Wilderness Campground ★★
407/824–2900

Fort Wilderness has campsites for tents and oversized, concrete parking pads for RVs as well as air-conditioned cabins. The cabins, which sleep six, rent for approximately the same nightly rate as a luxury hotel. The wide-open spaces of the campground are perfect for volleyball, biking, and exploring, making the resort a good choice for families with kids old enough to enjoy all the outdoor options. "Fort Wilderness lights two campfires

Helpful Hint
Fort Wilderness Camp-
ground is so sprawling
that many families rent
a golf cart to make it
easier to get around.

every night for marshmal-
low roastings and sing-
alongs," reports one mom
from Maine. "The s'mores
packages, which are $7 and
include toasting sticks, are a
real bargain, and after the
singing a Disney movie is shown in the amphitheater under
the stars. Perfect!"

Proximity to the Magic Kingdom: Good, via bus or launch
Proximity to Epcot: Fair, via bus
Proximity to Hollywood: Fair, via bus
Proximity to the Animal Kingdom: Fair, via bus

Pluses

+ Fort Wilderness offers tons of activities for kids: wagon
  rides, horseback and pony riding, and a petting zoo.

+ Hookups and tent sites, starting at $54, are your cheapest
  lodging options. The upgraded campsites start at $65 a
  night. Fort Wilderness Cabins start at $325 a night.

+ Groceries are available at the on-site trading post.

+ Fort Wilderness is pet-friendly; dogs have a playground at
  the "Waggin' Trails," an off-leash play area.

Minuses

– A large number of people are sharing relatively few facilities; the pools and the beach can get very crowded.

– This place is so spread out that it requires its own in-resort
  bus system to get you from one area to another. You can
  rent golf carts or bikes, but make no mistake: Fort Wilderness is huge and hard to navigate.

Overall Grade: ★★ If you like to camp and can put up with a
little inconvenience for great savings, this is a good option.

Grand Floridian Resort

★★
407/824–3000

Modeled after the famed Florida beach resorts of the 1800s, The Grand Floridian is possibly the prettiest of all Disney hotels, with 900 rooms ensconced beneath its gabled roofs and soaring ceilings, and off its broad white verandas. This elegant and stately lady is also the hub of many activities, including a variety of programs for children.

Proximity to the Magic Kingdom:	Excellent, via monorail or launch
Proximity to Epcot:	Good, via monorail with a change at the TTC
Proximity to Hollywood:	Fair, via bus
Proximity to Animal Kingdom:	Fair, via bus

Pluses

+ Convenient location on monorail line.

+ A private beach and marina on the Seven Seas Lagoon and numerous boating options.

+ On-site child-care center and programs for children.

+ On-site health club and full-service spa.

+ Exceptional dining. Citricos and Victoria & Albert's are among the finest restaurants in all of WDW. If you have the kids along, check out 1900 Park Fare, which hosts breakfast and dinner character buffets.

+ Lots of special little touches, such as afternoon tea and live music in the lobby each night.

Minuses

− Starting at $465, these are the most expensive rooms on Disney property.

— The elegance puts off some families who feel funny troop-
ing past a grand piano with squalling babies in their arms.

Overall Grade: ★★ Luxurious but expensive.

Polynesian Resort

★★★
407/824–2000

Designed to emulate an island village, the Polynesian is relaxed
and casual. Activities take place at the Great Ceremonial
House, where all the shops and restaurants encircle a beautiful
garden with orchids, parrots, and fountains. Guests stay in one
of the sprawling "long houses" along the lagoon. "The Polynesian was worth every penny," wrote one satisfied mom from
Connecticut: "The rooms were gorgeous and we sat on the
beach two magical nights in a row to catch the Magic Kingdom
fireworks." There's no spa, but the excellent Grand Floridian
spa is actually on a walkway between the Polynesian and the
Grand Floridian—close enough that it's easily accessible.

Proximity to the Magic Kingdom:	Excellent, via direct mono-rail, boat launch, or ferry
Proximity to Epcot:	Good, via monorail with one change at the TTC
Proximity to Hollywood:	Fair, via bus
Proximity to the Animal Kingdom:	Fair, via bus

Pluses

+ There's a private beach with an attractive pool, plus numerous boating options. Canvas shells shade napping babies and toddlers digging in the sand.

+ The Kona Café is one of the best places for desserts in all
of Disney World.

+ Excellent on-site child-care center.

+ The recently refurbished rooms are some of the prettiest
on Disney property.

Minuses

— Without a discount, expect to pay $425 a night and up.

— As of this writing, the Polynesian has no hot tub. Inexcusable!

Overall grade: ★★★ The Polynesian enjoys a loyal repeat clientele and that says it all.

Wilderness Lodge and Villas   ★★★
                                          407/824–3200

Starting at $290 a night, the Western-spirited Wilderness Lodge is aimed at filling the gap between the mid-price and luxury resorts. The theme of the Wilderness Lodge extends into every aspect of the hotel's design. The pool begins indoors as a hot spring and then flows through the lobby into a waterfall that tumbles over rocky caverns and culminates in the outdoor pool. The awe-inspiring lobby, which looks like a Lincoln Log project run amok, centers on an 82-foot fireplace that blazes all year round. The Native American–theme wallpaper, the staff dressed like park rangers, and even the stick ponies children ride to their tables in the Whispering Canyon Café all combine to evoke the feel of a National Park Service lodge built in the early 1900s.

Proximity to the Magic Kingdom:	Good, via launch
Proximity to Epcot:	Fair, via launch and monorail. You can also take the bus, but expect longer than average commute times.
Proximity to Hollywood:	Fair, via bus, but expect longer than average commutes.
Proximity to the Animal Kingdom:	Fair, via bus, but expect longer than average commutes.

Pluses

+ The lodge is heavily themed, and the pool area, with its erupting geyser and stone hot tubs, is especially dramatic.

+ On-site child-care facilities.

+ Tons of happy quasi-campers here. Families return to the Wilderness Lodge again and again.

+ The Wilderness Lodge Villas, starting at $395 a night, provide all the great amenities and a little more space.

Minuses

— Although it's one of the least expensive luxury options, it still isn't cheap.

— This is the only Magic Kingdom resort hotel without direct monorail service. The boat takes slightly longer than the bus. And bus service is frequently shared with Fort Wilderness, which means an extra stop on the way to Hollywood Studios, Epcot, and Animal Kingdom.

— The rooms are small and sleep only four people; the other luxury resorts sleep five. "It's a great resort once you get outside of your room," said a mom from Indiana. "But while inside the room we were practically on top of each other."

Overall Grade: ★★★ A great family-pleasing setting and a favorite with many of our readers.

Epcot Hotels

Most of the Epcot resorts—the Yacht and Beach Clubs, Board-Walk, Swan, and Dolphin—share their own "back-door" entrance into Epcot's World Showcase, accessed by water taxis and walkways. Unfortunately—and somewhat ironically, considering that these properties are marketed as "Epcot resorts"—it can be tricky to get to Epcot's front gates. The Future World section of Epcot usually opens at 9 am, but Epcot resort guests enter through the World Showcase, where the rides, shops, and restaurants don't open until 11 am. That means Epcot hotel guests have to walk through the World Showcase and enter Future World at a special rope-drop area. (Many people assume that the Epcot hotels offer bus service to the main entrance of Epcot. They don't.) The bad news is that this stroll through the World Showcase adds 10 minutes to your commute. The good news is that there are fewer people at this entrance point, so you can still get a jump on the crowds, a key factor if you're heading to a popular attraction like Soarin.'

By contrast, getting to Hollywood is a breeze. Water taxis leaving from the Epcot resort marinas will have you at the Hollywood gates within minutes. In addition, there are plenty of restaurants, clubs, and entertainment options around the lagoon. "We never left the Epcot resort area," wrote one mom from Texas. "Everything we wanted to do was right there."

The one Epcot hotel that doesn't follow this plan is the Caribbean Beach Resort, which is a mid-price property a bit apart from the others. It runs buses to both Hollywood Studios and Epcot; the Epcot bus lets you off at the Future World entrance.

BoardWalk Inn and Villas
★★★
407/939–5100

The BoardWalk Inn and Villas form the hub of a large complex with convention space, several restaurants and shops, the ESPN sports club, and a dance club and piano bar. The mood is turn-of-the-20th-century Atlantic City. Bright, attractive rooms are clustered above an old-fashioned boardwalk, and the action on the waterfront goes on until late at night.

"Once you stay at the BoardWalk, nothing else is good enough," wrote one enthusiastic grandmother of two in Ohio. "The location is perfect for both Epcot and Hollywood, and there's always free entertainment, like jugglers or comedians, to keep the kids happy."

Proximity to the Magic Kingdom: Fair, via bus
Proximity to Epcot: Excellent, via a short stroll
                                       or water taxi
Proximity to Hollywood: Excellent, via water taxi
Proximity to the Animal Kingdom: Fair, via bus

Pluses

+ Lots of entertainment: surrey bikes for rent, midway games, and a wider variety of restaurants and bars than you'd find at most resorts.

+ On-site health club.

+ On-site child-care facilities.

+ Great location for both Epcot and Hollywood.

+ Great restaurant choices, including the excellent Flying Fish Café.

Minuses

− Expensive, at $390 and up per night.

− Maybe too lively and hopping for families with very young kids. The boardwalk can get loud at night.

Overall grade: ★★★ You'll feel like you're right in the middle of the action—because you are.

Caribbean Beach Resort
★★
407/934–3400

This family-priced, 2,112-room resort is on 200 acres with a private lake surrounded by beaches. Each section of this mammoth hotel is painted a different tropical color and named for a different Caribbean island, and each "island" has its own shuttle-bus stop, beach, and pool with waterslide. The rooms, although small, are attractively decorated—some of the recently refurbished ones have either a *Pirates of the Caribbean* or *Finding Nemo* theme. There's a slight surcharge, $25–$50 depending on the season, for these rooms.

Proximity to the Magic Kingdom: Fair, via bus
Proximity to Epcot: Fair, via bus
Proximity to Hollywood: Fair, via bus
Proximity to the Animal Kingdom: Fair, via bus

Pluses

+ The price is right, starting at $149 a night.

+ The Pirate and Nemo rooms are absolutely adorable and themed to the max—for example, some of the furniture looks like cargo chests. "A little cheesy but our boys flipped out with joy," said a mom from Texas. "The excitement was well worth the extra $25 a night!"

+ Caribbean Cay, an artificial island with a playground, climbing fort, and small aviary, is fun for young kids.

+ The pirate-themed water play area, which offers small slides and fountains, is a hit with young kids.

+ A marina with watercraft is available.

Minuses

- Although the buses are regular, they must stop at all of the resort's many "islands." Expect a longer commute time to the parks.

- The place is huge. It may be a major hike from your hotel room to the food plaza or marina. If you have young kids, bring your own stroller.

Overall Grade: ★★ All the moderate-price resorts offer solid value for the money, but due to its size, Caribbean Beach is overwhelming. Try the others first.

★
Swan and Dolphin Resorts   407/934–4000
407/934–3000

This convention-resort complex made up of two side-by-side hotels is connected to Epcot and Hollywood by water taxis and bridges. The Swan and Dolphin are the only hotels not owned by Disney that are on Disney property and whose guests qualify for on-site perks. Sometimes called "twin" hotels (like the nearby Yacht and Beach Clubs), the Swan and Dolphin have separate check-ins but are alike in architecture and mood.

Proximity to the Magic Kingdom:	Fair, via bus
Proximity to Epcot:	Excellent, via water taxi
Proximity to Hollywood:	Excellent, via water taxi
Proximity to the Animal Kingdom:	Fair, via bus

Pluses

+ On-site child-care facilities.

+ The beach area has a playground, kiddie pools, water-slides, and a small marina with paddleboats.

+ Bike rentals, tennis courts, and a health club.

Minuses

— Somewhat expensive, with rates beginning at $219 per night, but if you can live without the full-throttle Disney ambience, this is the closest you'll get to Epcot and Hollywood Studios for the price.

— Conventioneers can erode the family feel.

— Since these resorts aren't owned by Disney, they don't qualify for the Magical Express Service and they don't have their own airport shuttles. In other words, you'll have to arrange for transportation from the airport to your hotel.

Overall grade: ★ A great place to go if the company is picking up the tab. Otherwise, try the Yacht and Beach Clubs first.

★★★
Yacht and Beach Clubs
407/934–7000
407/934–8000

Designed to resemble a turn-of-the-20th-century Nantucket seaside resort, the Yacht Club and Beach Club are side-by-side resorts that share many facilities. Both hotels are charming yet casual (think Polo Ralph Lauren), with sunny, airy rooms overlooking a freshwater lake and a wide variety of restaurants and sporting options.

Proximity to the Magic Kingdom:	Fair, via bus
Proximity to Epcot:	Excellent, via a short stroll or water taxi
Proximity to Hollywood:	Excellent, via water taxi
Proximity to the Animal Kingdom:	Fair, via bus

Pluses
+ Stormalong Bay, the water recreation area shared by the two resorts, is like a private water park. The sand-bottom "bay" contains pools of varying depths, whirlpools, waterslides, and a wrecked ship for atmosphere.

+ On-site child-care facilities.

+ Disney characters are on hand for breakfast at the Cape May Café in the Beach Club.

+ The two resorts share an on-site health club.

Minuses
— Price is the only real drawback. Rates begin at $340 per night.

Overall Grade: ★★★ These hotels enjoy a lot of repeat business from satisfied families.

Downtown Disney Hotels

These hotels are the first ones you encounter when you enter Disney property, and are a good choice for families who'll also be visiting Universal Studios, SeaWorld, or other Orlando attractions. Also, proximity to the action of Downtown Disney vastly increases your restaurant options.

Old Key West Resort

★★
407/827–7700

At the villas of Old Key West you'll get all the standard amenities of a Disney resort, plus a lot more room. The setting is pleasant, casual, and very Floridian in spirit. "We love the quieter atmosphere of Old Key West," wrote a mother of three from Maryland. "Our kids are young (ages 2, 5, and 7), so even with naps they're often too exhausted at night for us to take them to a restaurant and expect them to behave. We like being able to go 'home' to a villa and order pizza or make sandwiches. The villas are more like an apartment than a hotel room."

Proximity to the Magic Kingdom: Fair, via bus
Proximity to Epcot: Fair, via bus
Proximity to Hollywood: Fair, via bus
Proximity to the Animal Kingdom: Fair, via bus

Pluses

+ If you have more than two children and need to spread out or you'd like a kitchen to prepare your own meals, Old Key West is a good on-site option.

+ A water taxi provides swift transit to Downtown Disney.

+ Tennis courts, pools, bike rentals, shuffleboard, basketball, a marina, a sand play area, an arcade, and a fitness room are all on-site.

+ Prices run from $330 for a studio with kitchenette to $1,370 for a Grand Villa that can accommodate up to 12 people. If you're willing to swap proximity to the parks for more space, Old Key West may be just what you need.

Minuses
— Still pricier than off-site villas such as the Embassy Suites on Hotel Plaza Boulevard.

— Quieter, with less going on than at other resorts.

— No on-site child-care facilities, which is unusual in a resort at this price point.

— A longer-than-average commute to the theme parks. "We were impressed with the accommodations at Old Key West," reported a mom from Toronto, "but transport to the parks involved surprisingly lengthy trips."

Overall Grade: ★★ Very homey, with nice touches, and a great option for families seeking peace and quiet at the end of the day. But if you want lots of amenities and food choices, look elsewhere.

Port Orleans Resort
★★★
407/934–5000

This mid-price resort called Port Orleans has two sections. The French Quarter has manicured gardens, wrought-iron railings, and streets with cute names like Rue d'Baga. The Mardi Gras mood extends to the pool area, where alligators play jazz while King Triton sits atop a funky-looking waterslide, regally surveying his domain.

The Riverside section is a bit more down-home, with a steamboat-shaped lobby, general stores run by gingham-clad girls, and a swimming area themed on *Song of the South*. Schizophrenic in architecture, with white-column buildings encircling fishing holes and cotton mills, Riverside manages to mix in a variety of Southern clichés without losing its ditzy charm.

Insider's Secret

If you want to go all princess all the time, check out one of the 512 castle-themed Royal Guest Rooms in the Magnolia Bend section of Port Orleans Riverside. The concept is that Princess Tiana from *The Princess and the Frog* has invited her royal friends on vacation. Rooms have what one Imagineer described as "over-the-top" theming with fiber-optic art hanging over ornate gold-and-crystal beds, bright-colored banners on the walls, and elaborate draperies and bedcovers. A surcharge that can range from $25 to $50 will be added on, but families are already raving about these rooms. They are quickly sold out, so check availability before promising one to your personal princess.

If Huck Finn ever married Scarlett O'Hara, this is where they'd come on their honeymoon.

Since the French Quarter is only half the size of Riverside, it's a shorter walk to the lobby, pool, food court, and shuttle-bus station; at Riverside, getting around is a bit more of a headache. Both resorts have a fast-food court and a bar that offers live entertainment; Riverside also has a full-service restaurant called Boatwright's, which serves a mix of Cajun food and American classics and has a few nice extras such as a selection of specialty New Orleans microbrews.

Proximity to the Magic Kingdom:	Fair, via bus
Proximity to Epcot:	Fair, via bus
Proximity to Hollywood:	Fair, via bus
Proximity to the Animal Kingdom:	Fair, via bus

Pluses

+ Affordable, starting at $149 a night, and well designed.

+ Great pool areas (especially at the French Quarter).

+ Both hotels have marinas with a selection of watercraft as well as bike rentals. The Sassagoula Steamboat offers easy water transport from both resorts to Downtown Disney.

+ Refurbished rooms now have flat-screen TVs, queen-size beds, and upgraded amenities. Riverside-section upgrade includes 512 princess-themed Royal Guest Rooms.

+ Riverside has a two-hour pirate-themed adventure (young buccaneers seize a boat and follow clues to find treasure) three mornings a week for ages 4–12 ($34).

Minuses

— In the off-season these two resorts share a bus to all major parks, which means a slightly longer commute.

Overall Grade: ★★★ You get a good deal here in more ways than one.

Saratoga Springs Resort and Spa
★★
407/827–1100

Saratoga Springs recalls the posh upstate New York retreats of the 1890s, complete with a horse-racing theme. Villas here are numerous and roomy. The recently updated and very attractive Treehouse Villas, for instance, have raised decks and enough space to accommodate large families. They're truly a home away from home.

Proximity to the Magic Kingdom:	Fair, via bus
Proximity to Epcot:	Fair, via bus
Proximity to Hollywood:	Fair, via bus
Proximity to the Animal Kingdom:	Fair, via bus

Pluses

+ Proximity to the restaurants and entertainment of Downtown Disney via water taxi.

+ Access to the biggest and best health club in WDW and a full-service spa.

+ The location is great for golfers—Saratoga Springs is adjacent to the Lake Buena Vista course.

+ A good choice for family-reunion groups seeking larger accommodations and a relaxed atmosphere with plenty of space for the kids to play in.

+ The grotto pool, complete with man-made hot springs, is one of the most dramatic hotel pools in WDW. Even the auxiliary pools are beautifully themed, with great play areas for the kids.

Minuses

— With villas starting at $330, Saratoga Springs is more expensive than off-site villa accommodations. The larger, home-style villas can run as high as $1,370.

— Saratoga Springs is often used by corporations for retreats and conferences, so you may find yourself in the middle of a group of businesspeople.

— Since you're pretty far out of the Disney loop, expect a longer commute time via bus to any of the major parks.

— At 65 acres, Saratoga Springs is so spread out that you might find yourself in a room far from the food court and main pool. Request to be as close as possible to the main building when you make your reservation.

Overall Grade: ★★ Roomy and close to Downtown Disney. The trouble is it's not particularly close to anything else.

Animal Kingdom Hotels

These hotels are in a surprisingly central location vis-à-vis the four theme parks and Downtown Disney.

★★

All-Star Sports, All-Star Music,   407/939–5000
and All-Star Movies Resorts   407/939–6000
and 407/939–7000

The All-Star resorts have built such a loyal following that, despite having about 6,000 rooms, they fill up quickly. There are three reasons for this success—price, price, and price.

All-Star Sports has five sections, each decorated with a tennis, football, surfing, basketball, or baseball theme. At All-Star Music, you can choose between jazz, rock and roll, country, calypso, and Broadway tunes. All-Star Movies offers The Love Bug, Toy Story, Fantasia, 101 Dalmatians, and The Mighty Ducks.

The in-your-face graphics of the brightly colored buildings and the resort's general zaniness appeal to kids. There are giant tennis-ball cans and cowboy boots, a walk-through jukebox, and footballs the size of houses. At the diamond-shaped baseball pool at All-Star Sports, you'll find Goofy as pitcher; Mickey conducts sprays of water in the Fantasia pool of All-Star Movies; and show tunes play all day under the marquee in the Broadway district of All-Star Music. It may be budget, but it ain't boring.

Proximity to the Magic Kingdom:	Fair, via bus
Proximity to Epcot:	Fair, via bus
Proximity to Hollywood:	Fair, via bus
Proximity to the Animal Kingdom:	Good, via a short bus ride

Helpful Hint

If you don't care which All-Star Resort section you're in, request a room near the lobby when you book. It's a little more expensive, but this can save you lots of walking each time you leave your room to catch a bus or eat a meal.

Time-Saving Tip

The All-Star Resorts are enormous and check-in time is a madhouse. If you arrive before 3 pm, try to check in early. If your room isn't available, you can store your bags and return later, when you'll only have to wait in the shorter, swifter-moving "key pickup" line.

Pluses

+ In a word, cost. Rooms start at $82.

+ The 214 suites at All-Star Music are, along with those at the Art of Animation Resort, among the most affordable on-site suite options. Units that sleep six start at $225 a night. "We used to get two rooms side by side," reports a mom of three from North Carolina, "which meant a girls' room with me and our daughters and a guys' room with my husband and son. All staying together in a suite is endlessly easier and better, and the kitchen, while small, was an added bonus."

+ All the All-Stars have special rooms for people with disabilities. For $109 a night, you can have a slightly larger ground-floor suite with roll-in showers.

+ The free shuttle buses are a good transportation option, considering the price. When you get into this price range at off-site hotels, you often have to pay for a shuttle.

Minuses

— Food options are limited to fast-food courts and pool bars only, with no restaurants or indoor bars.

— Sports options are limited; swimming is it.

— The rooms are very small. They sleep four, but you'll be bunched.

— Long check-in lines.

— By breaking each resort into five separate sections, Disney is striving to eliminate that sleeping-in-the-middle-of-Penn-Station feel. But the bottom line is, it takes more effort to get around a huge hotel than a small one.

Insider's Secret

If your child adores *101 Dalmatians* or is a big football buff, you can indeed ask to be lodged in that section of the All-Star Resorts when you make your reservation. Disney won't guarantee you'll get your request, but they'll try.

Overall Grade: ★★ Lots of bang for the buck here. Just don't expect too many amenities.

Animal Kingdom Lodge and Villas

★★★
407/938–3000

Step inside the massive lobby of the Animal Kingdom Lodge and you'll be transported . . . outdoors. From the thatch roof to the enormous mud fireplace, and from the rope bridges to the tribal art to the lighting that's designed to simulate sunrise to sunset, the resort creates the feel of a game lodge in the middle of a wildlife preserve.

The Animal Kingdom Lodge is in the middle of a 33-acre savanna where more than 200 animals freely roam. Thirty-six species of mammals, including giraffes, zebras, and gazelles, and 26 species of birds, such as the sacred ibis and African spoonbill, live within the working wildlife preserve. The kopje, a series of rock outcroppings, serves as a natural barrier but is also an elevated walkway that offers panoramas of the landscape and the chance for you to come within 15 feet of the animals. If you'd rather engage in animal viewing from the comfort of your own balcony, many of the guest rooms have a savanna view.

The villas have their own animal reserve, check-in, and a cool Indian restaurant, and the rooms are lovely.

Proximity to the Magic Kingdom:	Fair, via bus
Proximity to Epcot:	Fair, via bus
Proximity to Hollywood:	Fair, via bus
Proximity to the Animal Kingdom:	Excellent, via a short bus ride

Pluses

+ A dramatic and exotic setting.

+ The Animal Kingdom Lodge has truly fantastic restaurants, including Boma, a buffet restaurant with especially good breakfasts, and Jiko, which serves excellent and authentic African food and an exclusively South African wine list.

+ Lots of extras for the kids, including tours that tell about the animals and "bush camp activities" such as African crafts, games, and folktales. You can even track the animals with night-vision goggles!

+ On-site child-care facilities, spa, and health club.

+ Some Animal Kingdom Lodge rooms have bunk beds, a good choice if your kids are older, different genders, or for some other reason balk at sleeping together.

+ The Animal Kingdom Lodge Villas are relatively new and very attractive.

Minuses

— Although not as expensive as many of the other luxury hotels, the Lodge can be pricey, with rates beginning at $290 a night. Villas begin at $335.

— The out-of-the-way location means a longer-than-average bus ride to the Magic Kingdom, Epcot, and Hollywood. Buses stop at both the resort and the villas, which adds five minutes to every commute.

— They save the architectural drama for the public spaces. Rooms are small and basic.

Overall Grade: ★★★ The most unusual resort on Disney property.

Coronado Springs Resort
★★
407/939–1000

Disney's only moderately priced convention hotel—rooms begin at $159—has a Mexican theme, with Spanish-tile roofs, adobe walls, and a pool area that is dominated by an imposing Mayan temple. The rooms are scattered around a 15-acre lake. There's a full-service restaurant called Maya Grill, a food court, and also an adult-oriented club called RIX with a bar and small dance floor.

Proximity to the Magic Kingdom:	Fair, via bus
Proximity to Epcot:	Fair, via bus
Proximity to Hollywood:	Fair, via bus
Proximity to the Animal Kingdom:	Good, via a short bus ride

Pluses

+ Dramatic pool area with waterslide, arcade, bar, fast-food stand, and theme playground.

+ Marina with standard boat and bike rentals.

+ Coronado Springs offers plenty of choices when it comes to food. In addition to the full-service restaurant, the food court provides far more options than the typical moderate resort, and RIX has a tasty bar menu.

Minuses

— Coronado Springs is a convention hotel, meaning it has more businesspeople and fewer families than is typical for a Disney resort.

— The resort is quite spread out, even by Disney standards. If you're in one of the more far-flung rooms, you face a 15-minute walk to the food court and shuttle-bus stop.

Overall Grade: ★★ Because of the convention trade, Coronado Springs has more amenities than are typical in this price range. But the conventioneer vibe can also be a turnoff.

ESPN Wide World of Sports Resorts

In Disney-speak, saying you're near the Wide World of Sports is another way of saying you're not near anything. The two value resorts here are less expensive partly because their out-of-the-way location means a longer commute to the parks. But if you have your own car or don't mind an extra 10 minutes on a bus, there are bargains to be found.

Pop Century Resort

★
407/938–4000

At Pop Century, each pair of buildings is themed to a different decade, from the 1950s to the 1990s. Expect the same larger-than-life icons that earmark the All-Stars. Cultural touchstones from each decade—including giant yo-yos, Big Wheel bikes, and Rubik's cubes—mark the entrances, and the roofs are lined with catchphrases from each era.

Insider's Secret

Request placement in the 1960s section when you make your reservation at Pop Century. It's a bit louder—and during the on-season they may charge you $10 more per night—but you're close to the bus stops, food court, and the fun Hippie Dippy pool. The '80s and '90s sections are a long walk from most of the hotel amenities.

Proximity to the Magic Kingdom: Fair, via bus
Proximity to Epcot: Fair, via bus
Proximity to Hollywood: Fair, via bus
Proximity to the Animal Kingdom: Fair, via bus

Pluses

+ The price is affordable, starting at $82 a night.

+ Free transportation, a rarity in this price range.

Minuses

− Food options are limited to a fast-food court.

− This resort is a special favorite for cheerleading competitions, bands, and other teenage groups. It can get loud and rowdy in the pool areas.

− Sporting options are limited to swimming.

− The rooms are small; they sleep four but you'll be crowded.

− The out-of-the-way location means a slightly longer commute by bus to all of the theme parks.

Overall Grade: ★★ The value resorts offer numerous perks at a reasonable price and are a great option for on-the-go families who primarily use their resort as a place to shower and sleep.

Art of Animation Resort

Rating N/A
407/934–7639

Based on the overwhelming popularity of the handful of family suites at All-Star Music Resorts, Disney is radically expanding the concept with the Art of Animation Resort. The resort will open in four stages, each themed around a popular Disney film.

The first three sections are Finding Nemo, Cars, and The Lion King, which collectively add almost 1,200 value-priced family suites to the Disney line-up. A fourth and final section,

The Little Mermaid, will have regular guest rooms. The Art of Animation is located adjacent to the Pop Century, and the two resorts are connected by a bridge.

The suites are popular because they offer a lot more space and comfort, and many families consider them a far more workable option than two adjoining rooms. There's a master bedroom, two bathrooms, a kitchenette, and three separate sleeping areas—meaning that six people can stay comfortably. The movie-based theming is also far more intense and immersive than in the older Disney resorts, making the Art of Animation tremendous fun for kids. Prices start at $250 a night.

Note: The Art of Animation is opening just after we go to press; thus, we are unable to rate it or survey families at this time. Stay tuned: next year's edition will have more details.

Proximity to the Magic Kingdom: Fair, via bus
Proximity to Epcot: Fair, via bus
Proximity to Hollywood: Fair, via bus
Proximity to the Animal Kingdom: Fair, via bus

Helpful Hint

So, which on-site hotel is best for you? It comes down to four questions:

How much are we willing to spend?

What park do we want to be closest to?

Are there must-have amenities (e.g., dining or sporting options, villa-style accommodations)?

What theme seems the coolest?

Pluses

+ This resort marks Disney's real commitment to value-priced on-site suites.

+ Free transportation, a rarity in this price range.

Minuses
- Food options are limited to a fast-food court.
- Sporting options are limited to swimming.
- The out-of-the-way location means a slightly longer commute by bus to all of the theme parks.

Off-Site Hotels: Which Location Is Best?

The three main off-site areas that Disney visitors frequent are Exits 62 and 68 off Interstate 4, and International Drive.

Exits 62 and 68 are within a 10-minute drive of the theme parks. Exit 68 (U.S. 535) has a vast number of chain hotels and eateries, and is your best bet if you want to get close to Disney without paying Disney prices.

Exit 62, which leads to U.S. 192, has similar chains represented, but the rates are about $30 less per night. Why? The hotels are, in general, older than the hotels of Exit 68. The whole area is a little less spiffy, but still close to Disney property.

International Drive is farther out, about 20 minutes from the Disney theme parks. This area has representatives from every chain restaurant and hotel you've ever heard of, as well as entertainment options like malls and miniature golf. International Drive is the conduit that runs between SeaWorld and Universal Orlando, so it's a smart central location if you're planning to visit those parks as well as Disney. Note that the more upscale end of International Drive is near SeaWorld and the convention center, to the south. As you head north toward Universal Studios, it gets a little shabbier, although it's still a safe and family-centric area.

How to Get the Best Deals on Off-Site Hotels

Orlando has more hotel rooms than any other U.S. city besides Las Vegas, so there are plenty of beds out there for the taking. Here are a few tips to make sure you're getting the most for your money.

Quick Guide to

Hotels	Style	Description
Comfort Suites at Maingate East	Budget	Inexpensive but close to Disney, free breakfast, best value for suites
Embassy Suites Lake Buena Vista	Moderate	Good location, free breakfast buffet, lots of sporting activities
Hyatt Regency Grand Cypress	Luxury	Luxury hotel, magnificent pool, camplike activities for kids
La Quinta International Drive North	Budget	Convenient location for all three parks, free breakfast and shuttles
Loews Universal Resorts: Hard Rock, Portofino Bay, Royal Pacific	Luxury	Three great options on Universal Orlando property
Magical Memories Villas	Condo-style	Private homes and condos for rent, good choice for large families
Residence Inn SeaWorld International Center	Moderate	Quiet and homelike suites, SeaWorld packages, free breakfast buffet
Sheraton Vistana Resort	Condo-style	Popular with our readers—well maintained and quiet
Sheraton Vistana Village	Condo-style	Popular with our readers—well-maintained and plenty of room

Off-Site Hotels

Phone and Web	Nearest Theme Park	Price Range
407/397–7848 choicehotels.com	Walt Disney World	$89 and up
407/239–1144 embassysuites.com	Walt Disney World	$113 and up
407/239–1234 hyattregencygrand cypress.com	Walt Disney World	$165 and up
407/351–4100 lq.com	Universal Studios, SeaWorld	$74 and up
407/363–8000 universalorlando.com	Universal Orlando	$219 and up
407/390–8200 magicalmemories.com	Depends on location	$109 and up most $144 and up
407/313–3611 residenceinn.com	SeaWorld	$119 and up
407/239–3100 starwood.com	Walt Disney World	$140 and up
407/238–5000 starwood.com	Equidistant from all	$140 and up

The Orlando Magicard is free and offers 20% to 30% discounts on area hotels, as well as restaurants and non-Disney attractions. You can download a card by visiting www.orlandoinfo.com/magicard.

Try calling both the hotel chain's toll-free number and the direct line to the particular hotel. You may be quoted different rates.

If you especially like a particular hotel chain, you can simply call their toll-free number and ask for the hotel nearest Disney World. This eliminates the element of surprise, because one Hampton Inn looks pretty much like another. Big chains have multiple Orlando locations, so stress that you'd like to be as close as possible to the Disney gates, preferably near Exit 62 or 68. Proximity to Disney raises the rate about 20%, but location is important; if you end up in a hotel near the airport or downtown, that means a major daily commute, and Orlando traffic can be brutal.

Finally, six little words can save you major bucks. When talking to a reservation clerk always ask, "Do you have any discounts available?" Remember that the reservation clerk works for the hotel, so if he can sell you a room at $95 a night there's no incentive for him to tell you how you can drop the rate to $79. But if you specifically inquire about discounts, he has to tell you.

Things to Ask When Booking a Room at an Off-Site Hotel

There's a wide range of amenities and perks among the hundreds of hotels in the Orlando area. To make sure you're getting top value for your dollar, take nothing for granted. Some $250-a-night hotels charge you for breakfast; some $75 ones do not. Some hotels count 12-year-olds as adults, others consider 19-year-olds to be children. Some relatively inexpensive hotels have kids' clubs; some larger and more costly ones are geared to con-

Time-Saving Tip

Many off-site hotels claim to run shuttles to the theme parks, but beware. Relying on off-site transportation can sometimes make for a long commute. The worst situations are when two or three hotels share a shuttle and you have to make stops at all of them. Even if a resort has its own shuttle, it may make stops at all of the major parks on each run, meaning commutes of up to an hour just to get from your hotel to the theme park of your choice. A lengthy bus ride is maddening in the morning when the kids are eager to get to the rides, and at night, when you're all exhausted, it can be disastrous.

A mother of three has this story: "We loved our resort along Highway 192 (Exit 62); very nice, with good amenities. But the shuttle was awful. It was hot, crowded, and took two hours to get back from the Magic Kingdom on a night after the fireworks. The hotel advertises that it is '4 miles from Disney' but it doesn't tell you that its shuttle stops at five other hotels and all four theme parks. We like the hotel well enough to go back, but next time we'll get a rental car."

To make matters worse, some off-site hotels charge you for shuttle rides. They may tell you that by buying shuttle tickets you'll save the "horrendous" cost of Disney parking, but the truth is Disney parking is $14 no matter how many people are in a car, and the shuttle-bus tickets can range from $5 to $12 per person. And it still may take you two hours to get there!

This is why I suggest that families staying off-site either drive to Orlando or get a rental car. If you do decide to use an off-site resort shuttle, be sure to ask if it's a private shuttle and if service to theme parks is direct. If you don't like what you hear, rent a car or call a cab.

vention and business travelers and don't even have an arcade. The moral is, always ask.

The following questions should help you ferret out the best deal.

- Does the hotel provide in-room babysitters? Is there an on-site child-care center or kids' club? What's the cost? How far in advance do you have to make reservations?

- Does the hotel provide direct shuttle service to the theme parks? How often do the buses run? How early do they begin and how late do they run? How many stops do they make? Do you share the shuttles with other hotels? Do they run to the theme parks directly or make a circuit of all four? Is there a fee?

- Do kids stay free? Up to what age?

- Do you have any suites with kitchens? If not, can we rent refrigerators or microwaves?

- Does the hotel provide a free buffet breakfast?

- What fast-food or family-style restaurants are nearby?

- Are laundry facilities on the premises?

- Can I buy tickets to area attractions through the hotels? Are the tickets discounted? (Note: Disney tickets are rarely discounted, but sometimes off-site hotels offer discounts to Universal Orlando, SeaWorld, and area dinner shows.)

Money-Saving Tip

If you're staying off-site and thus will be eating at least some of your meals outside of Disney property, pick up a few of those free tourist magazines that are available in the airport and all around Orlando. They're full of dining discount coupons, many of them for family-oriented restaurants near the theme parks.

Helpful Hint

One note of caution: An extremely cheap hotel rate, say $55 or less, generally means that the hotel is in a less desirable part of town than those I've listed, both in terms of theme-park proximity and general security.

Great Off-Site Hotels for Families

Orlando has plenty of hotel rooms, so how is a family to choose? The listed properties that follow are tried-and-true family favorites based on proximity to Disney World, amenities, and value. For descriptions of the Universal Orlando resorts, see Chapter 14.

Two notes: Since the hotels listed are all recommended as good family choices, we did not provide star ratings. And since Walt Disney World is so huge and spread out, our "proximity to Disney" rating is based on the distance between the hotel and Disney's main entrance gate.

There are plenty of great hotels in the Orlando area, but based on our visits and comments from readers, we've narrowed it down to two suggestions per category: luxury, midpriced, condos, and budget.

Recommended Off-Site Luxury Hotels

Hyatt Regency Grand Cypress   407/239–1234
www.hyattregencygrandcypress.com

This beautiful hotel has expansive grounds, lush landscaping, spiffy restaurants, and numerous sporting options. It's a serene oasis and a great choice for families who want the option to escape from Disney in the evening and yet remain conveniently close to the parks. Prices start at about $165 in the off-season, $225 in the on-season. There is a discount for advanced booking.

A $22 surcharge per room per day is automatically added, but it covers a plethora of extras: shuttle transportation to the TTC, where you can catch the monorail or buses to all Disney parks, bike and watercraft rental, poolside activities for the kids, Internet access, an elaborate pitch-and-putt golf course, a climbing wall, and access to the health club.

Proximity to Disney World:	Excellent, via a 5-minute drive or shuttle service
Proximity to Universal:	Good, via a 15-minute drive
Proximity to SeaWorld:	Good, via a 15-minute drive

Pluses

+ The pool area is gorgeous, with 12 waterfalls and several very secluded hot tubs. There's a terrific slide for kids and a section of the pool is heated, if you're traveling off-season.

+ You can golf, play tennis, and enjoy a far wider than normal range of resort activities. Pleasant trails wind through the grounds for walkers and runners. If you're looking to schedule a day "off" from theme-park touring, simply hanging around the Hyatt can keep you more than entertained.

+ Camp Hyatt has great activities for kids 3–12, such as pool games, nature walks, poolside movies, canoeing, tennis lessons, fire-pit marshmellow roasting, and pitch-and-putt golf. It runs daily during the summer and holidays as well as weekends throughout the off-season. Prices are $90 a day and $60 for evenings, and include meals. A half-day session with no meals is $45. (Children must be toilet trained; the resort will help you arrange in-room sitting if you need child care for babies or toddlers.) Check to make sure Camp Hyatt is running and confirm prices when you make your reservation.

+ Sophisticated dining options include Hemingway's, dramatically perched atop one of the pool waterfalls, and La

Coquina's Chef's Table, which offers a seven-course tasting menu served in a luxurious nook tucked back in the restaurant kitchen.

+ The Hyatt basically backs up to Disney World grounds and offers an easy commute to any Disney theme park.

Minuses

— Price: both the rooms and restaurants can be expensive, especially during the on-season or if you upgrade to suite-style accommodations.

— The Hyatt frequently hosts conventions and attracts a more adult crowd than other area hotels. But in the past two years, they have added more family-oriented activities and report that their leisure guests now outnumber their business guests.

The Loews Resorts at Universal Studios: Hard Rock Hotel, Portofino Bay Hotel, and Royal Pacific Resort
www.universalorlando.com   **407/363–8000**

If you want to go the luxury route, consider the three hotels located within the Universal Studios complex. They are reviewed in detail in Chapter 14. Although also affiliated with a theme park, they have a far calmer, elegant, and removed quality than the Disney properties, while still offering plenty of benefits for families.

Recommended Midprice Resorts

Embassy Suites Lake Buena Vista   **407/239–1144**
www.embassysuites.com

The Embassy Suites chain is very popular with our readers, especially this location. The suites include kitchenettes, the hotels are generally well maintained, and a bountiful breakfast is included in the price. There are five Embassy Suites in Orlando; rates at the Lake Buena Vista location, which is the closest to Disney World, range from $113 to $146 during the off-season and $147 to $177 during the on-season.

Note: The two International Drive locations—Embassy Suites International Drive South and Embassy Suites International Drive Jamaican Court—are also convenient to area theme parks, being reasonably close to Disney World and very close to Universal Studios and SeaWorld. Embassy Suites Lake Buena Vista South is under construction as we go to press, and will not only be brand-spanking new but also very well located in relation to Disney. Look for more details of the revamped hotel in our next edition.

Proximity to Disney World:	Good, via a 10-minute drive
Proximity to Universal:	Fair, via a 15-minute drive
Proximity to SeaWorld:	Good, via a 10-minute drive

Pluses

+ You can access Disney property through the Downtown Disney gate without the hassle of getting on I–4.

+ Complimentary breakfast buffet with made-to-order pancakes and an omelet station.

+ Kitchenettes make it easy to keep snacks and sandwich supplies on hand.

+ A shopping center with a grocery and fast-food restaurants is nearby. And there's a Pizza Hut Express in the lobby.

+ The heated indoor-outdoor pool is an asset in the winter.

+ Lots of sports options: a gym, tennis courts, basketball, shuffleboard, and volleyball.

+ Although the resort isn't new, the grounds have been well maintained.

Minuses

— Proximity to I–4 means a consistently high noise level.

— This Embassy Suites is on Palm Parkway surrounded by many other hotels, which means you may hit traffic getting to the parks—another reason to start early.

Residence Inn SeaWorld International Center
www.residenceinn.com   **407/313–3611**

The suites at the Residence Inn are especially homelike, and you can choose between one- to three-room units, all with separate areas for eating and relaxing. Plus, the hotel is practically at the back door of SeaWorld and Discovery Cove. Disney World and Universal Studios are each about 5 miles away. Prices begin at $110 for a studio, $149 for a one-room suite with sofa bed, and go up to $229 for a three-room (two bedrooms and a living room with sofa bed) suite. During peak times the prices rise about $20 a night. The property features a heated outdoor pool, a game room, a sports court with basketball and tennis, a health club, and a children's playground. "My husband hates crowds and noise and was very skeptical about taking a vacation in Orlando," a woman from Michigan wrote to us. "But even he had to admit that the Residence Inn was very relaxing and that SeaWorld was a wonderful theme park."

Proximity to Disney World:	Good, via a 10-minute drive
Proximity to Universal:	Good, via a 10-minute drive
Proximity to SeaWorld:	Excellent, via a 5-minute drive or shuttle ride

Pluses

+ Suites are spacious and the kitchens are well equipped.

+ Complimentary hot breakfast buffet.

+ Packages including SeaWorld tickets are available.

+ Complimentary theme-park transportation.

Minuses
- The bigger the suite, the higher the price.

- The hotel is a bit off the main drag of International Drive. For families seeking peace and privacy, that actually may be a plus, but you'll have to drive for every meal unless you're eating in your own kitchen.

Recommended Condo Properties

Magical Memories Villas   407/390–8200
www.magicalmemories.com

One can only imagine how thrilled Disney is that this independent rental agency has adopted the word "magical"—perhaps the most frequently employed word in Disney promotional materials. But Magical Memories, while having no affiliation with Disney, can offer good deals for families. The company handles both condo and house rentals in nine different neighborhoods throughout Orlando. If you want to pay for a home with a private pool in a gated community, that's certainly available, but most of the rentals are clean, simply furnished, safe apartments in condo complexes. Rates start surprisingly low: during the off-season you'll pay $109 for a two-bedroom condo and $179 for a five-bedroom house with a private pool. During the on-season, condos begin at $129 a night and houses at $224 a night. Be sure to browse the website to see all your options. There's a substantial range of amenities and prices.

But the benefits can be substantial as well, as outlined by a mother from Canada. "Because we have a family of six, we would have had to rent two hotel rooms, so renting a house was ideal for our situation—not to mention that we split the cost with another family. We ended up with a five-bedroom, five-bath house with all the perks. They said it was minutes from Disney, and it really was."

Proximity to Disney:	Minimum 5 miles, maximum 8 miles
Proximity to Universal:	Maximum 16 miles
Proximity to SeaWorld:	Maximum 13 miles

Pluses

+ Good choice for large families and groups, since you can get a multi-bedroom house or condo with a well-equipped kitchen and all the conveniences of a hotel.

+ If you're staying at one of the condo-style Magical Memories villas, you'll also have use of the villa clubhouse. Some have amenities such as Wi-Fi, exercise rooms, larger pools, etc. The Magical Memories Villas encompass 15 different villa sites, and each clubhouse is different, so if you're seeking a specific amenity, be sure to ask when reserving.

Minuses

— This isn't like a familiar hotel chain where you know what to expect. There's a range in the quality of accommodations.

— For rentals of four nights or fewer you'll be charged a cleaning fee based on the size of your unit.

— A stay of three nights is required for the villas and five nights for the houses.

— There's a very strict reservation and payment policy. This isn't something you can cancel at the last minute, like a hotel, so make sure your plans are firm before you book.

Sheraton Vistana Resort and	407/239–3100
Sheraton Vistana Resort Villages	for the resort,
www.starwood.com	407/238–5000 for the Villages

Both of the Sheraton Vistana properties have been perpetual favorites with our readers since we first began doing resort surveys. One mom wrote, mirroring many other letters, "We found the Villages to be very pretty, very quiet, and very clean. And it took us only 15 minutes to drive to Disney World."

The two properties are located fairly close to each other, with the older Sheraton Vistana Resort being slightly more convenient to Disney and the Villages being on International Drive. The Villages is the newer and more upscale of the two, but the Resort is the favorite of many families with older children, who report they have more activities. One grandfather of five, who stayed at both properties in the course of a single week, distinguishes them thusly: "Both properties were a good value, but when we had all the kids down we preferred the Resort, which had a lot going on. When we put the kids on the plane and settled down to relax by the pool, the Villages were the better choice."

Unusually well decorated and maintained, these villas supply almost anything a family could require. One-bedroom villas begin at $140 in the off-season and $189 in the on-season; two-bedroom villas begin at $177 off-season and $219 on-season.

Proximity to Disney World: Good, via a 15-minute drive
Proximity to Universal: Good, via a 15-minute drive
Proximity to SeaWorld: Good, via a 15-minute drive

Pluses

+ Activities offered in the game room during the day and in-room babysitting at night allow parents to have some private time. Some of the activities have modest fees, but many are free.

+ A central location near both International Drive and I-4 makes it easy to get to all the theme parks and to family-friendly restaurants and minor attractions along International Drive.

+ The villas are larger and more comfortable than those in most other all-suites hotels.

Minuses

− On-property food options are limited, although there's a casual deli-style restaurant and pool bar. Since most families take advantage of the villa kitchenettes and there are plenty of family-friendly restaurants in the area, the lack of on-site dining options is rarely a problem.

− The condos are spread out at both locations, so it really does feel like you're more "at home" than "on vacation." This is an advantage for families who are seeking normalcy at the end of an active day, but a disadvantage for families who like to keep the rah-rah vacation feel going 24/7.

Recommended Budget Hotels

Comfort Suites at Maingate East   407/397–7848
www.comfortsuitesfl.com

This hotel is cheaper than most of the area suite-style hotels, largely because of its location off Route 192. Also called the Irlo Bronson Memorial Highway, Route 192 isn't as upscale as International Drive, but the hotel is clean and comfortable, the staff are pleasant, and the price is definitely right. Maingate East is a mere 2 miles from Disney property, and if you're looking for a location that's both affordable and close enough to be able to return to your hotel for a midday break, the Comfort Suites at Maingate East is a good option. Prices range from $89 to $149 during the off-season and $119 to $189 during the on-season.

Proximity to Disney World:	Excellent, via a 5-minute drive
Proximity to Universal:	Fair, via a 20-minute drive
Proximity to SeaWorld:	Fair, via a 20-minute drive

Pluses

+ Starting at $89 for the smallest suite, it's hard to beat the price.

+ Suites have either partial dividers or separate rooms, plus microwaves, refrigerators, coffeemakers, and sleeper sofas.

+ A deluxe continental breakfast is included.

+ This is as close as you'll get to Disney property at this price point; and the Maingate East entrance means you can skip I-4 traffic altogether.

Minuses

− The one-bedroom suites are comfortable for families of four or fewer. While the website says the suites can accommodate a family of six, you'll be cramped.

− Route 192 may be the least scenic part of Orlando. You're close to a funky little amusement park, endless chain restaurants, and big-box discount stores. But one of the reasons we recommend the Comfort Suites over other properties in the area is that it's pretty far off the main drag and thus quieter and more secluded than the others. In fact, keep your eyes peeled, since it's easy to miss the hotel entrance altogether.

La Quinta International Drive North
www.lq.com   **407/351–4100**

There are plenty of La Quintas in Orlando, but this location is especially appealing to families who are headed to Universal Studios. Rooms begin as low as $74 in the off-season. During peak times prices climb to the $79–$120 range. Still a deal.

Proximity to Disney:	Fair, via a 20-minute drive
Proximity to Universal:	Excellent, via a 5-minute drive
Proximity to SeaWorld:	Good, via a 10-minute drive

Pluses

+ It's an easy drive to SeaWorld and Universal and a bit farther to Disney. The hotel runs complimentary shuttles to the theme parks.

+ There are plenty of family-friendly chain and budget restaurants along I-Drive.

+ Complimentary breakfast is included and there are laundry facilities on-site.

Minuses

– The commute to Disney can be problematic if you're traveling at peak traffic times.

– The I-Drive location, while bringing you close to services, means you'll also have to deal with traffic and noise.

CHAPTER

3

Once You Get There

Bare Necessities: Strollers, Babies, and First Aid

Whether you're pregnant, traveling with a baby, or nursing a sore ankle, Disney World is prepared to accommodate your needs.

Strollers

Strollers are available for rent at each theme park for $15 (single) and $31 (double). (If you book for multiple days, the price per day drops to $13 for a single and $27 for a double.)

At these rates, if you need a stroller every day it's obviously most cost-effective to bring one from home. But if you have an older child who will only need a stroller at Epcot, a rental isn't a bad option.

> If you're renting a stroller for more than one day, you don't have to get in line every morning. On your first park visit, tell them you want, for example, a four-day stroller rental, and they'll give you coupons for four days. After that you can skip the rental line and go directly to the stroller pick-up booth.

- All kids 3 and under need a stroller, for napping as well as riding and resting.

- For kids 4 to 6, the general rule is this: Strollers are a must at Epcot, nice in the Magic Kingdom, and less needed at the Animal Kingdom or Hollywood, where the walkable areas of the parks are smaller and you spend a lot of time sitting in shows.

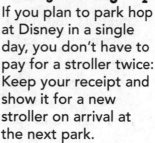

Money-Saving Tip
If you plan to park hop at Disney in a single day, you don't have to pay for a stroller twice: Keep your receipt and show it for a new stroller on arrival at the next park.

- On busy days the Magic Kingdom opens an additional stroller-rental stand outside the main gate, before you enter the bag-check area. This location is never as crowded as the rental stand inside the park.

- Tie something like a bandanna or a balloon to your stroller to mark it; otherwise, when you emerge from a ride it may be impossible to find your stroller in a sea of look-alikes. Also, people sometimes just grab the nearest

Helpful Hint
Just because your stroller isn't where you left it doesn't mean it's been taken—it may simply have been moved aside. Families often stop in midstride when they see an appealing attraction and abandon their stroller in the middle of the sidewalk. There are Disney cast members whose sole duty is to collect and rearrange these strollers, lining them up outside rides and packing them as close together as possible. Keep looking—you'll likely find your stroller a few yards away from where you left it.

stroller without checking the name tag, but most people stop short of taking a personal belonging.

@ Still can't find your stroller? In the Animal Kingdom replacement strollers are at Mombasa Marketplace, and in Hollywood they can be found at Tatooine Traders. In the Magic Kingdom, check in at Tinker Bell's Treasures in Fantasyland, the Frontierland Trading Post in Frontierland, or Buzz Lightyear's Space Ranger Spin in Tomorrowland. At Epcot you can get a new stroller at the World Traveler shop between France and the United Kingdom or the Glas und Porzellan shop in Germany. As long as you've kept your receipt there's no additional charge for a new stroller; however, the shops don't have many spare strollers and those they do have are given out on a first-come, first-served basis.

@ If at 8 am your 5-year-old swears she doesn't need a stroller but at noon she collapses in a heap halfway around Epcot's World Showcase, head for the World Traveler shop. The World Traveler is also the place to rent a stroller if you're coming from the Yacht and Beach Clubs, Board-Walk, or the Swan and Dolphin hotels and using the "back-door" entrance.

@ Families staying at one of the more sprawling resorts, such as Pop Century, Caribbean Beach, Coronado Springs, Art of Animation, Port Orleans, Fort Wilderness, or the All-Star resorts, should bring a stroller from home for any child under 4. You'll need it just to get from your room to the food court or shuttle-bus stop.

Baby Care

Each park has a Baby Care Center where rockers, bottle warmers, high chairs, and changing tables are available; diapers, formula, and jars of baby food are also for sale.

In the Magic Kingdom, Baby Care is beside the Crystal

Palace Restaurant. In Epcot it's on the bridge that connects Future World to the World Showcase. At Hollywood it's in the Guest Relations (aka Guest Services) building; and in the Animal Kingdom it's behind the Creature Comforts gift shop.

Disposable diapers are available in the larger shops, but they're kept behind the counter, so you'll have to ask for them. Changing tables are provided in most women's restrooms and some men's as well. If fathers have trouble locating a changing table in a men's room, they can always make a stop in Baby Care.

Nursing Moms

Disney World is so casual and family oriented that you shouldn't feel self-conscious about using a towel or blanket and discreetly nursing anywhere that's comfortable. If you're too modest for these methods, or your baby is easily distracted, try the rockers in the Baby Care Center.

First Aid

First-aid clinics are beside the Baby Care Center in each park. Although the clinics mostly treat patients with minor problems such as sunburn, motion sickness, and boo-boos, they're equipped for major emergencies and, when necessary, can provide ambulance service to an area hospital.

If you do suffer a medical emergency, take comfort in the fact that hundreds of families that I've interviewed have given ringing endorsements to Disney cast members in times of crisis. I've gotten dozens of e-mails and letters from people who have broken their arms, fainted from heat, gone into premature labor, come down with

Helpful Hint
Seek medical advice the moment you suspect there may be a problem. Waiting it out only makes the solution more painful and more expensive.

Insider's Secret

If anyone in your family has a recurring medical condition—your son often gets ear infections, for example—bring a prescription from home in case you need medication while in Orlando.

the chicken pox, and everything else you can imagine—and each person has lauded the Disney cast members for their quick medical response and emotional support. One mother of two from Maryland wrote, "We visited Walt Disney World with our son, who has cystic fibrosis, and found everyone there to be extremely helpful and aware of what our needs might be. In fact, they often anticipated our needs before we did."

General First-Aid Tips

- If someone begins to feel ill or suffers an injury while in the parks, head for the nearest first-aid clinic. If the nurses there can't fix the problem, they'll find someone who can.

- All on-site hotels and many off-site hotels have physicians on call 24 hours a day. Contact either the Guest Relations desk at your own hotel or Centra Care Walk-In Medical Care (www.centracare.org), which, as the name implies, accepts walk-in patients and has in-house pharmacies. There are two locations near Disney World. Most area hotels provide courtesy transport to medical clinics and pharmacies for guests in need.

- If you need a pharmacy, try the Walgreens (407/253–6288) on Kirkman Road or the CVS (407/390–9185) on U.S. 192. Both are open 24 hours a day.

- Of course, in a true emergency call 911. Within the parks, any cast member can summon an ambulance for you.

@ ECVs ($50 with an additional $20 deposit) and wheel-chairs ($12 a day or $10 a day for multiday use) are available at all theme parks, so if you're traveling with an older family member, a woman in the late stages of pregnancy, or anyone who might be laid low by the heat, don't hesitate to rent a little mechanical assistance—especially at Epcot, which has the largest walking areas of any Disney park.

More Things You Don't Want to Think About

A Rainy Day

Unless there's a full-out hurricane headed inland, the parks operate as usual. If there's an electrical storm, outdoor rides and shows are suspended until the weather clears, and water parks may close down for the day.

But if you just run into one of those afternoon cloudbursts so common to Florida, soldier on. Rain slickers are available throughout the parks for $7, and they're much more practical than umbrellas because your hands are free to hang on to your kids. The only problem is that on a rainy day half the people in the park are wearing the slickers and thus everyone looks alike. It makes it easier to lose your kids in the crowd, so stay especially alert.

Here are some tips to make sure that a rainy day doesn't turn into a total washout.

@ Disney's Hollywood Studios is a good choice when the weather is iffy because most of the rides and shows are indoors. The Animal Kingdom has mostly outdoor attractions, but if it's just misty and not pouring, it can also be a good choice because the animals are more active when a little rain cools off the air. The Magic Kingdom, where many rides are outside, and Epcot, which requires a lot of walking, are a bit tougher to navigate.

⊜ There's always plenty to do at Downtown Disney: shopping, movies, Cirque du Soleil, and DisneyQuest. But be forewarned—DisneyQuest is especially swamped when the weather turns bad.

⊜ Remember, a rainy morning doesn't necessarily mean a rainy day. Weather conditions can change rapidly in Orlando, and if it clears up later in the day the parks will be less crowded than usual. If you see a storm approaching, duck into a show or indoor attraction and give it some time. You may walk out to find sunny skies.

"My advice is to pray for rain," wrote a father of two from Pennsylvania. "We were standing in a long line for Dumbo, and it began to shower. Everyone left, but we just went into a nearby shop and it stopped raining after just a couple of minutes. When we emerged, Fantasyland was practically empty, and we got on Dumbo with no wait at all."

Lost Kids

Obviously, your best bet is not to get separated in the first place. Savvy families set up prearranged meeting places.

If you do get separated and your kids are too young to understand the idea of a meeting place, act fast. Disney employees are well briefed about what to do if they encounter a lost child, so the odds are good that if your preschooler has been wandering around on his own for more than a couple of minutes, he's been intercepted by a Disney cast member. The cast member has been trained to walk around the area with the child for about 10 minutes and, if they don't find you, take the child to the Baby Care Center in that park. So if you've been wandering around looking for longer than 10 minutes, flag down the nearest person you see wearing a Disney name tag,

Insider's Secret

Where and when are kids most apt to get lost? During character signings, in play areas, and just after parades.

and ask them to call Baby Care and see if the child has been reported found. You can also make things easier if you wear colorful clothing and explain to any child old enough to remember that "Mom is wearing a bright blue shirt today." This increases the chances the cast member will be able to spot you in the crowd.

The one glitch in the system is that lost kids are often so interested in what's going on around them that they aren't crying and they don't look lost, and, thus, no Disney employee intercepts them. Explain to your kids that if they get separated from you to approach the nearest person wearing a Disney name tag. That person can call in the child's name to Baby Care and, assuming you've also called in to report the child as missing, the attendant can tell you where your child is.

In real emergencies—when the child is very young or disabled, or when you're afraid she's been nabbed—bulletins are put out among employees. So if you lose a child, don't spend a half hour frantically searching on your own. Contact the nearest Disney employee and let the system take it from there.

Insider's Secret

Stop by Disney's Guest Relations in the morning and get a tag where you can put your cell phone number on the inside of your child's clothing.

Parking

It's embarrassingly easy to forget where you parked, so be sure to write down your row number (or take a picture of it with your phone) as you leave your car in the morning. Pluto 36 seems easy to remember at 8 am, but you may not be able to retrieve that information 14 brain-numbing hours later. If you forget to do this and can't find your car, tell a parking attendant the approximate time you arrived. Since the trams service parking lot sections in a predictable sequence, if the attendant knows the general time you arrived, he or she can help you at least narrow the search.

Auto Breakdowns

As the tram drops people off at the end of the day, security vehicles are parked at the end of rows in anticipation of the fact some unlucky family is going to find that their battery is dead, a tire's gone flat, or they've locked in their keys. This recently happened to me on a rainy night, and I returned to the tram drop-off site and flagged down security to tell them our battery was dead. The young woman inside followed me back to the car and had the battery recharged within seconds. Then she was off to help a frantic family who couldn't remember what their rental car looked like. It's these little "we take care of you" touches that make Disney so special.

Closed Attractions

Because Disney World is open 365 days a year, there's no downtime for repainting and repairing rides. Ergo, two or three attractions throughout Disney World may be closed for refurbishment on any given day. They try hard to keep major attractions up and going for summer and holidays, so refurbishment is more likely to be an issue in the off-season. You can check to see which attractions are scheduled to be closed for maintenance during the time you'll be in Orlando by visiting www.disneyworld.com. There's still a slight chance that a ride will be malfunctioning and thus temporarily closed when you visit, but this is relatively rare, and the rides usually come back on line quickly.

Unexpected Problems

No matter how carefully you plan your vacation, the unforeseen can always occur. Your best bet when trouble brews is to go straight to the nearest Disney cast member and report your problem. There's a reason you're paying these high prices and one of the biggest is that Disney has created a very responsive team of cast members whose highest priority is to help you have a great experience. Our mail is absolutely full of stories about Disney cast members who have gone above and beyond the call of duty. Here are some examples:

"My father lost his cell phone in the Animal Kingdom, and a cast member called every single attraction we had ridden that day until they found the phone. I can't say enough about the helpfulness of Disney employees!"

"Our family missed the last bus leaving the Fantasia Gardens miniature golf course, and we had no idea how we were going to get back to Fort Wilderness. Panic was setting in when an out-of-service bus passed by. My dad flagged him down, and, to our surprise, the driver told us to get aboard, and he would take us there himself. He even calmed my little sister down by singing to her through the loudspeaker. It was the end of his shift, and he could have easily driven by, but that's not the Disney way."

"We had a Princess dinner at Epcot scheduled for our first night, and my daughter's princess dress was packed in our luggage, which hadn't yet been delivered through Magical Express. We called the bell captain at our hotel, who was able to track the bag and get it to our hotel. He had it waiting for us when we got to the bell desk and let my daughter change in the luggage holding room! Then, since by that time we were running late, he even arranged for a special car to take us to Epcot so we wouldn't have to wait on the bus. It was a shining example of Disney customer service."

"One day our 4-year-old was crying hysterically—I think it was because his sister drank the last of the pineapple juice. A street sweeper on Main Street asked us what was wrong, and then said 'Follow me' and led us into Casey's where he got my son a Sprite. I was blown away. Such a kind gesture, especially considering how many crying kids that man probably sees in a day."

"We had arranged to attend the Perfectly Princess Tea Party to celebrate my daughter's birthday. They called our room to tell us the event had been cancelled at the last minute—evidently Sleeping Beauty called in sick—but my daughter overheard the phone call and collapsed into tears. It was too late to get into any other character meals, but I remembered reading in an earlier version of your book that you should ask for help when you need it. We were staying at the Caribbean Beach Resort and a wonderful woman in Guest Relations not only got us into a Princess Breakfast at Epcot, which we all enjoyed, but sent a special little gift to the room for our daughter every single day for the rest of our trip."

Got the picture? If a problem develops, let the Disney cast members try to sort it out. And even if things are going smoothly, stop and chat with them. Many of our readers report that cast-member interactions are some of the highlights of their Disney stay.

Saving Money

Saving money at Disney World is somewhat of an oxymoron, but there are ways to contain the damage.

- Be aware that once you cross the Florida state line, there's an inverse relationship between time and money. You have to be willing to spend one in order to save the other.

It's worth taking a few minutes to really analyze if cost-cutting measures are worth it; given the high cost of tickets, it doesn't make sense to spend hours trying to save a few bucks.

@ How should you spend your arrival day at Disney World? It's tempting to rush straight to the parks, but that's rarely the best use of your money. Since it will probably be at least afternoon before you arrive and settle into your hotel, you'll be using a full day of your expensive ticket for only a few hours in the park. Instead, relax around your resort pool or spend the evening at Downtown Disney, which offers lots of Disney-theme fun but doesn't require a ticket. Then you can start your first full day rested and raring to go.

@ Staying hydrated is essential—and expensive—so bring your own bottles, and keep refilling them at fountains. All fast-food places also provide free cups of ice water on request. Also, on-site hotels offer a deal where you can buy a souvenir beverage mug the first day of your trip and get free refills at the resort for the remainder of your stay. Because soft drinks and coffee are so costly, families who plan to eat a lot of meals at their hotel can save as much as $20 per person with the souvenir mugs.

@ If you're not on the dining plan, try to eat at least some of your meals outside the parks. If you get a suite, it's easy to keep breakfast food and snacks in your room. Many off-site Orlando hotels offer free breakfast buffets to their guests, and there are numerous fast-food and family-friendly chain restaurants along the I-4 exits that flank Walt Disney World.

@ Dining in Epcot's World Showcase can be very special, but book those restaurants for lunch, when prices are considerably lower than at dinner. And remember that portions are huge, even for kiddie meals. Consider splitting a meal with a family member. Or toss a few Ziploc bags in your tote and save some of those chips or grapes for a later snack.

@ The dinner shows are expensive, costing a family of four about $150; even a character breakfast can set you back $70 or more. If the budget is tight, skip those extras and concentrate on ways to meet the characters inside the parks.

@ Except for maybe an autograph book and a T-shirt, hold off on souvenir purchases until the last day. By then the kids will really know what they want and you won't waste money on impulse buys.

@ Buy memory cards or film, blank videotapes, diapers, and sunscreen at home before you leave. These things are all for sale in the parks, but you'll pay dearly for the convenience.

@ If you move from park to park in the course of a day, save your parking receipt so you'll only have to pay the fee once. Also, remember that parking is free for on-site guests.

@ Buy your tickets when you make your hotel reservations, so you'll have them before Disney decides it's time for another price increase.

Meeting the Disney Characters

Meeting the characters is a major objective for some families and a nice diversion for all. If your children are young, prepare them for the fact that the characters are big and, therefore, often overwhelming in person. I once visited Disney World with a toddler whose happy babble of "my Mickey, my Mickey" turned into a wary "no Mickey, no Mickey" the minute she entered the Magic Kingdom gates and saw that everyone's favorite mouse was much, much larger than he appears on TV.

That reaction isn't unusual. Many kids panic when they first see the characters, and pushing them forward only makes matters worse. The characters are trained to be sensitive and sensible (in some cases more so than the parents) and will always wait for the child to approach them.

On the other hand, some kids fall in love with the characters from the start. A father from Ohio said, "We were really surprised at how fast our 3½-year-old daughter became a character groupie. Even when in her stroller she could spot them from a mile away, and she loved getting autographs. This took a lot of time but was worth it just to see the excitement on her face." And a mom from Tennessee reported that the first thing her 4-year-old son said upon entering the Magic Kingdom gates is "I see the real Mickey and he is awesome."

Many children, even older ones, enjoy getting character autographs, and an autograph book can become a cherished souvenir. Before lining up, prepare the kids for the fact that the characters don't talk. (With, that is, the exception of characters without masks.) As many as 30 young people in Mickey suits (mostly women, because the suits are pretty small) might be dispersed around Disney World on a busy day, and they can't all be gifted with that familiar squeaky voice. So the characters communicate through body language.

Times and places for meeting the characters are listed on theme-park maps, tip boards, and entertainment schedules.

Our Top 10 Tips for Hanging with the Characters

1. Short on time? The character meals are a low-stress way to meet several characters at once. They're popular, so make reservations in advance, and if you can't get a reservation at Cinderella Castle, don't despair. There are princesses aplenty at the Akershus Royal Banquet Hall in the Norway pavilion at Epcot and that's much easier to book.

2. And what about the guys? In response to princess fever, Disney has done more to emphasize the pirates, especially at the Pirate League, where swashbuckling kids can get in face paint, eye patches, and costumes, and the Pirate Tuto-

rial Session starring Captain Jack Sparrow. Both are located near the Pirates of the Caribbean ride in Adventureland.

3. If you're scheduling a character breakfast, save it for the last day of your vacation. By this time kids have seen the characters plenty of times in parades and shows and even the most nervous toddler has usually relaxed enough to give Mickey a hug. If you choose a restaurant inside a resort you can see the characters without having to burn a day of your multiday ticket and it's a great send-off for the trip home.

4. Let the kids wear their costumes to the character meals, especially little girls with their princess regalia. What could be cuter than a miniature Belle meeting the real thing?

5. Character dining can be pricey, so if money is an issue, skip the meals and use your entertainment schedule to find out where the characters will be inside the parks. The characters are usually available in greeting locations for about 20 minutes before they're whisked away to another spot. There's always an escort close at hand, so if the line to meet a certain character is long, check with the escort before you line up. He or she can tell you approximately how much longer the character will be there and save you from waiting patiently only to have the heartbreaking experience of having Woody and Buzz leave just as your child makes it to the front of the line.

6. If your child is nervous about meeting the characters, start with the so-called "face" characters, like Aladdin or Cinderella, who don't wear masks and who can talk. They're far less intimidating to young children than "mask" characters like Goofy and Mickey.

7. If the kids are still freaked out, remember not to push them forward. The characters are good at gently urging

shy children to approach them. That said, because of the construction of their costumes, the mask characters can't always see what's happening beneath them too clearly. Donald and Daisy, for example, have a hard time looking over their bills, and small children standing at their feet might be ignored. If this appears to be happening, lift your child to the character's eye level. You can also make Mickey's day a little easier if you provide a thick marker for him to grasp and hold the pen and autograph book right in front of his face.

8. Older kids especially love chances to actually interact with the characters, such as at the Jedi Training Academy outside of Star Tours in Hollywood or the aforementioned Pirate Tutorial Session in the Magic Kingdom.

9. Don't assume that the best place to meet the character is the Magic Kingdom. The stars of Disney-Pixar films and Playhouse Disney are exclusively available at Hollywood Studios. The lines at the Animal Kingdom are rarely unmanageable and the characters are doubly adorable, outfitted in their picnic gear. And the World Showcase at Epcot can be a character bonanza; meeting Mulan in China, Belle in France, Aladdin in Morocco, or Mary Poppins in the UK makes the experience just that much more special.

10. Wherever you are, don't get so involved in the hoopla that you lose your kids. When the kids are excited and dashing from one character to the next and parents are preoccupied with getting the perfect photo, it's easy to look up and realize little Jeremy has slipped out of sight.

CHAPTER

4

Touring
Tips and
Plans

General Disney World Touring Tips

The size of Walt Disney World is often a shock to first-time visitors, many of whom arrive with vague notions that they can walk from Epcot to the Magic Kingdom or even that they are separate sections of the same theme park. There can also be confusion over the names: Some people use "Walt Disney World" and "Magic Kingdom" synonymously, where in reality the Magic Kingdom is a relatively small part of the much larger Disney World complex. There's more to this place than Cinderella Castle and Space Mountain. Thus it's vital that you have at least a basic understanding of the Disney World layout and transportation system before you leave home.

The tips in this chapter encourage you to visit more than one park a day—to follow a morning hitting the waterslides at Blizzard Beach, for example, with an afternoon taking in the shows at Hollywood. The best way to avoid overstimulation and burnout is to work a variety of experiences—some active, some passive, some educational, some silly—into each day. (Note that this strategy requires you to have a Park Hopper Pass.)

When it comes to touring, families tend to fall into three groups. The first group sleeps in, has a full-service meal at their hotel, and lollygags over to the parks around 11 am. They wander around, finding the lines for major rides to be so long that their only choices are either to wait 90 minutes for Splash Mountain or to spend the whole afternoon riding minor attractions. By the time they begin to get in a groove (i.e., they figure out time-saving systems like Fastpass), it's 5 pm, and they're exhausted. They retreat to their hotel room frustrated at how little they've seen, irritated by how much they've spent, and carping at each other. This is a vacation?

The second group is what I call Disney World Commandos. These hyper-organized types have elaborate tour plans and march determinedly from ride to ride, checking off their "to do" list as they go. Amanda wants to ride Dumbo twice in a row? No way! It'll throw them off schedule. Jeffrey wants to hang out at Innoventions? Sorry, it's not on the list. If anything unforeseen happens—Space Mountain opens late or there's a glitch in the bus system—the whole group goes into a psychological meltdown. This is a vacation?

Disney-savvy families find the sweet spot between the two extremes. They have an overall plan, but make sure to leave empty spaces in the day to allow for spontaneity. They get an early start each morning, but factor in plenty of downtime to rest, particularly in the afternoon. Most important, they're familiar enough with each park and its attractions that they arrive with a clear idea of what they want to see, but they don't feel compelled to do it all. One father of four from Washington wrote, "Disney World is so big and so overwhelming that the first time we went down we spent hours just aimlessly drifting around. People need some kind of plan."

The following tips should help you make the most of your time without pushing anyone, parents or kids, past their endurance level.

For families with kids, it's especially important to avoid the exhaustion that comes with just trying to get there. If you're staying off-site, it can easily take two hours from the time you leave your hotel until you board your first ride, which is enough to shatter the equanimity of even the most well-behaved kid. Your children have been waiting for this vacation a long time, and now they've been flying and driving for a long time. You owe it to them to get into the parks quickly.

Insider's Secret

Come early! If you follow only one tip in the whole book, make it this one. Although in recent years the mornings have become more crowded than they used to be, you'll still find far shorter waits for big-deal rides than you will in the afternoon.

Every Disney World guidebook on the market tells people to come early, so it's no shock that in the 24 years since I wrote this book's first edition, the mornings have become more crowded. However, the good news for you is that most people visiting Disney World still arrive between 10 and 11 am, many of them proudly announcing that this is their vacation and they'll sleep in if they want. (These same people seem to take a strange inverse pride in bragging about how long they stood in line and how little they saw.) Arriving early is like exercising regularly: everyone knows you should do it, but most people don't. So an early start is still the best way to ride major attractions with little or no wait time.

If, for example, the Magic Kingdom is scheduled to open at 9 am, be at the gate by 8:30. At least part of the park is usually open early and you can be at the end of Main Street awaiting the rope drop while the other 50,000 poor saps are still crawling along I-4.

@ If you're indeed allowed to enter the first section of the park early, use your time wisely. Take care of any business—get maps and entertainment schedules, rent strollers, take a potty break—before the main park opens. If you haven't had breakfast, there's always a kiosk where you can grab juice and muffins. The characters are usually on hand to greet kids, which is a fun way to start the day. But be sure to be at the ropes about 10 minutes before the stated opening times.

@ Because people were practically stampeding after the rope drop, Disney is now controlling how fast you can enter the main body of the park. Once the whole park opens, proceed quickly but calmly (they'll nab you if you run) to the first ride you'd like to board. Sometimes the Fastpass system doesn't start working until 20 or 30 minutes after the park opens, so it's definitely better to ride your top-priority attraction first and get your Fastpass second.

@ Plan to see the most popular attractions either early in the day, late at night, or during a time when a big event siphons off other potential riders (such as the afternoon parade in the Magic Kingdom).

Time-Saving Tip

To maximize your time in the parks, either eat breakfast at your hotel or buy fast food while you're waiting for the rope drop. There's always at least one sit-down place to get breakfast in each park, but you don't want to waste the relatively uncrowded morning hours in a restaurant.

- Eat at "off" times. Some families eat lightly at breakfast, have an early lunch around 11 am, and supper at 5 pm. Others eat a huge breakfast and then a late lunch around 3 pm and have a final meal back at their hotel after the parks close. If you tour late and you're really bushed, all on-site hotels and many off-site hotels have in-room pizza delivery service.

- Kids usually want to revisit their favorite attractions, and parents who overschedule to the point where there's no time for this risk a mutiny. One way to handle this is to save the entire last day of your trip as a "greatest hits" day and go back to all your favorites one more time, even if this means maximum park hopping.

Time-Saving Tip

The single most important thing you can do to make your Disney visit go more smoothly? Use Fastpass for the most-popular attractions.

- Use the touring plan to cut down on arguments and debates. It's a hapless parent indeed who sits down at breakfast and asks, "What do you want to do today?" Three different kids will have three different answers.

- When making plans, keep the size of the parks in mind. Hollywood is small and can be easily crisscrossed to take in various shows. Likewise, the Animal Kingdom can be toured in five or six hours. The Magic Kingdom has more attractions and more crowd density, slowing you down; although some cutting back and forth is possible, you'll probably want to tour one land fairly thoroughly before heading to another. Epcot is so enormous that you're almost forced to visit attractions in geographic sequence or you'll spend all your time and energy in transit.

@ If your kids have the stamina for it, try park hopping. Families with a multiday pass might figure: We'll spend Monday at the Magic Kingdom, Tuesday at Hollywood, Wednesday at Blizzard Beach, Thursday at Epcot, and Friday at the Animal Kingdom. Sounds logical, but a day at the Magic Kingdom is too much riding, 14 hours at Epcot is too much walking, the Animal Kingdom simply doesn't require that much time, a whole day at Hollywood is too many shows, and anyone who stays at Blizzard Beach from dawn to dusk will wind up waterlogged. Mix it up a bit.

@ If you're trying to predict how crowded a ride or show will be, four factors come into effect:

The newness of the attraction. In general, the newer it is, the hotter it is, especially if it's an attraction that's gotten a lot of media attention like Toy Story Mania.

The quality of the attraction. Space Mountain, Fantasmic!, and other Disney classics will still be mobbed years from now.

Speed of loading. Continuous-loading attractions such as Pirates of the Caribbean, Spaceship Earth, and It's a Small World can move thousands of people through in an hour. The lines at start-and-stop rides such as Dumbo, TriceraTop Spin, and the Mad Tea Party move much more slowly.

Capacity. Shows like Muppet*Vision 3D, Captain E-O, and Mickey's PhilharMagic have theaters that can accommodate large crowds at once. For this reason, theater-style attractions are good choices in the afternoon, when the park is at its most crowded and you need a rest.

© Take some time to familiarize yourself with the sprawling WDW transportation system. If you're staying on-site you'll be given a transportation map at check-in, and Guest Relations (a.k.a. Guest Services) can help you decide the best route to take to out-of-the-way locations.

© For families with young children, seeing the characters is a major part of what makes Disney World special, so don't overplan to the point where you don't have time to hang with Mickey and the gang. Your theme-park map indicates when and where they'll appear, but the one place you probably won't see them is just walking down the street. At Disney, the characters are the equivalent of rock stars, and security around them is tight. If you want that photo, autograph, or hug, you'll need to either line up or schedule a character meal.

© In the off-season, the Magic Kingdom, Hollywood, and the Animal Kingdom sometimes close at 5 or 6 pm, but Epcot always stays open later, even during the least crowded days of the year. So spend your days at one of the parks that closes early, and evenings at Epcot. This buys you more hours in the parks for your money, and besides, many of the best places for dinner are at Epcot.

© If there's a wide gap in the ages of your kids, check out the maps and develop some strategies in advance. There are plenty of places throughout all four parks where Disney has put kiddie attractions next to rides that appeal to older kids. For example, the Beauty and the Beast show at Hollywood Studios is just down the block from the Tower of Terror and Rock 'n' Roller Coaster. One parent can take the younger kids to the show while the other parent takes the older kids to the thrill rides. Likewise, at the Animal Kingdom, the Dinosaur ride scares the willies out of youngsters, but the nearby Boneyard is a great place for them to play while their older siblings are on the ride. Be aware of which attractions are so intense that you'll need to split up and which—such as Mickey's PhilharMagic, Soarin,' and Kilimanjaro Safaris, to name a few—are designed for all ages to experience together.

@ If you'll be at Disney World for more than four days, consider planning a "day off" in the middle of your vacation. A day in the middle of the trip devoted to sleeping in, hanging around the hotel pool, shopping at Downtown Disney, and maybe taking in a character breakfast at an on-site hotel can make all the difference. Not only will you save a day on your multiday ticket, but you'll also start the next morning refreshed and energized.

@ You need a strategy for closing time. Except for the Animal Kingdom, the major parks all have nighttime extravaganzas that result in huge logjams as nearly every guest in the park convenes for the show and then mobs the exits en masse when it's over. See the "Tips for Leaving" sections in each park for specific information on how to best exit each one.

@ Go digital. Disney's official Mobile Magic app (currently free) provides real-time info about line lengths, Fastpass return times, and even the locations of the characters for meet-and-greets. It's also GPS-enabled to keep you oriented and to help when you need to find a character, a hamburger, or a restroom—and you need to find them fast. The only drawback is that this app is available solely to Verizon customers. Not a Verizon customer? There are six (and counting) unofficial apps for the iPhone priced between $0.99 and $3.99. Collectively they provide maps, park information, hotel-and-restaurant-reservation tracking, and more. And a basic iPhone app with real-time, ride-line lengths is free.

Money-Saving Tips

It isn't easy to save money at Disney, but the following tips will help.

- Consider the Disney Dining food plan. By turning your vacation into more of an all-inclusive, it helps you better gauge the cost of your trip in advance, a planning tool that some families prefer to showing up and "winging it."

- Choose wisely when it comes to your hotel. A more expensive hotel with lots of family-friendly perks might end up being more cost-effective than a hotel with a lower nightly rate but no extras.

- Tickets are expensive, so use them only on days when you can maximize your hours in the park. This might mean not visiting a park on the first or last day of your vacation when your travel schedule cuts into your available time; instead, use these days for a character breakfast at a Disney hotel, a visit to Downtown Disney, miniature golf, or just to relax at the hotel pool.

- Be aware of how little things add up. Bring strollers, sunscreen, water bottles, video supplies, diapers, etc., from home. Make lunch your big meal of the day. Let two family members share a drink or a meal. Ask for a cup of ice water instead of buying bottled water at quick-service venues. And bring resealable plastic bags so that you can save leftover chips and fruit for a later snack.

- One savvy mom from Wisconsin suggests that you hold souvenir shopping to a minimum by giving each child a gift card with a reasonable amount of money on it the first day you arrive. "If they know they have $40 to spend for the whole trip," she writes. "They may decide on their own that they don't really need that $20 toy. It keeps them from begging and whining for every little thing you pass."

When it comes to character mania, cut corners where you can. If you figure out ways to meet the characters inside the park, you won't have to pay for a character breakfast. One mother from Florida reported that she bought her daughter's Cinderella dress on sale at The Disney Store before they left home and then did her own version of the Bibbidi Bobbidi Boutique in their hotel room on the morning of their character lunch. "I dabbed on a little makeup and put her hair in an updo with glitter hairspray," she said "and this alone saved us a hundred dollars."

On the other hand, when faced with a toddler determined to have one of those $15 balloons, there are times that you just have to take a deep breath and get over it. "Choose your battles carefully" advised an Oklahoma mom. "It's their vacation too. Buy them the balloon already."

Touring Tips for Visitors Staying On-Site

By far the greatest advantage of staying on-site is the shortened commute to the theme parks, making for an easy return to your hotel for a mid-afternoon nap or swim. You can reenter the parks in the early evening. Remember the mantra: Come early, stay late, and take a break in the middle of the day.

Take advantage of the Extra Magic Hour program. You're given a brochure at check-in telling you which park is featured on which day of your visit. If you want to use this information in your pre-trip planning, visit www.disney world.com to verify which park will have extended hours on which day.

Touring Tips for Visitors Staying Off-Site

- Time your commute. If you can make it from your hotel to the theme-park gates within 30 minutes, it may still be worth your while to return to your hotel for a midday break. If your hotel is farther out and your commute is longer, it's doubtful you'll want to make the drive four times a day.

- If it isn't feasible to return to your hotel, find afternoon resting places within the parks. (See the sections headed "Afternoon Resting Places.") Sometimes kids aren't so much tired as full of pent-up energy. If that's the case, take them to the play areas in each park (Tom Sawyer Island in the Magic Kingdom; the play fountains in Epcot; the Honey, I Shrunk the Kids Adventure Zone at Hollywood; and the Boneyard at the Animal Kingdom) and let them run around for a bit.

- The restaurants in the Magic Kingdom resorts are rarely crowded at lunch, and dining there is much more relaxed and leisurely than eating lunch in the parks. An early dinner can also effectively break up a summer day, when you'll be staying at the park until late. If you do take the monorail to a Magic Kingdom resort, be sure to line up for the train marked "Resort Monorail" and not the express back to the Transportation and Ticket Center (TTC).

- Off-site visitors tend to tour all day, so either bring or rent strollers for preschoolers. Few 4-year-olds can walk through a 14-hour day.

- If you have the Park Hopper option on your ticket, spend the morning in a park where you'll be active (like the Animal Kingdom or Magic Kingdom) and in the afternoon transfer to a park (such as Epcot or Hollywood) that has more shows and thus more places to sit and rest.

Tips to Save Your Sanity

Use Your Time Wisely

This boils down to one thing: Avoid the lines.

Head for the most crowded, slow-loading attractions first. In the Magic Kingdom that's Splash Mountain, Space Mountain, and Big Thunder Mountain—although some Fantasyland attractions, such as Peter Pan and the Many Adventures of Winnie the Pooh, can also draw long lines. In Epcot it's Soarin' and Test Track. At Hollywood it's Toy Story Mania, Rock 'n' Roller Coaster, and the Tower of Terror. At Animal Kingdom it's Expedition Everest and Kilimanjaro Safaris.

Ride as many of the big-deal rides as you can in the morning, when waits are shorter. In general, save theater-style attractions for the afternoon. And if you can't get to all the big-deal rides during the first couple of hours the park is open, try again during the parades, or during the last hour before closing.

Be Willing to Split Up

By this point in the planning process, it's probably beginning to dawn on you that every single member of the family expects something different from this vacation.

Discuss which attractions you'll enjoy as a family; some rides, shows, restaurants, and parades will be a blast for everyone. But there are also bound to be some attractions that won't have such universal appeal, and this is especially true if there's a significant gap in the ages of your children.

If only one or two members of the family are into a certain show or ride, there's no need to drag the whole crew along.

Preteens and teenagers, in fact, often like to split off for an hour or two and simply shop, hang out in arcades, or ride a favorite over and over. Security in Disney parks is tight, so this is an option worth considering. Just make sure to have a clearly designated meeting time and place or remind them to keep checking their cell phones for your calls or texts.

About splitting up, one mother of three from Ohio wrote, "Disney Junior is a wonderful attraction for young children, but my preteen son wasn't that thrilled with the idea of standing in line for an hour to see the Little Einsteins. We let him walk around on his own for an hour while we took the younger kids. Normally, I would worry about letting him be on his own, but at Walt Disney World we felt pretty safe about it. And he was in a much better mood after a break from his little sisters."

Master Fastpass

Disney World's Fastpass system is designed to reduce the time you spend waiting in line. Attractions offering Fastpass are listed in each theme-park chapter.

Here's how it works: Let's say you enter the Animal Kingdom at 10 am and find that a long line has already formed for Kilimanjaro Safaris. Rather than standing in line for an hour, go to the Fastpass kiosk and insert your theme-park ticket. You'll get the theme-park ticket back, along with a small paper

Insider's Secret

Only a limited number of Disney Fastpasses are available for each attraction. At the most popular rides on crowded days, Fastpasses can run out by mid-afternoon. So if you want to guarantee you'll get a Fastpass for Toy Story Mania or Space Mountain, visit the kiosk as soon as possible after you enter the park.

Helpful Hint

Disney's Fastpass kiosks are most often located outside of the attraction in question, meaning that getting a Fastpass from, say, Soarin,' and then returning to use it two hours later can involve a lot of walking, especially in a park as huge and sprawling as Epcot. You might want to send one parent to get the Fastpasses for the whole family while the other supervises the kids in a play area or takes them on a less crowded attraction.

Fastpass that looks like a movie admission stub. The Fastpass (along with a digital clock at the kiosk) will tell you when to return. There's usually an hour-long window of opportunity, which in this case might be between 11:30 am and 12:30 pm.

Go on to tour the rest of the Animal Kingdom and return to Kilimanjaro Safaris sometime within that one-hour period. Show your Fastpass to the attendant and you'll be allowed to enter a much shorter line and proceed directly to the boarding area. The waits with Fastpass average 10 to 15 minutes, a vast improvement over the 90-minute waits that big attractions can post on crowded days.

Helpful Hint

Four family members will need four Disney Fastpasses, but that doesn't mean you all have to line up at the kiosk. Let one person be in charge of holding on to all the tickets and all the Fastpasses. (Maybe in a little Ziplock bag?) That way you won't find that Tyler has somehow managed to lose his Fastpass just as you're set to board Test Track.

Insider's Secret

Fastpass is so popular that Disney is always looking
for ways to expand the system, and you never know
when they'll be offering some new perk. Check the
information flyers you get with your park maps for
anything new about the Fastpass program. Disney
has already experimented with giving out bonus
Fastpasses, wherein a second Fastpass for a different attraction is automatically distributed when you
get your first Fastpass of the day. There's also talk
that Disney hotel guests may be able to order Fastpasses before they even get to the park through an
in-room ordering system. At the very least they may
be shortly creating kiosk locations distributing multiple Fastpasses to help cut down on walking.

When You Don't Need Fastpass

As great as Fastpasses are, you don't always need one. Don't use
the Fastpass system if (a) the wait time in the general-admit-
tance line is 20 minutes or less, (b) the attraction in question is
a theater-style show that admits hundreds of people at once, or
(c) you plan to later ride an even more popular attraction. Essentially, you want to use your Fastpass privilege where it's most
effective, for big-deal rides that get the most crowds.

Tips for Big Families

Disney offers plenty of help to groups, such as family reunions.
If you have more than eight guests over the age of 3 in your
party, a specialist can help you arrange rooms, tickets, and dining for the whole party, and they handle details such as individual payment. Call 407/934–7639 or visit Magical Gatherings
on the website (disneyworld.disney.go.com/planning-guides) for
details.

Insider's Secret

If your older kids want to go on a big-deal Disney attraction such as Expedition Everest or Space Mountain over and over, use the theme-park tickets of younger siblings to obtain multiple Fastpasses. "Our twin 4-year-olds just wanted to hang around the play areas and meet the characters," said one father of four. "So we used their tickets to get Fastpasses for our older two children, who were determined to ride the coasters as many times as possible."

Also, as an Ohio mom said, "Be careful when you're getting your Fastpass to make sure you retrieve your park ticket. We left our multiday tickets in a Fastpass machine in Epcot and didn't realize it for hours. Disney eventually got it straightened out, but it took awhile and it was very stressful."

"We copied the backs and fronts of our tickets when we got them," added a mom from Canada. "And this turned out to be invaluable when we realized on day three that we had somehow managed to lose one of our seven-day passes! The lady at Guest Relations was very kind and because we had the numbers written down she was able to reissue us a new ticket in minutes. She said we probably left one of the tickets in a Fastpass machine and that it happened all the time."

There are ways to max out the power of Fastpass. Get the Fastpass for the attraction you most want to see as soon as you can. You can get another (a) once you've used the first one, (b) after the time indicated at the bottom of your first Fastpass ticket, or (c) after the time on your first Fastpass ticket has expired, so clever families keep them rolling. For example, if you've gotten a 10:30 Fastpass for Kilimanjaro Safaris the bottom of your ticket will indicate you're able to get another Fastpass around 10:15. Grab a Fastpass for another big-deal ride like Expedition Everest at 10:15 and then return to ride Kilimanjaro Safaris.

The following tips may also make things a little less hectic.

@ If you're all on the Dining Plan, there are certain special experiences designed for Dining Plan groups of eight or more. These experiences vary, but in the past have included an IllumiNations reception at Epcot, a safari-theme meal at the Animal Kingdom, and a character breakfast at the Magic Kingdom. Your options will be explained to you when you add the dining plan to your package.

@ It's approximately, um, three times harder to get a table for twelve than one for four, so make dining reservations early. If you have trouble getting bookings, eat at off times (say 3 pm for lunch or 5 for dinner or stick to resort restaurants, which are generally less crowded than those in the parks. Note: A gratuity of 18% is added for parties of eight or more—even at buffet restaurants).

@ Consider renting a villa or condo. Many have kitchens, so you can save on eating out. On-site resorts with villa-style lodging include Old Key West, Saratoga Springs, Board-Walk Villas, the Beach Club Villas, and the Villas at Wilderness Lodge. There are also plenty of off-site condos and villas for rent; check out the Off-Site Hotels section in Chapter 2 for ideas.

@ If you'd like a little less togetherness, book as many rooms as you need at a resort, but ask for adjoining rooms.

@ Transportation can be an issue, especially if there's a wide variation in the ages, stamina, and risk tolerance of the family members. Older kids will probably want to stay at

Money-Saving Tip

If the adults plan to head out for a night, an in-room sitter is generally less expensive than drop-off child care when three or more children are involved.

the park all day, while the toddlers and grandparents might be burned out and ready to rest by noon. Either way, stay on-site so you can use the Disney transportation system at your leisure, or, if you're driving, bring more than one vehicle to the parks so that family members have the option to leave early.

@ Bring your cell phones to the theme parks. Large groups tend to scatter and you don't want to spend half your time trying to get the group reassembled.

@ Have everyone wear the same color T-shirt or hat each day. A tour operator passed along this tip, which makes it easier to spot "your people" in a sea of faces.

Tips for Guests with Disabilities

@ Special boarding passes allow people with disabilities, including Down syndrome and autism, to enter their own queues, which are often shorter than the general lines. Attendants are on hand to help. You can pick up a pass at any Guest Relations window. The passes—not unlike the birthday buttons you can also pick up at Guest Relations—guarantee you a little special treatment. One mother of a special-needs child wrote that her 4-year-old son was nervous about meeting Captain Hook, but she told him to show the villain his "special card." Hook rose to the occasion, dramatically blowing his nose on the card before returning it to the child with great ceremony. "Andrew was laughing by then," the mother said "and didn't worry about meeting characters for the rest of the trip."

@ Download a copy of the official *Guidebook for Guests with Disabilities* at www.disneyworld.com when you book your room. It offers detailed information on how to approach each attraction. You can also get the guidebook at any Disney hotel and Guest Relations window, but having it in advance will help you know what to expect.

@ You can rent wheelchairs ($12 per day or $10 per day for multiday use) and ECVs ($50 plus an additional refundable $20 deposit) on a first-come, first-served basis. We regret to report that every year it seems there are more able-bodied people than ever who rent ECVs simply to avoid walking and for the free front-of-the-line access. This glut of ECVs, often badly driven by theme-park guests who are clearly using them for the first time, can really hold up the system, especially on buses, where it takes considerable time to load and unload them. But Disney does not challenge anyone claiming a disability, so there's really no way to avoid the ECV army.

@ Now back to the good stuff. People with disabilities give the Disney resorts high marks for convenience at reasonable prices. The All-Star resorts, for example, have several wheelchair-accessible rooms that begin as low as $109 a night. Most of the on-site resorts offer rooms with specially equipped bathrooms and extra-large doors, and if you request it, you can have a complimentary wheelchair waiting for you upon check-in. Plus, life jackets are available at all the pools and water parks.

@ The monorail, buses, boats, and other forms of transportation are all wheelchair accessible.

@ You can refrigerate insulin and other medications at first-aid stations, all on-site hotels, and most off-site hotels.

@ Guests with visual disabilities should be aware that guide dogs are welcome at all parks and many area hotels. You can also rent a tape recorder and cassette describing the attractions at each park and a braille guidebook with a refundable deposit. Just visit Guest Relations.

@ Guests who are deaf can pick up a handheld captioning device at Guest Relations. This device works on many attractions.

- Guests with some hearing loss can rent listening devices that amplify attraction music and words through Guest Relations with a refundable deposit.

- TTYs are available throughout Disney World, and guests can also contact Disney Reservations via TTY at 407/939–7670.

- For more detailed information on hotel options for people with disabilities, call Central Reservations at 407/934–7639 (407/W–DISNEY) and ask for the Special Reservations Department.

Finally, not a tip, but a word of reassurance. If you're traveling with someone who has a chronic health problem or disability, rest assured that the Disney World cast members will help you in any way they can. Because Disney World is frequently visited by children sponsored by the Make-A-Wish Foundation and other programs like it, the Disney staff is accustomed to dealing with a wide range of situations, even cases in which visitors are seriously ill. The key is to make sure that Disney employees both at your hotel and within the parks are aware of your presence and that you may need assistance. With a few preliminary phone calls, you'll find that Disney World is one of the best possible travel destinations for such families.

A dad of three, including a special-needs 8-year-old, wrote, "We heard how Disney cast members go out of their way to accommodate special children. We found this to be absolutely true. For any ride that William could go on, we got front-of-line privileges. We also were escorted to special viewing areas for shows and parades."

A mom from Connecticut wrote, "We informed our hotel (the Contemporary), in advance, of our daughter's health problems and when we checked in, we were delighted to learn that our family had been invited to ride in the first car of the afternoon parade at the Magic Kingdom. The cast member told us that there is no way to guarantee such an invitation, but that if they know a special-needs child is visiting, they try to offer some treats. Riding in the convertible and waving to the crowd was the highlight of our daughter's week."

"My 6-year-old daughter has some usable vision but is legally blind," wrote another mom. "We knew she wouldn't be able to enjoy most of the shows, so we stopped by Guest Relations, and they gave us a Guest Assistance Card. Any time we approached a show, she held out the card and a cast member would escort us to special front seating. This meant the world to all of us. She was able to actually *see* Belle dancing with the Prince."

Tips for Pregnant Guests

I've personally toured Disney World twice while pregnant and not only lived to tell the tale but honestly enjoyed both trips. However, a few precautions are in order.

- Make regular meal stops. Instead of buying a turkey leg from a vendor, get out of the sun and off your feet at a sit-down restaurant.

- If you aren't accustomed to walking as much as 7 miles a day, begin getting in shape a couple of months before the trip by taking 30- to 40-minute walks at home.

- Dehydration is a real danger. Keep water in your tote bag and sip frequently. You can refill your bottle at water fountains throughout the parks.

- Consider staying on-site so that you can return to your room in the afternoon to rest.

- Mothers-to-be are welcome to rest in the rocking chairs inside Baby Services.

Helpful Hint
The most important tip of all if you're pregnant: check out restroom locations in advance.

Helpful Hint

Walt Disney World has always been a popular destination for grandparents vacationing with their grandkids, but here's one word of warning: Don't be so eager to make the week magical that you let discipline and routine go totally out the window. Grandparents rarely have their grandkids full time and thus might be more likely than parents to "cave," that is, let them skip naps, eat sugary treats, and buy way too many souvenirs. So the overwhelm factor that comes into play at a high-stimulation place like Disney World is even more likely to happen with grandparents. Even the best-behaved kids can have a meltdown if they're given too much leeway, so set ground rules in advance.

@ Standing stock-still can be more tiring than walking when you're pregnant, so let your husband stand in line for rides. You and the kids can join him as he's about to enter the final turn of the line.

Birthdays and Special Occasions

Celebrating a birthday? Anniversary? Graduation? Is it your first visit? Drop by Guest Relations in each park and pick up a free pin announcing your status. Cast members keep an eye out for special visitors and will make an extra effort to acknowledge them, especially a child wearing a birthday pin. One mother reported that when the characters in the afternoon parade saw her daughter's birthday pin, they made a point to come over and high-five her or shake her hand.

If you're celebrating a special occasion, the general rule is "Ask and you shall (probably) receive." If you're staying at a

Insider's Secret

If you're a single parent, consider vacationing with one of your siblings or another single parent. "My daughter is 11 and my son is 4," wrote one mother from Texas. "They like totally different things, and it would have been impossible to give them both the Disney experience they wanted if we'd gone to Orlando by ourselves. So we went with my sister and nephew, rented a nice condo, and had a great time. I did the wild rides with my daughter and meanwhile my sister, who is so prone to motion sickness that she once threw up in an elevator, took the boys around to meet all the characters."

"It's never a good idea to let the kids outnumber the adults," adds another single mother from New Jersey. "My friend Jenny, who doesn't have kids but who loves being an unofficial aunt, has gone down to Disney with us twice. Otherwise, I don't think I'd have the guts to try it."

Disney resort, inform Guest Relations or the concierge in advance if you'd like flowers or a gift delivered on a special day. Rooms can also be decked out with confetti, balloons, and banners while you're in the park so that the celebrant returns to find things fit for a party. If you want to celebrate with a special meal, make reservations at your restaurant of choice weeks in advance and let the manager know your preferences. You can arrange for a special cake that's themed to the occasion and the likes of the birthday boy or girl. (And if you want to have a full birthday party on-site, there are locations for that as well.)

One mother wrote that her son celebrated his birthday at a character breakfast featuring Pooh and friends. The cake was delivered to the table by Tigger, the child's favorite character, who then led the birthday guests in an impromptu parade around the restaurant. Another young birthday girl was sere-naded by the doo-wop group preshow at Beauty and the Beast. Or consider the young man who proposed to his girlfriend at the Coral Reef in the Living Seas pavilion at Epcot. The couple was having dinner next to the mammoth glass aquarium when, at the key moment, one of the divers swam by the table carrying a sign that read, "Will you marry me?" When the girl turned to look at her boyfriend, he was on one knee with the ring—and the whole restaurant stood up and cheered when she said yes.

What do these stories have in common? They were arranged in advance. So if you'd like to add some treats and sur-prises to a special occasion, contact the management at the hotel or restaurant. With their help, you should have no trou-ble finding a way to make the day memorable.

How to Customize a Touring Plan

Get Some General Information

Disney's website, www.disneyworld.com, is a good source of preliminary information, including theme-park hours during the time that you'll be visiting.

Ask Yourself Some Basic Questions

Consider how long you'll want to stay at each park. If your kids are under 8, you'll probably want to spend more time in the Magic Kingdom. Older kids? Plan to divide your time fairly equally among the major parks, and save some time for the water parks and Downtown Disney.

The time of year you'll be visiting is a major factor, too; al-though you may be able to tour Hollywood thoroughly in a single day in October, it will take you twice as long to see the same number of attractions in July. In summer the combina-tion of the crowds, the heat, and extended park hours means you'll need to build in more downtime.

Plan at least one evening each in the Magic Kingdom, Hollywood, and Epcot, so that you can see all the closing shows.

Set Your Priorities

Next, poll your family on what attractions they most want to see and build these priorities into the plan. I'd let each family member choose three must-sees per park. For example, at Hollywood, 10-year-old Jeremy wants to ride Toy Story Mania, the Tower of Terror, and Rock 'n' Roller Coaster. His 6-year-old sister, Elyce, chooses Muppet*Vision 3-D, Star Tours, and Voyage of the Little Mermaid. Mom thinks the '50s Prime Time Café sounds like a hoot and wants to ride The Great Movie Ride and Toy Story Mania. Dad is all over the Tower of Terror/Rock 'n' Roller Coaster thing and thinks the Lights, Motors, Action! stunt show sounds interesting.

Okay, because of some overlap you have nine items on this family's personal must-see list. They should make sure that they experience these attractions even if they don't do anything else. With any luck, they'll have some extra time and may be able to work in a few other things as well, but the key is to make sure you honor everyone's top three choices.

Cut Some Deals

Building each family member's must-sees into the touring plan has many advantages. You're seeing the best of the best, you've broken out of that "gotta do it all" compulsion, and the kids feel that they're giving input and are full partners in the vacation planning.

There's another huge advantage: A customized touring plan minimizes whining and fights. Your 12-year-old is more apt to bear a character breakfast with good grace if she knows that you'll be spending the afternoon at Blizzard Beach, one of her top choices. Kids understand fair. They might fidget a bit in Chefs de France, but if you've already covered Soarin' and Mission:

SPACE, you're perfectly justified in saying, "This is Mom's first choice in Epcot, so be quiet and eat your croquette de boeuf."

Break Up the Days

Divide each day of your visit into three components: morning, afternoon, and evening. It isn't necessary to plan where you'll be every hour on the hour—that's way too confining—but you need some sense of how you'll break up the day.

Pencil in things that have to be done at a certain time. You have a character breakfast for Wednesday morning, for example, or you must be in the Magic Kingdom on Friday night because that's the only time the evening parade is scheduled during your visit.

Monday
Morning: Magic Kingdom
Afternoon: Rest by hotel pool
Evening: Epcot

Tuesday
Morning and afternoon: Animal Kingdom
Evening: Hollywood

Wednesday (rest day)
Morning: Character breakfast
Afternoon: Downtown Disney, then early to bed

Thursday
Morning and afternoon: Blizzard Beach
Evening: Epcot

Friday
Morning: Hollywood
Afternoon: Rest by pool
Evening: Magic Kingdom

Note: This plan assumes you have the Park Hopper option on your tickets.

Favorite Attractions for Kids 5-8

IN THE MAGIC KINGDOM
Aladdin's Magic Carpet
Buzz Lightyear's Space Ranger Spin
Country Bear Jamboree
Dumbo
It's a Small World
Jungle Cruise
Mad Tea Party
The Many Adventures of Winnie the Pooh
Mickey's PhilharMagic
The parades
Peter Pan's Flight
Pirates of the Caribbean
Monsters, Inc.

IN THE ANIMAL KINGDOM
The Boneyard
Festival of the Lion King
Tree of Life—It's Tough to Be a Bug!
Kali River Rapids
Kilimanjaro Safaris
TriceraTop Spin
Expedition Everest (if they're daredevils)
Finding Nemo

AT EPCOT
Innoventions
Journey into Imagination
The Seas with Nemo and Friends
Soarin'
Turtle Talk with Crush

AT HOLLYWOOD
Beauty and the Beast
Honey, I Shrunk the Kids Movie Set Adventure
Muppet*Vision 3-D
Disney Junior
Toy Story Mania
Voyage of the Little Mermaid

Whatever you do, save plenty of time to meet the
characters. It's a major thrill for kids this age.

Favorite Attractions for Kids 9–12

IN THE MAGIC KINGDOM
Big Thunder Mountain Railroad
Buzz Lightyear's Space Ranger Spin
Haunted Mansion
Mickey's PhilharMagic
Pirates of the Caribbean
Space Mountain
Splash Mountain
Monsters, Inc.

IN THE ANIMAL KINGDOM
Dinosaur
Expedition Everest
The exploration trails, including Gorilla Falls and
Maharajah Jungle Trek
Festival of the Lion King
Tree of Life—It's Tough to Be a Bug!
Kali River Rapids
Kilimanjaro Safaris
Primeval Whirl
Finding Nemo

AT EPCOT
IllumiNations
Live entertainment around the World Showcase
Mission: SPACE
The Seas with Nemo and Friends
Turtle Talk with Crush
Soarin'
Spaceship Earth
Test Track

AT HOLLYWOOD
Beauty and the Beast
Fantasmic!
The Great Movie Ride
Lights, Motors, Action! Extreme Stunt Show
Muppet*Vision 3-D
Rock 'n' Roller Coaster
Star Tours
Toy Story Mania
Twilight Zone Tower of Terror
Voyage of the Little Mermaid

IN THE REST OF DISNEY WORLD
Blizzard Beach
Cirque du Soleil
DisneyQuest
Typhoon Lagoon
Water Sprite boats

Favorite Attractions for Teens

IN THE MAGIC KINGDOM

Big Thunder Mountain Railroad
Buzz Lightyear's Space Ranger Spin
Haunted Mansion
Mickey's PhilharMagic
Pirates of the Caribbean
Space Mountain
Splash Mountain

IN THE ANIMAL KINGDOM

Dinosaur
Expedition Everest
The exploration trails
Tree of Life—It's Tough to Be a Bug!
Kali River Rapids
Kilimanjaro Safaris

AT EPCOT

IllumiNations
Live entertainment around the World Showcase
Mission: SPACE
Soarin'
Test Track

AT HOLLYWOOD

Toy Story Mania
Fantasmic!
The Great Movie Ride
Lights, Motors, Action! Extreme Stunt Show
Rock 'n' Roller Coaster
Star Tours
Twilight Zone Tower of Terror

IN THE REST OF DISNEY WORLD

Blizzard Beach
Cirque du Soleil
DisneyQuest
Downtown Disney
Surfing Lessons at Typhoon Lagoon
Typhoon Lagoon
Water Sprite boats

CHAPTER

5

The Magic
Kingdom

The Magic Kingdom

Ft. Sam
Clemens

Rivers of America

Big Thunder
Mountain
Railroad **8**

12 Haunted
Mansion

it's a
small
world **13**

FANTASYLAND

× Pinocchio's
Village Haus

19 Dumbo

LIBERTY
SQUARE

Peter Pan's Flight **14**

Mickey's
Philharmagic

15

16 Prince
Charming Regal
Carrousel

WDW
Railroad
Frontierland
Depot

Tom Sawyer
Island

9

Liberty
Square
Riverboat

10

Columbia
Harbour
House

Cinderella's
Royal Table

×

The Hall of
Presidents **11**

17

Splash
Mountain **7**

FRONTIERLAND

Castle
Forecourt **18** Cinderella
Stage Castle

Th
o

Pecos Bill **×**
Café

6 Country Bear
Jamboree

Liberty Tree **×**
Tavern

Central
Plaza

ATM

Sunshine
Tree
Terrace **×**

Agrabah
Bazaar

Tip
Board

Plaza
Restaurant

Mons
Laug

Tortuga **×**
Tavern

4

5 Aloha Isle **×**

Casey's
Corner **×**

Walt Disney's
Enchanted
Tiki Room **3**

The Magic
Carpets of
Aladdin

Tomorrowlan
Terrace
Noodle Static

Pirates of the
Caribbean

2 Jungle
Cruise

1
Swiss
Family
Robinson
Treehouse

Crystal
Palace

First Aid
& Baby Care

MAIN
STREET
U.S.A.

ADVENTURELAND

Emporium
Parade Route

Tony's
Town Square
Restaurant

×

Town
Square

City Hall

WDW
Railroad

Town Squ

◆ ATM

Lockers/Wheelchair R

Newsstand

Stroller Shop

Monorail
Station

Guest Relations **◆**
Entrance Turnstiles

Seven Seas
Lagoon

KEY

×	Restaurants
	Restrooms
	Rail Line
	Monorail
•••	Parade Route

Mad
Tea Party
21

20
The Many Adventures
of Winnie the Pooh

Tomorrowland
Indy Speedway
22

Cosmic Ray's
Starlight Café

TOMORROWLAND

Monsters, Inc. **24** Stitch's
Laugh Floor   Great Escape

29

morrowland
Terrace
odle Station   **25** Buzz
Lightyear's
Space Ranger
Spin   Astro Orbiter
26

27
Tomorrowland
Transit Authority

28
Carousel of
Progress

ny's
Jare
rant

Town Square Theatre

heelchair Rentals

Shop

WDW Railroad
Mickey's
Fantasyland
Depot

ATM

23
Space
Mountain

Ferry Landing

Getting to the Magic Kingdom

If you're staying off-site, prepare for a complicated journey. Either drive or take your hotel shuttle to the Transportation and Ticket Center (TTC) inside the Magic Kingdom parking lot. From the TTC you can cross the Seven Seas Lagoon by ferryboat or monorail. Both deliver you to the Magic Kingdom front gates.

If you're staying on-site, getting to the Magic Kingdom is a lot easier. From the Contemporary Resort, you can bypass the TTC and take the monorail to the Magic Kingdom or walk to the park. From the Grand Floridian, you can either take the monorail or the ferry. From Fort Wilderness Campground or Wilderness Lodge, take the ferry. Polynesian guests have all the options: the monorail, a water taxi, or the ferry.

Guests at Disney hotels that aren't Magic Kingdom resorts will take shuttle buses that deliver them directly to the Magic Kingdom gates, bypassing the TTC. Sometimes families who stay on-site but have a car prefer to drive to the parks, which can save time at every park except the Magic Kingdom. If you're headed for the Magic Kingdom, take Disney transportation even if you have your own car just so you can avoid the TTC.

Helpful Hint

Driving? The Magic Kingdom parking lot is the most confusing of the four parks. Even if you come early enough to park near the gate, still take the tram just to make sure you wind up at the right place.

Through the Turnstiles

If you're staying off-site, each of your park tickets will be a different color and have a different scene or character on the front. When you get your tickets, assign each one to a different family member and have everyone write his or her name on the back of the ticket. If you're staying on-site with a package, your plastic room key will also be your theme park ticket. Either way, copy and carry with you the identifying numbers on your tickets in case they're lost—a problem that has become more pressing in the last few years, because using the Fastpass system requires people to take out their tickets several times during the day, increasing the risk of dropping one. Plus, in the heat of the moment it's all too easy to forget to retrieve one or more of your theme-park tickets from the Fastpass machine.

You can designate one person (i.e., Mom) to hold on to all the tickets, but when you get to the turnstiles, everyone will need to hold his or her own ticket. Disney's security system, called Ticket Tag, requires ticket holders to place their second finger into an electronic reader as they slide their ticket through a machine at the turnstiles. Disney makes a quick electronic measurement of the finger, allowing the system to link your park ticket to you and you alone.

Getting Around the Magic Kingdom

The Disney World Railroad leaves from Main Street with stops in Frontierland and Fantasyland. A lap around the park takes

20 minutes; trains depart from Main Street every four minutes at busy times and 10 minutes at slower times. Even so, this isn't your fastest way to get around the park. In the morning, when crowds are heaviest, you may have to wait for a second or even third train; by that time, you could have walked.

Walking, in fact, is the fastest means of transport in the Magic Kingdom. The train, vintage cars, and horse-drawn carriages are cute, but think of them as rides, not as a serious means of getting around the park.

Tips for Your First Hour in the Magic Kingdom

- Be through the gates 30 minutes earlier than the stated opening time. Get strollers and pick up a map and entertainment schedule as you enter. The entertainment schedule is crucial, because it gives you showtimes and character meeting times for that day.

- Early morning is a great time to visit Guest Relations (aka Guest Services) inside Town Hall. If anyone in your party has something to brag about—a birthday, an anniversary, or just being a first-time visitor—you can pick up a pin announcing the news. This also guarantees you a little extra attention from cast members.

- There are usually characters waiting to interact with you in the Town Square section of Main Street. If the park

Helpful Hint

Be prepared to make frequent rest stops in the Magic Kingdom. You won't walk as much as you do in Epcot, but you're likely to spend more time standing in line. This is ultimately harder on the feet—and the nerves—than walking.

hasn't officially opened and the ropes haven't dropped, let the kids stop by and say "hi." But if the park is open, you need to move ahead to the rides, which will draw long lines later in the day. You can always return to Main Street in mid-afternoon to meet the characters. Since Toontown has been closed down, the Mickey meet and greet has been moved into the Town Square Theatre. You'll also find a separate queue leading you to princesses like Cinderella, Aurora, and Belle. The Mickey and princess meet-and-greet lines will have Fastpasses.

@ On Extra Magic Hour mornings, Fantasyland and Tomorrowland open first. Older kids should head straight for Space Mountain and Buzz Lightyear, while younger kids should start with Dumbo, Peter Pan's Flight, and the Many Adventures of Winnie the Pooh. When Under the Sea—Journey of the Little Mermaid opens, head there first.

Helpful Hint

On days that are anticipated to draw large crowds, you can travel the length of Main Street before the Magic Kingdom officially opens. On less crowded days, people are usually held in the Town Square just in front of the railroad. Either way, several characters will be on hand to give the kids something to do while you're waiting for the ropes to drop.

@ On regular mornings the whole park opens at once. If your kids are up for it, head for Splash Mountain when the ropes drop, then on to Big Thunder Mountain Railroad. Both may have long lines even by 9:15—if there's more than a 20-minute wait, get a Fastpass. Again, when the Under the Sea—Journey of the Little Mermaid attraction opens, head there first.

Quick Guide to Magic

Attraction	Location	Height Requirement
Astro Orbiter	Tomorrowland	None
Barnstormer	Fantasyland	35 inches
Big Thunder Mountain Railroad	Frontierland	40 inches
Buzz Lightyear's Space Ranger Spin	Tomorrowland	None
Carousel of Progress	Tomorrowland	None
Country Bear Jamboree	Frontierland	None
Dumbo	Fantasyland	None
The Enchanted Tiki Room	Adventureland	None
The Hall of Presidents	Liberty Square	None
Haunted Mansion	Liberty Square	None
it's a small world	Fantasyland	None
Jungle Cruise	Adventureland	None
Liberty Square Riverboat	Liberty Square	None
Mad Tea Party	Fantasyland	None
The Magic Carpets of Aladdin	Adventureland	None
Prince Charming Regal Carrousel	Fantasyland	None

Scare Factor
0 = Unlikely to scare any child of any age.
! = Has dark or loud elements; might rattle some toddlers.
!! = A couple of gotcha! moments; should be fine for school-age kids.
!!! = You need to be pretty big and pretty brave to handle this ride.

Kingdom Attractions

Speed of Line	Duration of Ride/Show	Scare Factor	Age Range
Slow	2 min.	!	5 and up
Moderate	1 min.	!	4 and up
Moderate	3 min.	!!	5 and up
Fast	6 min.	0	3 and up
Fast	22 min.	0	10 and up
Moderate	15 min.	0	All
Slow	1 min.	0	All
Fast	20 min.	0	All
Fast	20 min.	0	10 and up
Slow	9 min.	!!	7 and up
Fast	11 min.	0	All
Slow	10 min.	0	All
Fast	15 min.	0	All
Slow	2 min.	0	4 and up
Moderate	1 min.	0	All
Slow	2 min.	0	All

(continued)

Quick Guide to Magic

Attraction	Location	Height Requirement
The Many Adventures of Winnie the Pooh	Fantasyland	None
Mickey's PhilharMagic	Fantasyland	None
Monsters, Inc. Laugh Floor	Tomorrowland	None
Peter Pan's Flight	Fantasyland	None
Pirates of the Caribbean	Adventureland	None
Space Mountain	Tomorrowland	44 inches
Splash Mountain	Frontierland	40 inches
Stitch's Great Escape	Tomorrowland	40 inches
Swiss Family Robinson Treehouse	Adventureland	None
Tomorrowland Indy Speedway	Tomorrowland	None
Tomorrowland Transit Authority	Tomorrowland	None
Tom Sawyer Island	Frontierland	None

Scare Factor

0 = Unlikely to scare any child of any age.
! = Has dark or loud elements; might rattle some toddlers.
!! = A couple of gotcha! moments; should be fine for school-age kids.
!!! = You need to be pretty big and pretty brave to handle this ride.

Kingdom Attractions

Speed of Line	Duration of Ride/Show	Scare Factor	Age Range
Moderate	5 min.	0	All
Moderate	20 min.	0	All
Moderate	22 min.	0	All
Moderate	3 min.	0	All
Fast	8 min.	!!	6 and up
Moderate	3 min.	!!!	7 and up
Moderate	10 min.	!!	5 and up
Moderate	15 min.	!!!	7 and up
Slow	n/a	0	4 and up
Slow	5 min.	0	2 and up
Fast	10 min.	0	All
Slow	n/a	0	4 and up

@ If there's a gap in the ages of your children and the 9-year-old is ready for a coaster but the 5-year-old isn't, split up during this crucial first hour, when popular attractions have relatively short waits. Mom can take one child, Dad the other, and you can meet back up in an hour.

@ Want to ride lots of big-deal rides? Get your first Fastpass early, but only after you take advantage of the usually un-crowded first hour to ride your first-choice attraction.

Attractions in the Magic Kingdom Offering Fastpasses

Big Thunder Mountain Railroad

Buzz Lightyear's Space Ranger Spin

The Many Adventures of Winnie the Pooh

Peter Pan's Flight

Space Mountain

Splash Mountain

Jungle Cruise (seasonally)

Under the Sea—Journey of the Little Mermaid

Main Street

Main Street is where the stage is set. With its pristine sidewalks, Victorian shops, flower stalls, and antique cars, strolling down Main Street is like walking through an idealized circa-1890 American town. It also provides a transition from the unglamorous parking lots and buses to the charms of the park, and people visibly relax as they move closer toward Cinderella Castle. Usually by the time they arrive, they're thoroughly Disney-fied.

The Magic Kingdom Don't-Miss List

IF YOUR KIDS ARE 8 OR OLDER

Any Fantasyland rides that catch their fancy

Big Thunder Mountain Railroad

Buzz Lightyear's Space Ranger Spin

Haunted Mansion

Mickey's PhilharMagic

The parades

Pirates of the Caribbean

Space Mountain

Splash Mountain

IF YOUR KIDS ARE UNDER 8

Buzz Lightyear's Space Ranger Spin

Country Bear Jamboree

Dumbo

"it's a small world"

Under the Sea—Journey of the Little Mermaid

Mad Tea Party

The Magic Carpets of Aladdin

The Many Adventures of Winnie the Pooh

Mickey's PhilharMagic

The parades

Peter Pan's Flight

Pirates of the Caribbean

Splash Mountain and Big Thunder Mountain, if they're
bold enough and if they pass the height requirement

Enchanted Tales with Belle

Main Street Touring Tips

@ Although you might spend a few minutes mingling with characters as you enter, don't take too much time in the shops of Main Street. One mom, who made the mistake of shopping too early, said, "We bought souvenirs on the way into the park, and I spent the whole day dragging things around. I looked like a Disney bag lady!" Instead, focus on getting to the major rides.

@ A tip board posted near the end of Main Street provides information about the approximate wait times of the major attractions, plus showtimes and character meeting places. Consult it whenever you're unsure about what to do next.

@ On Main Street, you may be waylaid by a Disney photographer wanting to snap a family shot with the castle in the background. Let him. He'll then hand you a PhotoPass, which looks like a credit card. You can have more shots added to it throughout the week, even photos taken with characters or on rides. Once you get home, use the number on the card to access all the pictures at www. disney-photopass.com. This allows you to peruse your photos at leisure. After deciding what you like, consolidate all of your pictures into a PhotoCD or order individual prints.

@ You might want to return to Main Street around noon for lunch or shopping when the stores are relatively uncrowded. But if you're not planning to see the parade, be off Main Street by 2:30 pm. After that, it's a mob scene.

@ The Magic Kingdom has interactive parades throughout the day. The parade theme changes periodically, but the daytime parades are designed to get you into the action, sometimes inviting you to dance or interact with the characters. It's all great fun, but keep an eye on your kids. It's easy to lose track of them in the celebration.

Helpful Hint

"Take a picture of your PhotoPass ID with your iPhone or home camera," a dad from Michigan advises. "That way, if you lose the card, you can still find your pictures online."

If you're touring the Magic Kingdom late and your party splits up, choose a spot on Main Street as your meeting place. Disney cast members clear people out of other sections of the park at closing time, but Main Street stays open at least an hour after the rides. It's the best place to reassemble the family before heading home.

Insider's Secret

After shopping in the Magic Kingdom, either stow your purchases in the lockers beneath the Railroad Station, or have them sent to Package Pick-Up next to Guest Relations. Disney resort guests can have packages sent directly to the gift shop in your resort.

Fantasyland

Fantasyland, directly behind Cinderella Castle, is home to many of the Magic Kingdom's classic kiddie rides. It's also the most congested section of the park, and, to make things even more complicated, Disney is wrapping up a major Fantasyland expansion.

Highlights of the new Fantasyland include (1) an attraction based on *The Little Mermaid* dubbed Under the Sea; (2) a *Beauty and the Beast*–themed meet and greet that culminates in an interactive storytime with Belle and Lumiere, called Enchanted Tales With Belle; (3) a new double-Dumbo attraction on the site of the old Mickey's Toontown (Never fear. Dumbo is so popular that Disney has promised not to close down the

Helpful Hint
Because the kiddie rides tempt them to wander off, Magic Kingdom's Fantasyland is the most likely spot in all of Disney World to lose your children.

existing ride before the new one is up and operative); and (4) a full-service restaurant themed around Beauty and the Beast's "Be Our Guest" and an adjacent quick-service restaurant that's a nod to Gaston's Tavern (Despite the term "tavern," the Magic Kingdom will remain an alcohol-free zone); (5) a fountained play area based on Casey Junior from *Dumbo*; (6) A new coaster, the Seven Dwarfs Mine Train, will be the last to come online, and is slated for 2014. You can find updated information regarding changes and openings at www.disneyworld.com.

Fantasyland Touring Tips

- Visit Fantasyland either before 11 am, after 7 pm, or during the parades.

- Wait times for Dumbo, Peter Pan's Flight, and the Many Adventures of Winnie the Pooh are always longer than for other Fantasyland rides. Visit these first or use Fastpass. When Under the Sea—Journey of the Little Mermaid and Enchanted Tales with Belle open, expect them to be mobbed.

- Don't eat or shop in Fantasyland. Similar foods and souvenirs are available elsewhere in less crowded areas.

Fantasyland Attractions

Mickey's PhilharMagic
A 3-D show projected onto a mammoth screen, Mickey's PhilharMagic, which rates high with all age groups, is one of the best attractions in Walt Disney World.

The story begins when maestro Mickey is called away from

The Scare Factor

Although the Mickey's PhilharMagic theater is dark and some special effects startling—Donald leaps right out of the screen at you—the presence of beloved Disney characters usually calms the kids. Unless you have a baby or toddler who's afraid of loud noises, children of any age will love the show.

the stage and Donald steps in as conductor. He promptly loses control of the orchestra and is whisked away on a madcap journey. A slew of other Disney characters gets into the act—you see Donald falling in love with Ariel, dancing with Simba, and sailing through the skies with Aladdin. The show is funny, the animation is breathtaking, and the music is stirring; in short, it's a great introduction to the 3-D experience for kids. "It was our 4-year-old's favorite attraction at the Magic Kingdom," concurs one dad from Ohio. "We were surprised at how much she enjoyed all the shows (even more than the rides), but this was the best."

it's a small world

During this 11-minute boat ride, dolls representing children of all ages greet you with a song so infectious that you'll still be humming it at bedtime. (Which may or may not be a good thing.) The line moves steadily, even during the most crowded

Helpful Hint

Although beloved by preschoolers, it's a small world can be torture for older siblings. One 10-year-old wrote that Disney should offer an "I Survived it's a small world" T-shirt similar to those they sell outside of Splash Mountain or the Twilight Zone Tower of Terror. In other words, if older kids opt to skip the ride, don't press the point.

parts of the afternoon. Babies, toddlers, and preschoolers seem to be especially enchanted.

Peter Pan's Flight

Tinker Bell flutters overhead as you board miniature pirate ships and sail above Nana's doghouse, the night streets of London, the Indian camp, and Captain Hook's cove. Of all the Fantasyland attractions, this one is most true to the movie that inspired it, and the level of detail is so captivating that even older kids tend to enjoy the ride. It lasts only three minutes, though, so if the wait's longer than 30 minutes, use Fastpass or come back during the parade.

Helpful Hint

Upon entering Fantasyland, immediately get a Fastpass for either the Many Adventures of Winnie the Pooh or Peter Pan's Flight. Both attractions draw longer-than-average lines. But when Under the Sea—Journey of the Little Mermaid opens, the ride will be the hottest thing in town, so get a Fastpass for it first.

The Many Adventures of Winnie the Pooh

This upbeat attraction follows Pooh and friends through a "blustery" day, so be prepared for your honey pot–shaped car to swirl and sway along the way. Designed especially for younger kids,

Insider's Secret

Many Disney purists mourned the passing of Mr. Toad's Wild Ride, an original Fantasyland attraction that was torn down to make way for Pooh. In a nod to the dear departed amphibian, there's a painting inside the ride that shows Mr. Toad passing along a deed to Owl.

the ride is gentle and fine for any age. Make sure to pick up your Fastpass for Pooh in front of Mickey's PhilharMagic. Hundred Acre Goods, at the exit, has great souvenirs for Pooh fans.

Prince Charming Regal Carrousel
Seventy-two white horses prance while a pipe organ toots out "Chim Chim Cheree" and other classic Disney songs. The carousel is especially gorgeous at night.

Insider's Secret
Heigh ho! Rumor has it that as part of the Fantasyland expansion, Snow White's Scary Adventures will be closing down to make way for a new princess meet-and-greet area. A new ride will feature the Seven Dwarfs, a mine, and rickety mining cars.

Dumbo
There's something very special about Dumbo. Although the lines move slowly—you could wait an hour for the 90-second ride—most kids seem willing to wait for a chance to ride in one of the iconic flying elephants. Come first thing in the morning to cut the wait time way down. And if all you want is the Dumbo shot, there's an earthbound elephant beside the ride, just for photo ops. After the Fantasyland expansion is complete, two identical rides (dueling Dumbos?) will be in what once was Toontown. This should make lines more manageable.

The Scare Factor

You control the height of your Dumbo flight via a joystick, so the ride is appropriate for any age. All the elephants do rise for a couple of high-flying laps at the end, but by then kids are generally used to the sensation.

Mad Tea Party

Spinning pastel cups, propelled by their riders, swirl around the Soused Mouse, who periodically pops out of his teapot. Because you largely control how fast your teacup spins, this ride can be enjoyed by all ages. Just don't go right after lunch.

Time-Saving Tip

Rider volume ebbs and flows at the Mad Tea Party. If the line looks daunting, grab a drink or make a bathroom stop. By the time you return, the crowd may have dispersed.

Castle Stage Show

The characters come out in full force for these 20-minute stage shows, which run several times daily in front of the castle. While the premise changes every year or so, the productions are always full of songs, dancing, and fun. Consult your map for show times, and if you want the best view, try to arrive 15 minutes in advance. Everyone stands, and it can be tiring, especially on a hot day, so don't worry if you arrive late and have to watch from the sidelines. These shows are entertaining, but it's not worth missing other Magic Kingdom attractions to see them.

Tomorrowland

Tomorrowland has a 1930s sci-fi look of "the future that never was." We're talking metal, chrome, robots, and neon.

Tomorrowland Touring Tips

- Ride Space Mountain early—by 9:15 it has substantial lines. If there's a 30-minute wait, get a Fastpass.

- Looking for fast food during peak dining hours? Tomorrowland stands are rarely as busy as those in other lands. Cosmic Ray's Starlight Café, the largest such place in the Magic Kingdom, moves you in and out fast.

Insider's Secret

Princess alert! The Bibbidi Bobbidi Boutique, fashioned on the popular Downtown Disney location, is appropriately situated inside Cinderella Castle. A variety of packages starting at $50 let young princesses receive fairy-tale makeovers: glittery new hairstyles, shimmering makeup, and sparkly nails. The complete Castle Package includes all of the above plus a costume and photos starting at $190. (Note: Several parents have written to complain that it's nearly impossible to get the glitter out of their children's hair afterwards.)

One mother got a little snippidi snappidi at my suggestion, in a previous edition of this book, that parents would have to have lost their minds to spring for the full package. "Yes, we paid almost $200 to have our daughter transformed into Princess Tiana," she wrote, "but they did it like only Disney can do it, and it was her favorite experience of the trip. Besides, they gave me all the leftover hair and makeup supplies, and I was able to reuse them when we got home. She ended up with the best Halloween costume ever."

In a gesture toward gender equality, boys can get the $15 Knight Package, which translates to hairstyling and a plastic sword and shield. Children must be at least 3 years old and, for the Magic Kingdom salon, theme-park admission is required. Reservations, which can be made 180 days in advance, are a must. Call 407/939–7895 (407/WDW–STYLE).

One thing for cost-and-time-conscious parents to note: It takes a while for the hairstyling and makeup, and that's an hour that you won't be riding rides and exploring the park. Considering the price of Disney tickets, you might want to let the girls get the princess treatment at the Bibbidi Bobbidi Boutique in World of Disney at Downtown Disney. You don't need a theme park ticket for that.

Tomorrowland Attractions

Space Mountain

This three-minute roller-coaster ride through inky blackness is one of the few scream-rippers in the Magic Kingdom. The cars move at a mere 32 mph, a tame pace compared to other monster coasters, but since the entire ride takes place in the dark, it's almost impossible to anticipate the turns and dips. Following a refurbishment, the special sound-and-light effects inside the mountain have been jazzed up. Best of all, they added some video games to the queue area to make the long waits more bearable. Nonetheless, use Fastpass if you can.

The Scare Factor

Space Mountain is the most intense ride in the Magic Kingdom, with a 44-inch height requirement. Most kids in the 3 to 8 age range find it too scary, but the 9 to 11 age group gives it a solid thumbs-up. It's the highest-rated attraction in the park among teens.

Buzz Lightyear's Space Ranger Spin

This attraction is an "interactive fantasy in which riders help Buzz save the world's supply of batteries." Huh? The ride transports you into the heart of a video game, where you pass

Insider's Secret

Attention Space Ace wannabes: The tougher the target, the higher the points, so don't waste all your time taking cheap shots. There are 100,000-point targets on the palm of the orange robot's left hand in the Robot Attack scene and another on the bottom Z of the spaceship in Zurg's Secret Weapon. Also, if you hit a target multiple times, it gives you more points.

through various scenes, spinning your cars and shooting at targets. Your car tallies your score and you learn whether you're a Space Ace or a lowly Trainee. Buzz is addictive, but the lines do move swiftly and Fastpass is available. "Buzz Lightyear is great for all ages," wrote a mother from Texas. "Our family members ranged from 2 to 83, and this was one ride everybody got into. Of course, we all got a little too competitive . . ."

Astro Orbiter

A circular thrill ride similar to Dumbo, Astro Orbiter is a bit too much for preschoolers and a bit too little for teens. If you ride at night, the astro-ambience is more convincing.

The Scare Factor

Astro Orbiter is a good choice for children ages 5 to 10 who might not be quite up to Space Mountain. But it's not for anyone prone to motion sickness.

Tomorrowland Indy Speedway

Tiny sports cars circle a nifty-looking racetrack, and although the ride itself isn't anything unusual, kids under 11 rate it highly, perhaps because young drivers can steer the cars themselves. (Kids 52 inches and taller can drive solo; others must be at least 32 inches tall and accompanied by an adult.)

Helpful Hint

Persuade your child not to rush through the Indy Speedway; loading and reloading the cars takes time—better to drive slowly than sit for five minutes in the pit waiting to be unloaded.

Tomorrowland Transit Authority

This little tram circles Tomorrowland and provides fun views, including a glimpse inside Space Mountain and the Buzz Lightyear attraction. The trip lasts 10 minutes, and the ride is never crowded, so the attendant usually lets you stay on for more than one cycle. The rocking of the train has lulled many a cranky toddler into a nap; cast members report that the ride is often full of parents holding sleeping youngsters.

Carousel of Progress

This is a fairly long show (22 minutes) and a high-capacity attraction, so it's good for the crowded times of the afternoon. Kids might be bored by this salute to modern inventions, especially once they've seen the more high-tech presentations of Epcot. That said, it has a nostalgic appeal; Carousel of Progress was one of Walt's contributions to the 1964 World's Fair. Note: Carousel of Progress is often closed during the off-season.

Stitch's Great Escape

Stitch's Great Escape tells the story of what Stitch was like before he came to Earth in the hit movie *Lilo & Stitch*. Stitch is captured by the Galactic Federation and taken to a prisoner processing facility. Since Stitch's reputation as a troublemaker precedes him, visitors to the attraction are recruited to provide additional security. But you can't keep a good alien down, and Stitch eludes security, causing mayhem everywhere he goes. The show features sophisticated Audio-Animatronics, including the remarkable, three-dimensional Stitch figure. It's also loud, dark, and far more forbidding than the advertisements indicate.

Monsters, Inc. Laugh Floor

This show lets you laugh, joke, sing, and interact right along with your one-eyed "monster of ceremonies" Mike Wazowski and other characters from *Monsters, Inc.* While the show technology is highbrow, the humor is lowbrow. Children as young

The Scare Factor

We receive a lot of mail about Stitch's Great Escape—most of it negative. While the height requirement to see Stitch is only 40 inches, the prevailing complaint is that the darkness and volume of the ride are simply too scary for many preschoolers. It seems Disney missed the boat here; they named an attraction after a familiar movie character and then created an experience so intense that it scares the daylights out of the age group it attracts. While Disney is constantly tinkering with the Stitch attraction (e.g., raising the light level during the most intense scenes), it remains, as one 7-year-old put it, "scary scary, not fun scary."

A mom from Delaware echoed the sentiment. "The worst thing about shows like Stitch (and Tree of Life—It's Tough to Be a Bug! in the Animal Kingdom) is that they take beloved Disney characters and make children afraid of them. My son wanted to ride Stitch, but now he's telling everyone at home that he would never go on it again." Unless you have brave preschoolers and you love Stitch, you should have your young ones skip this attraction.

as 5 should be able to enjoy the silly jokes and slapstick, and even if they miss a joke here or there, they'll still have fun. Oh, and even if the spotlight doesn't fall on you, you can still get in on the action—while you're waiting in the preshow area, you can text-message jokes for possible use in the show.

Monsters, Inc. was created in response to the way-popular Turtle Talk with Crush in the Living Seas at Epcot. Kids love shows in which characters on-screen interact with people sitting in the audience. It's high-tech with heart.

Adventureland

Thematically the most bizarre of all the lands—sort of a Bourbon Street meets Trinidad by way of Congo—Adventureland definitely conveys an exotic mood.

Adventureland, Frontierland, and Liberty Square Touring Tips

- If you have two days to spend touring the Magic Kingdom, begin your second day in Frontierland, at Splash Mountain. Move on to Big Thunder Mountain, then the Haunted Mansion in Liberty Square. All three attractions are relatively easy to board before 10 am.

- These lands stay crowded between noon and 4 pm, when the crowds line up to watch the afternoon parade finally disperse. If you miss Splash Mountain, Big Thunder Mountain Railroad, or the Haunted Mansion early in the morning, wait until early evening to visit them.

- Should you find yourself stuck in these lands in the afternoon, you'll find a bit of breathing space on Tom Sawyer Island or in the Enchanted Tiki Room or the Hall of Presidents. Surprisingly, Pirates of the Caribbean can be a smart choice even when the park is crowded. At least you wait inside, and this is one of the fastest-loading attractions in Disney World.

Time-Saving Tip

If you hustle to Frontierland only to find that Splash is posting a 30-minute wait, get a Fastpass and ride Big Thunder Mountain Railroad first.

Adventureland Attractions

Jungle Cruise

You'll meet up with headhunters, hyenas, water-spewing elephants, and other varieties of frankly fake wildlife on this 10-minute boat ride. It's dated-looking in comparison to the attractions in the Animal Kingdom, but it's still fun, thanks largely to the amusing patter of the tour guides, who somehow manage to tell jokes and puns so corny that you're groaning and laughing in the same breath.

The cruise isn't at all scary and is fine for any age. Fastpass is available seasonally but is rarely necessary.

Hidden Mickey

When you and the kids are keeping an eye out for Mickey Mouse, you may not realize that you're walking right past him. No, we're not talking about the life-size Mickeys, we're talking about those silhouettes and abstract images that are cleverly tucked throughout Walt Disney World. These "Hidden Mickeys" began as an inside joke among the Imagineers and artists who design theme-park attractions. Spotting a Hidden Mickey is a real treat.

Ready for your first test? When you pass a group of three beached canoes halfway through the Jungle Cruise, look carefully at the carvings. You'll see not only Mickey, but Donald and Goofy, too.

The Magic Carpets of Aladdin

This colorful, appealing attraction is a circular aerial ride similar to Dumbo. The twist is that you can make your carpet tilt, rise, or drop on command—evasive maneuvers that are necessary if you wish to avoid the spitting camels that guard the ride.

The Scare Factor

Because the carpets pitch around a bit, the Aladdin ride is slightly more intense than Dumbo, but most kids love it.

Walt Disney's Enchanted Tiki Room

Due to a vast number of guest complaints, the Enchanted Tiki Room has recently gone through an "anti-refurbishment"—in other words, Imagineers have now removed Zazu and Iago and returned the Tiki Room to its original show. The singing and talking Tiki Room birds represent Disney's first attempt at the Audio-Animatronics that are now such an integral part of theme-park magic. While not the most exciting show in the Magic Kingdom, it's an easy place to sit and rest for a few minutes on a hot afternoon. Grab a Dole pineapple whip at the nearby Aloha Isle first to help you get in a tropical mood.

The Scare Factor

The Enchanted Tiki Room show is loud. When the Tiki gods are angered, the theater darkens and lightning and thunder begin. The noise level frightens some toddlers.

Pirates of the Caribbean

This attraction inspires great loyalty and since the success of the movie series of the same name the pirates are hotter than ever, especially Captain Jack Sparrow. If you've been on the ride before, you'll notice an updated twist to the story line as Sparrow races to a cache of plundered treasure. It's a kick to see the new figures interacting with some of the older animatronic buccaneers. All the Audio-Animatronics figures are remarkably life-

The Scare Factor

The Pirates of the Caribbean queue winds through a dark drafty dungeon, so many kids are nervous before they even board. After that, the scariest elements of the ride occur in the first three minutes—there are skeletons, cannons, periods of shadowy darkness, and a manifestation of Davy Jones in the mist. When you get to the mangy-looking and politically incorrect buccaneers themselves, however, the mood is up-tempo, as evidenced by the cheerful theme song. This ride is fine for most kids over 6, unless they're afraid of the dark.

Insider's Secret

If you can't get enough of Captain Jack Sparrow and crew, stop by the Pirate League in Adventureland. Partly a boy-friendly alternative to the Bibbidi Bobbidi Boutique and partly an interactive adventure, the Pirate League experience begins with the spin of a chest to reveal your official pirate name. (I'm Charlotte Crestpaddler.) From there, young buccaneers can choose the Pirate Package for $30 that includes beards, eye patches, and gnarly-looking makeup. Johnny Depp wannabes can go for the full-throttle Captain Package, which adds on dreadlocks, a costume, and professional photography for $125. After suiting up, the freshly minted pirates are taken into a private room for the swearing of an oath, the presentation of their pirate credentials, and a picture-taking session before being released back into Adventureland. The cool thing about the Pirate League is that it isn't just an imitation of the Bibbidi Bobbidi Boutique; the setting is terrific and the cast members working the attraction enter into the pirate theme with great enthusiasm. Call 407/WDW–CREW for reservations.

Insider's Secret

Kids can become a pirate at the fun, lively, interactive Captain Jack Sparrow's Pirate Tutorial in Adventureland. A Johnny Depp lookalike and his mangy sidekicks pull young volunteers from the audience and give them a crash course in everything it takes to be a swashbuckling buccaneer. Check your entertainment schedule for showtimes.

like, right down to the hair on their legs, and the theme song is positively addictive. Even though the story is dark, violent, and brutal, in the hands of Disney it all somehow manages to come off as a lighthearted happy adventure.

Swiss Family Robinson Treehouse

There's a real split of opinion here—some visitors revel in the details and love climbing through this replica of the ultimate tree house, while others rate it as dull. Kids who have seen the movie tend to like it a lot more. Note: There are lots of steps, and this can be an exhausting attraction to visit with preschoolers, who often start out with enthusiasm and then clamor to be carried.

Insider's Secret

There's been a rumor that the Swiss Family Robinson Treehouse is due for a major revamp to tie the theme into a more contemporary movie and make it more interesting to the younger set. Stay tuned.

Frontierland

Kids love the rough-and-tumble Wild West feel of Frontierland, which is home to several of the Magic Kingdom's most popular attractions.

Frontierland Attractions

Big Thunder Mountain Railroad

A roller coaster designed as a runaway mine train, Big Thunder Mountain is one of the most popular rides in the park with all age groups. The glory of the ride is in the setting. You zoom through a deserted mining town and although the details are best observed by day, the lighting effects make this an especially atmospheric ride after dark. Be warned that the ride is very bouncy and jerky, but the effects are more apt to make you laugh than to scream.

The Scare Factor

When it comes to coasters, Big Thunder Mountain is more in the rattle-back-and-forth style than the lose-your-stomach-as-you-plunge style. Most children over 7 should be able to handle the dips and twists, and many preschoolers adore the ride as well. The height requirement is 40 inches. If you're debating which of the three mountains—Space, Splash, or Big Thunder—is most suitable for a child who has never ridden a coaster, Big Thunder is your best bet.

Splash Mountain

Based on *Song of the South* and inhabited by Br'er Rabbit, Br'er Fox, and Br'er Bear, Splash Mountain takes riders on a winding watery journey through swamps and bayous.

The Scare Factor

The intensity of Splash Mountain's last drop, which gives you the feeling that you're coming right out of your seat, along with the 40-inch height requirement, eliminates some preschoolers. Watch a few cars make the final drop before you decide. Our mail indicates that most kids over 5 love the ride.

Helpful Hint

Just because your toddler can't ride Splash Mountain doesn't mean she can't get a thrill. There's a certain place you can stand to watch the log boats on their final drop. The shrieks combined with the sprays of water will delight any child. A father of three from Florida agreed. "Our 2-year-old's favorite ride was Splash Mountain. She couldn't ride it, of course, but she stayed outside with Dad while Mom and her brothers rode and she loved watching the boats splash down. Water shoots up after the boats and she squealed every time."

Because it's the first thing you see as you approach, most of the attention is given to that 40-mph drop over a five-story waterfall, but there's a great story to the ride as well. You get into a log boat and follow Br'er Rabbit's adventures throughout the attraction, and each time he gets into trouble, you get into trouble, too. In other words, each dangerous moment is followed by an escape through a water drop, and the ultimate danger culminates in the ultimate water drop. The interior scenes are delightful, and "Zip-a-Dee-Doo-Dah," perhaps the most hummable of all Disney theme songs, fills the air.

Splash Mountain can get very crowded; ride early in the morning or in the last hour before closing. You can get soaked, really soaked, especially if you're in the front-row seats of the log, and especially if you're sitting on the right. This can be

Hidden Mickey

In the final scene of Splash Mountain, as you pass the Zip-a-Dee-Lady paddleboat, look for a pink cloud floating high in the sky. It's a silhouette of Mickey lying on his back.

great fun at noon in June, less of a kick at 9 am in January. Some people bring ponchos or big black garbage bags for protection and then discard them after the ride.

Country Bear Jamboree

Younger kids usually enjoy the furry, funny, Audio-Animatronics critters featured in this 15-minute show. From the coy Trixie, who enters via a ceiling swing, to the wincingly off-key Big Al, each face is distinctive and lovable.

The Jamboree seats large numbers of guests for each show, and it's a good choice for the afternoon when you'll want to sit and rest. Kids 10 and up often think the bears are hokey, so parents can take younger kids to the Jamboree while their older siblings visit Splash Mountain and Big Thunder Mountain Railroad. A clock outside the Country Bear Jamboree tells you how long you have until the next show. Don't enter the waiting area until the countdown is 10 minutes or less.

Tom Sawyer Island

A getaway playground full of caves, bridges, forts, and windmills, Tom Sawyer Island is the perfect destination for kids full of pent-up energy who just need to run wild for a while. You'll want to accompany them through the Mystery Cave and Injun Joe's Cave, however; both can be dark, confusing, and a little scary. Across the bouncy suspension bridge is Fort Sam Clemens, the perfect spot to play cowboy.

The big drawback is that the island is accessible only by raft, so you often have to wait to get there and back. If your kids are under 5, don't bother. The terrain is too wild and widespread for preschoolers without careful supervision. Likewise, there's little on the island for teenagers and adults. But for kids 5 to 12, a trip to Tom Sawyer Island is the ideal afternoon break. "Tom Sawyer Island was my 6-year-old's favorite place in the Magic Kingdom," wrote a mom from Texas. "It's so detailed with a lot for a boy his age to do. We definitely thought it was worth the wait to catch the raft."

Liberty Square

As you walk between Frontierland and Fantasyland, you find yourself transported back in time to colonial America, strolling the cobblestone streets of Liberty Square.

Liberty Square Attractions

Haunted Mansion

More apt to amuse than to frighten, the recently revamped mansion is full of clever special effects—there's a fascinating ballroom scene where spirits waltz, and, at one point, a ghost hitchhikes along in your doom buggy. The cast members have great costumes (including the bat-in-a-hat that ladies wear), and they add to the fun with their mortician-like behavior and such instructions as, "Drag your wretched bodies to the dead center of the room." The mansion is full of clever insider jokes. For example, the tombstones outside feature the names of Imagineers who designed the ride; keep watching Madame Leota's face and you may be surprised. And be sure to take a glance at the pet cemetery when you leave.

The Scare Factor

Many kids 7 to 11 list the Haunted Mansion as a favorite attraction. While some kids in this age group are frightened by the opening story, the setting, and the darkness, once they get going, they're usually okay. The attraction is richly atmospheric, but the spooks are mostly for laughs. In contrast, many toddlers are intimidated. One mother said that her daughter, age 3, referred to "that ugly house with the bad people" for weeks after their Disney visit.

Hidden Mickey

Look at the arrangement of dishes on the table in the Haunted Mansion banquet scene. Do any of the place settings look like you-know-who?

The mansion draws long lines in the afternoons, especially just before and after the parade. Try to see it mid-morning, or—if you have the courage—after dark.

Liberty Square Riverboat

The second tier of this paddle-wheel riverboat offers nice views of the Rivers of America, but the 15-minute cruise is a bit of a snooze for kids. It would be fine if they could really nap, but there are few seats on the boat, so most riders stand. Board only if you have time to kill and the boat is at the dock.

Note: The riverboat is sometimes used for special shows, such as the Princess Tiana's Jubilee during the release of the Princess and the Frog. During these times, of course, it's much more fun and a worthwhile stop on your tour.

The Hall of Presidents

The residents of the Hall of Presidents are so lifelike that it's a bit eerie (and Disney cast members report that this is a very "interesting" attraction to clean at night). The show opens with a film about the history of the presidency (otherwise known as

Insider's Secret

If you've visited the Magic Kingdom before and want to try something a little different, consider the Family Magic Tour. This adventure is designed for kids 4 to 10 and their families. You follow clues throughout the park and end by solving the mystery and finding a character. See Chapter 10 for details.

"nap time" for the preschool set) and moves on to the highlight, the presidential roll call. Each chief executive responds to his name with a nod or similar movement, while in the background the other presidents fidget and whisper.

The hall seats 700, with shows every 20 minutes, and thus is a good choice during the most crowded parts of the afternoon. Ask an attendant at the lobby doors how long it is before the next show and amble in five minutes early.

Food Choices in the Magic Kingdom

Let's face it, the Magic Kingdom isn't known for fine dining. Even so, some options are better than others.

If you want to have a sit-down meal and see the characters, consider Cinderella's Royal Table, which is inside the castle. The princess breakfasts and lunches are especially popular with young girls (generally ages 10 and under) who want to meet Cinderella, Snow White, Belle, and some of the other princesses. (Characters vary in the evening; check when you book.) Reservations are always snapped up months in advance, so be sure to reserve early, preferably 180 days ahead of time, by calling 407/939–3463 (407/WDW–DINE). Little girls like to wear their princess regalia when they dine in the castle, so pull

Helpful Hint

We thought the following note from a conscientious mom of two hit the nail on the head. "The one thing we learned about the Magic Kingdom princess breakfast is not to promise this treat unless you already have reservations. It took us six days of getting up at 6:30 AM to start trying to get through the phone line at 7 before we got lucky enough to get seats. I was already trying to figure out how to tell my then-5-year-old daughter there wasn't room for us at the castle."

Insider's Secret

In terms of fast food, your choices abound, but Cosmic Ray's Starlight Café in Tomorrowland is the largest fast-food spot in the park, and the lines move fast. For snacks, try the fruit cobblers at Sleepy Hollow in Liberty Square or the pineapple whips at Aloha Isle in Adventureland.

out those tiaras and magic wands before you go. One mother reported that she brought her daughter's princess gear with her and let her change in a nearby bathroom just before her character meal. "I noticed a lot of families doing the same," she said. "It makes sense because afterwards you can change your child back into play clothes for the rest of the day."

Other character options include the Crystal Palace, where Winnie the Pooh and his friends circulate among diners for breakfast, lunch, and dinner. There's a wide debate on the quality of the Crystal Palace experience; while one mom considered it, "perfect for our family since we love the Pooh characters, and the food selection was really nice," another mom described the food as "inedible, even by theme-park standards." The food is served buffet style, so at least there's no waiting and plenty of variety.

Insider's Secret

Closed out of the princess character meals at Cinderella Castle? Try the lesser-known princess meals at Akershus Royal Banquet Hall in the Norway Pavilion of Epcot.

Willing to dine without the characters? At Liberty Tavern, expect an all-you-can-eat dinner with down-home cooking like turkey, pork chops, mashed potatoes, and macaroni and cheese. The Plaza Restaurant on Main Street, thematically the plainest of all Magic Kingdom restaurants, offers a variety of salads and sandwiches, along with elaborate ice cream–based desserts. Tony's Town Square, also on Main Street, offers generous servings of Italian food and a charming *Lady and the Tramp* theme.

Afternoon Resting Places

- Country Bear Jamboree
- The Disney World Railroad (you can rest while you ride)
- The Enchanted Tiki Room
- Hall of Presidents
- Mickey's PhilharMagic
- Monsters, Inc.
- The small shady area across from Sleepy Hollow in Liberty Square

New Attraction

Sorcerers of the Magic Kingdom is a new interactive experience that encourages guests to collect magic spell cards and fight Disney villains. Visit one of the training centers in Fantasyland, Liberty Square, or Main Street to receive a packet of six magic cards and a specialized key card. Then travel around to different locations throughout the Magic Kingdom, hold up your key card, and use the spell cards to fight off villains. Sound complicated? Don't worry, cast members are all around to help, and kids always pick it up faster than the adults. Be warned though, this game can become addictive, and will take away from valuable time in the parks. Try to steer the kids clear if this is your first time.

Best Vantage Points for Watching the Parade

The Magic Kingdom has two basic parades: the afternoon parade (usually 3 pm), which runs daily, and the evening parade, which runs nightly in the on-season and periodically during the off-season. All parades begin by City Hall and finish beside the gate just to the left of Splash Mountain.

Insider's Secret

The evening fireworks include a nifty little extra called Tinker Bell's Flight. Look toward the castle and you'll see a young gymnast dressed like Tink descend via wire from the top of the castle.

Stake your curb space about 30 minutes before the parade is due to start. If you show up an hour early, you might snag a seat on the second floor of the railway station. For some families the bird's-eye view more than makes up for not being able to interact with characters.

Tips for Your Last Hour in the Magic Kingdom

- Some rides—most notably Big Thunder Mountain Railroad, Prince Charming Regal Carrousel, Astro Orbiter, Dumbo, and Splash Mountain—are particularly beautiful at night.

- If you're visiting on an evening when the parade is scheduled, make sure you're stationed as close as possible to the beginning of Main Street. This way you can turn in your strollers and make a final potty run before the parade

Insider's Secret

The best place to watch the Magic Kingdom fireworks isn't in the Magic Kingdom at all. It's the California Grill, high atop the Contemporary Resort. The California Grill is a beautiful upscale restaurant, with some of the best cuisine in all of Orlando. Despite the restaurant's reputation, it isn't formal or stuffy. Kids are welcome.

To see the fireworks, reserve a time about 30 minutes before the parade is due to start. (This needs to be done before you leave home. First call 407/824–4321 to determine the evenings and times the parade is scheduled, and then reserve a table by calling 407/WDW–DINE.) Since so many guests have been showing up at the restaurant just to see the fireworks, the restaurant has been forced to implement the policy that only diners are allowed to view the show. (Can't get a perfectly timed reservation? If you dine at California Grill earlier that evening, ask if you can return at fireworks time. Some families have reported that if they kept their dining receipt they were allowed back at fireworks time for the viewing. A large outdoor walkway area keeps the restaurant from getting too packed.)

Once the fireworks begin, the restaurant dims its lights and pipes in the theme music from the fireworks show. You have a fabulous view of the pyrotechnic display and a bona fide magical moment.

While the vantage point isn't quite as perfect, you can also see the fireworks from Narcoossee's and Citricos, two restaurants in the Grand Floridian.

And if you're willing to part with a few doubloons, there's even a pirate-themed cruise on the Seven Seas Lagoon that gives you a perfect view of the fireworks and lots of fun extras besides. See Chapter 12 for details.

begins and make a quick exit after the fireworks end. Otherwise you risk being stuck in the exiting crowds, which can be really difficult to navigate, especially if you're trying to carry small children or push a stroller.

@ Not watching the evening parade? It pulls almost everyone in the park to one place at one time, so about an hour before the parade starts you'll notice a definite shift in the crowd. This is a great time to squeeze onto a couple of rides that had long lines earlier in the day.

@ "People who aren't watching the evening parade really do need to get out before it begins," confirms one mother from New York. "The kiddie rides in Fantasyland get less crowded before the parade starts so we decided to ride a few one night and then slip out before the parade began. Bad idea. We lost track of time and it took us literally 45 minutes to get from Fantasyland to the front gate, pushing two strollers through crowds of people who were standing still in the middle of the sidewalks, looking up at the fireworks. After that we started setting our phone alarm to ring for 30 minutes before the parks were scheduled to close."

@ Wishes, the present manifestation of the fireworks display in the Magic Kingdom, is beautiful, with pyrotechnics perfectly synchronized to a musical score. It's presented nightly at closing time, even when the parade isn't scheduled to run, and it's visible from any location.

@ The rides stop running at the park's official closing time, but Main Street stays open for up to an hour longer. If the crowd looks bad here, you can be sure it looks even worse at the bus stop or monorail station. Pause, have a snack, and let the crowds thin before you exit.

Tips for Leaving the Magic Kingdom

@ Upon exiting, visitors staying off-site should pause and survey their options. If a ferry is in dock at your far left, that's your fastest route back to the TTC. Otherwise, queue for the express monorail back to the TTC.

@ Guests of the Contemporary Resort should either take the monorail or, if stamina permits, the footpath. Guests of Wilderness Lodge and Fort Wilderness should take the water-taxi launch. Guests of the Polynesian or Grand Floridian resorts should glance down at the launch dock. If a water taxi is in sight, take it back to your hotel. Otherwise, head for the resort monorail. Guests of other Disney hotels should return to the shuttle-bus station.

CHAPTER
6
Epcot

Epcot

WORLD SHOWCASE

ITALY
Via Napoli ✕

AMERICAN ADVENTURE
✕ Liberty Inn

JAPAN

GERMANY
✕ Tutto Italia

MOROCCO
✕ Marrakesh

✕ Teppan Edo

Biergarten ✕ 🚻

America Gardens Theatre ◆

AfricaOutpost

World Showcase Lagoon

FRANCE
Les Chefs de France ✕

Stroller & Wheelchair Rental 🚻

CHINA
Nine Dragons ✕

INTERNATIONAL GATEWAY 🚻

NORWAY
Akershus ✕ 🚻
◆ Maelstrom

Rose & Crown ✕

UNITED KINGDOM

✕ San Angel Inn

CANADA

MEXICO

WORLD SHOWCASE PLAZA

Le Cellier ✕

Odyssey Center (First Aid & Baby Care) ◆ 🚻

◆ Agent P Booth

Captain E-O ◆ Journey into Imagination

Tip Board

FUTURE WORLD

Test Track

Fountain of Nations

THE LAND
Living with the Land ◆ ◆ Soarin'
◆ Circle of Life
✕ Garden Grill

Mission:SPACE

Agent P Booth ◆ **INNOVENTIONS**
East   West

WONDERS OF LIFE

THE SEAS WITH NEMO & FRIENDS
✕ Coral Reef Restaurant
◆ Lockers ◆ Turtle Talk with Crush

UNIVERSE OF ENERGY

SPACESHIP EARTH 🚻

◆ Guest Relations

◆ Stroller & Wheelchair Rental

Entrance Plaza

Ⓨ

PARKING

Monorail

KEY
✕ Restaurants
🚻 Restrooms
Monorail
🚢 Ferry

Getting to Epcot

Many off-site hotels and all on-site hotels offer shuttle buses to Epcot, and it is also easy to reach by car. If you arrive early in the morning, you can park close to the entrance gate and forgo the tram. If you arrive a bit later, however, the trams do run quickly and efficiently. Just be sure to note the number of the row where you parked your car.

If you're staying at the Contemporary, Polynesian, or Grand Floridian resorts, your fastest route is to take the monorail to the Transportation and Ticket Center (TTC) and then transfer to the Epcot monorail.

The Yacht and Beach Clubs, and the BoardWalk, Swan, and Dolphin resorts are connected by bridge to a special "back-door" entrance into Epcot's World Showcase. You can get there either by water taxi or by walking.

Getting Around Epcot

Epcot is an acronym for Experimental Prototype Community of Tomorrow—although some Disney insiders insist that Epcot really stands for "Every Person Comes Out Tired."

Epcot is indeed sprawling—more than twice the size of the Magic Kingdom. It's composed of two circular sections, Future World and the World Showcase, which form a basic figure-eight shape. The only in-park mode of transportation is the FriendShip (there are actually two) that crosses the World Showcase Lagoon; most of the time, you'll walk.

Tips for Your First Hour at Epcot

- If you're an on-site guest and visiting Epcot on an Extra Magic Hour morning, only a few attractions will be open, but those will have a significantly reduced wait time.

- On regular mornings, you're usually allowed into the entrance plaza around Spaceship Earth before the rest of the park officially opens. You'll have time to get a map and entertainment schedule, and rent a stroller before the ropes drop.

- If you're staying at the Yacht and Beach Club, BoardWalk, Swan, or Dolphin and thus entering through Epcot's back-door entrance, walk through the United Kingdom and Canada until you get to the rope. It's a bit of a hike to start the day, but the payoff is that you're in a good position to beat the main crowd to Soarin' once the ropes drop.

- Once you're allowed into the main body of the park, ride Soarin' first. This attraction, popular with literally all age groups, can draw such long lines that Fastpasses frequently run out by midday. If you think you might want to ride again later in the day, go ahead and get a Fastpass. Next, assuming your kids are up for it, cross Future World and head for Test Track. If you didn't get a Fastpass at Soarin,' get one for Test Track. If you did use your Fastpass option back at Soarin,' ride Test Track first and then nearby Mission: SPACE. Confused? The main issue is that these three rides are the ones most apt to get crowded later in the day so you want to ride them relatively early and use your Fastpass option judiciously.

@ Next, visit the Seas with Nemo & Friends; after you disembark, head for Turtle Talk with Crush.

Attractions at Epcot That Offer Fastpass

Mission: SPACE

Soarin'

Test Track

Maelstrom (during the on-season)

Epcot Touring Tips

@ Take Epcot in small doses if you're traveling with young kids; four hours at a time is enough.

@ In the off-season, Epcot hours are often staggered. Future World is generally open from 9 am to 7 pm (although Soarin,' Test Track, and Mission: SPACE generally remain operative until Epcot closes), and the World Showcase is open from 11 am to 9 pm.

@ Tour Future World in the morning and then drift toward the World Showcase in the afternoon. You can escape to the films and indoor exhibits during the hottest and busiest times of the day.

- On entering a World Showcase pavilion that has a show or film—France, Canada, America, or China—ask the attendant how long until the show begins. If your wait is 10 minutes or less, go on inside. If the wait is longer, browse the shops or take a bathroom break and return 10 minutes before showtime. Epcot theaters are so large it's rarely a problem to get in.

- Innoventions provides a nice break from the enforced passivity of the rides. But ride first and save the exhibits for the afternoon.

- Check out your entertainment schedule and save time for some of the shows that take place in the pavilions of the World Showcase. Shows like Off-Kilter or the Chinese acrobats have major kid-appeal.

- If you miss Soarin,' Mission: SPACE, or Test Track in the morning, return in the evening. Although they're packed throughout the afternoon, it's often easier to slip onto these popular rides while everyone else is eating dinner in the World Showcase or watching IllumiNations.

- If you're touring off-season and plan to spend mornings in the other parks and evenings at Epcot, make your dinner reservation times early, like around 5 pm. That leaves you several hours to tour after dinner.

- Another alternative: If the kids have had a good afternoon nap and can keep going until 11 pm, arrange your reservations for 8:30. The restaurants keep serving as the park closes down, so eating late buys you maximum hours in the park—assuming your kids can handle the schedule, that is, and assuming that you'll be seeing IllumiNations on another night.

- If you're not staying for IllumiNations, begin moving toward the exit gates while the show is in progress.

Time-Saving Tip

A morning at Epcot is best spent moving among continuous-loading attractions such as Mission: SPACE, Test Track, the Seas with Nemo & Friends, and especially Soarin.' Save theater-style attractions for the afternoon.

Future World

Future World comprises nine large pavilions, each containing at least one major attraction, and is very much like a permanent World's Fair, mixing educational opportunities with pure entertainment. Most visitors are drawn first to the rides with their spectacular special effects, but don't miss Innoventions and the chance to play with the smaller interactive exhibits. These hands-on exhibits encourage young visitors to learn while doing and help kids avoid what one mother termed "Audio-Animatronics overload."

The Epcot Don't-Miss List

IllumiNations

Innoventions

Mission: SPACE (if the kids are old enough and
pass the 44-inch height requirement)

Soarin' (if the kids pass the 40-inch height requirement)

Spaceship Earth

Test Track (if the kids pass the
40-inch height requirement)

Turtle Talk with Crush

World Showcase entertainment

Future World Attractions

Spaceship Earth

Whatever their age, few travelers can remain blasé at the sight of Spaceship Earth, the most photographed and readily recognizable symbol of Epcot. Even preschoolers rate it highly, probably because of the excitement of actually entering the "big ball."

The ride inside, which coils toward the top of the 17-story geosphere, traces developments in communication from cave drawings to computers. You climb past scenes of Egyptian temples, a Greek classroom, and the invention of the Gutenberg press. A simple interactive game near the end lets you answer some questions and then see your own "future"—complete with your own face.

Take a few minutes to check out the post-show as you exit the ride. Most of the exhibits are technology based and geared toward older kids, but children of any age will enjoy watching their image flash on the screen and their hometown light up on a global map that indicates the hometowns of past guests.

Hidden Mickey

We all know Mickey is a star, and he actually has his own constellation in Epcot's Spaceship Earth. Look for him in the starry sky at the beginning of the ride, just after you load.

The Seas with Nemo & Friends/Turtle Talk with Crush

The Seas saltwater aquarium is so enormous that Spaceship Earth could float inside it. The Finding Nemo ride within is a hit with preschoolers. You board "clamobiles" (similar in shape to the Haunted Mansion "doom" buggies) and travel through a coral reef looking for Nemo. On the way, you meet Dory,

Insider's Secret

If you really want to experience the Living Seas, a program called DiveQuest ($175) lets visitors 10 and over scuba dive in the aquarium, while the Epcot Seas Aqua Tour ($140) lets guests 8 and up snorkel. Whether you go under the sea or stay on top, these three-hour programs give you bragging rights and a cool T-shirt. Call 407/WDW–TOUR if you're interested.

Bruce, and other stars from the film. At the end of the ride, you disembark at Sea Base, with its interactive exhibits.

Don't miss the lighthearted and funny Turtle Talk with Crush, in which the laid-back animated turtle interacts with the kids in the audience through real-time animation technology. Encourage your child to sit up front on the floor and ask Crush questions. We get tons of positive mail about this show. "Adorable," wrote a mom from Canada. "Our children considered it one of the highlights of the day."

Helpful Hint

Turtle Talk with Crush is far more popular than its out-of-the-way location and small seating area would indicate. If you have preschoolers, try to get here before 11:30 am. Afternoon shows can be crowded.

The Land

This cheerful pavilion, devoted to the subjects of food production and the environment, is home to three attractions, a rotating restaurant, and one of Epcot's most elaborate fast-food courts. Because there are so many places to eat here, the Land

Quick Guide to

Attraction	Location	Height Requirement
The American Adventure	World Showcase	None
Captain E-O	Future World	None
Circle of Life	Future World	None
Gran Fiesta Tour	World Showcase	None
Impressions de France	World Showcase	None
Innoventions	Future World	None
Journey Into Imagination	Future World	None
Living with the Land	Future World	None
Maelstrom	World Showcase	None
Mission: SPACE	Future World	44 inches
O Canada!	World Showcase	None
Reflections of China	World Showcase	None
The Seas with Nemo and Friends	Future World	None
Soarin'	Future World	40 inches
Spaceship Earth	Future World	None
Test Track	Future World	40 inches
Universe of Energy	Future World	None

Scare Factor

0 = Unlikely to scare any child of any age.
! = Has dark or loud elements; might rattle some toddlers.
!! = A couple of gotcha! moments; should be fine for school-age kids.
!!! = You need to be pretty big and pretty brave to handle this ride.

Epcot Attractions

Speed of Line	Duration of Ride/Show	Scare Factor	Age Range
Fast	30 min.	0	All
Fast	17 min.	!	5 and up
Fast	20 min.	0	All
Fast	9 min.	0	All
Fast	20 min.	0	10 and up
n/a	n/a	0	3 and up
Fast	13 min.	!	3 and up
Fast	10 min.	0	All
Moderate	15 min.	!!	4 and up
Slow	15 min.	!!!	7 and up
Fast	20 min.	0	10 and up
Fast	20 min.	0	10 and up
Moderate	8 min.	0	All
Moderate	15 min.	!	5 and up
Moderate	15 min.	0	All
Slow	25 min.	!!!	7 and up
Slow	30 min.	!!	3 and up

is crowded from 11 am to 2 pm, when everyone heads in for lunch.

@ *Living with the Land.* You travel by boat past scenes of farming environments, ending with a peek at fish farming, drip irrigation, and other innovative agricultural technologies. It's a fairly adult presentation, but it moves swiftly, so kids shouldn't be too bored. If you have older kids who might benefit from doing a school project on the subject of futuristic farming, consider the hour-long "Behind the Seeds" greenhouse tour. The sign-up booth is tucked away near the entrance to Soarin,' and the price is $18 for adults and $14 for kids.

@ *Circle of Life.* This 20-minute film stars Simba, Pumbaa, and Timon from *The Lion King,* and the beloved characters do a terrific job of pitching the conservation message. Simba explains how humans affect, both positively and negatively, their environment, so the show is both educational and entertaining. And because the Harvest Theater is large, with comfortable seats, Circle of Life is the perfect choice for afternoon.

@ *Soarin.'* Soarin' provides a bird's-eye view on an exhilarating flight above the beautiful state of California. It works like this: you're lifted 40 feet off the ground inside a giant dome. The interior of the dome is actually an enormous screen with images of redwood forests, Napa Valley,

Time-Saving Tip

Soarin' is madly popular and likely to remain that way. Use Fastpasses whenever you can and remember that on busy days all the Fastpasses may be gone by noon.

Yosemite, and the Golden Gate Bridge. You'll feel like you're hang gliding as you gently climb, bank, and descend your way through the scenery. The details make the ride: you'll feel the wind blowing through your hair and smell orange blossoms and pine trees. One mother of three from New York raved about the experience: "Soarin' was the favorite of everyone in our family, including our 5-year-old. She is normally afraid of heights but insisted on riding it three times, and the last time she actually wanted to sit on the highest row so she could see better!"

@ An interesting fact is that Soarin' is the most popular ride in all of Walt Disney World, both in terms of being highly rated and in terms of the ride volume. Perhaps it's because the ride appeals to all age groups, preschoolers to grandmas.

Journey into Imagination

The ride's premise is that Dr. Nigel Channing (Eric Idle), the rather stuffy head of the Imagination Institute, must be broken out of his shell and taught the true meaning of imagination, and the lovable purple creature known as Figment is just the dragon for the job. The ride is pretty simple, especially in contrast to other Future World attractions, but younger kids like it and there's rarely a wait.

After the ride, stop off at the interactive exhibits in the ImageWorks Lab.

Captain E-O

In 2010, *Captain E-O*, a circa-1986 film starring Michael Jackson, returned to the Disney parks for the first time in 15 years. The 17-minute presentation—which has silly characters, great dancing, and seat-grabbing 3-D effects—appeals to all ages. The basic plot is that Captain E-O, as a down-on-his-luck space commander with a misfit crew, uses music to transform a colorless planet into a world of peace and happiness. But it's really all just an excuse to remember what a phenomenal performer Michael Jackson was.

The Scare Factor

In Captain E-O volume is loud, the seats rumble a bit, and the supreme commander starts out pretty darn ugly, but there's little doubt that Michael and the gang will ultimately carry the day, so the show won't scare most kids.

Test Track

Test Track is the fastest ride in all of Disney World—we're talking 34 separate turns, 50-degree banking, and speeds of 65 mph.

The cars replicate tests at the General Motors proving grounds, and each vehicle is independently powered and controlled. In other words, this isn't the Tomorrowland Speedway. Thanks to an onboard computer, the cars are constantly adapting to road conditions, vehicle weight, and the location of the other 28 cars on the track.

You begin the ride inside, checking out how your vehicle responds to cold, heat, sharp turns, rough roads, and other stresses. The stress level of the passengers soars when you move to the impact test, break through a barrier, and then zoom outside the building to the track. Here cars reach their top speeds—well, actually, they could go higher than 65 mph, but Imagineers didn't think it would be prudent to break the Florida speed

The Scare Factor

Children must be 40 inches tall to ride Test Track. It's all about speed, with no flips or plunges, so kids 5 and up should be fine.

limit—as they go through a mile of curves, hills, and turns. It's one powerful ride.

Test Track can draw long lines, and a new interactive queue area will debut in 2012. A whole day's supply of Fastpasses is often gone by early afternoon. If the Fastpasses are all gone and your kids are old enough to handle the intensity, consider going through the Singles Line. You won't get to ride together, but your wait time will be cut significantly.

Mission: SPACE

Epcot's most technologically advanced thrill ride launches guests into a simulated space adventure, from the excitement of liftoff to the wonder of flight. To develop the story and design, Disney Imagineers worked with 25 space experts from NASA, and the result is completely immersive and interactive.

You're grouped into teams of four and each person is given a crew position—Commander, Navigator, Pilot, or Engineer—and assigned the tasks that go along with that role. Once you board your pod, everything happens fast. If you've opted for the spinning version of the ride, the motion is so rapid that it really feels like flight. The sustained g-forces during the launch are by far the most intense part of the ride. And before you fully recover, you're required to take on your crew role and push a few buttons (made somewhat more difficult by the gravitational pull of the ship's movement) as directed by mission control. (These "tasks" engage the kids, especially if they're a bit nervous

Time-Saving Tip

"I wasn't sure my kids could handle the g-forces [of Mission: SPACE] so I talked them into going into the green non-spinning line," said one mom. "An added bonus is that the green line is much shorter. We waited five minutes on a day when the regular line had a 40-minute wait."

The Scare Factor

There was tremendous concern over Mission: SPACE after two people died on the ride shortly after it debuted. It was ultimately shown that the victims had preexisting conditions, and the ride was not to blame, but Disney decided to offer a tamer—in other words, non-spinning—version of the ride for younger children and anyone with health concerns. As you approach the attraction, signs direct you toward either the orange team, which boards the spinning capsules, or the green team, which boards the non-spinning capsules. If you opt not to spin you have the same engaging preshow and postshow, and the same visual effects; the main difference is you don't feel the dramatic g-forces during the liftoff portion of the ride. That said, there's a fair amount of bouncing around in both sets of capsules.

The height requirement is 44 inches for either version. Take Disney's safety recommendations seriously: no pregnant women, children under 7, or anyone with high blood pressure or back, neck, or motion-sickness problems, especially on the spinning version of the ride.

about flying, but if you mess up, not to worry. You'll land safely back in Orlando just the same.)

In motion simulators you can avoid motion sickness by looking away from the screen, but on the spinning version of Mission: SPACE, where your cabin is actually moving, the opposite is true. If you begin to feel queasy, keep your head back against the seat and focus intently on the screen. Shutting your eyes is the worst thing you can do.

As you exit, there's a small Space Base crawl area for younger kids and a cool competitive group game called Space Race for older kids.

Universe of Energy

The Universe of Energy features Ellen DeGeneres, Alex Trebek, and Jamie Lee Curtis. Ellen has a dream in which she's a contestant on the game show *Jeopardy!*, and when she's thoroughly skunked by smarty-pants Jamie Lee, she realizes she needs to know a lot more about energy. Luckily for her, neighbor Bill Nye the Science Guy is happy to help.

The Disney twist comes when the 97-seat theater begins to break apart in sections that align themselves in sequence and form a train. A curtain lifts and you begin to move through a prehistoric scene that carries you back to the era when coal deposits first formed on Earth. All around you are those darn dinosaurs, among the largest Audio-Animatronics figures Disney has ever created. After your train has once more morphed into a theater, there's a final film segment in which a newly educated Ellen gets her *Jeopardy!* revenge. Note: The Universe of Energy is often closed in the off-season, and there are rumors that it might close permanently.

Despite its proximity to the front gate, Universe of Energy isn't a good choice for the morning; save it for the afternoon, when you'll welcome the chance to sit down for 30 minutes.

Time-Saving Tip

When entering the Universe of Energy, ask the attendant how long it is until the next show begins, or check the digital clock. Don't enter sooner than 10 minutes before showtime; this is a 30-minute presentation, and there's no point in wearing out the kids before you begin. The theater can seat many people, so there's rarely a reason to line up and wait.

Helpful Hint

Don't be overwhelmed by the options at Innoventions—just wander over to a kiosk and start playing. Cast members can answer questions or help you get the hang of the games and experiments. Exhibits change frequently, keeping things fresh, and many of the stations are kid-friendly. Even preschoolers will find plenty to do.

One of Innovention's exhibits, the "Sum of All Thrills" lets theme-park guests play the role of Imagineer and build their own ride. The experience begins with a tutorial in a design room. A few lessons on math and engineering are snuck in along the way as participants use a touch-screen computer to pick a vehicle shape and determine how fast the ride can and should go. The information is saved on a magnetized card that is fed into a simulator; visitors then get to experience the track they just created. Kids get to take the cards home where they can be used at a website sponsored by attraction developer Raytheon to access more fun math and science games.

Innoventions

Innoventions is the arcade of the future, where you can try out new video games before they hit the market, experience virtual reality, and play with beyond-state-of-the-art technology. The wizards at Innoventions have even found ways to make fire safety, recycling, and personal finance into fun interactive games.

World Showcase

Pretty by day and gorgeous by night, the World Showcase comprises the pavilions of 11 nations: Mexico, Norway, China,

Germany, Italy, America, Japan, Morocco, France, the United Kingdom, and Canada. The countries are like links in a chain that stretch around a large lagoon. Really large. Making a full circle is a 1.2-mile trek.

Some of the pavilions have full-scale attractions, while others have only shops and restaurants. Wonderful live entertainment is also available; check your entertainment schedule for showtimes.

Each pavilion is staffed by citizens of the country it represents. Disney goes to great pains to recruit, relocate, and if necessary, teach English to the shopkeepers and waiters here, bringing them to Orlando for a year and housing them with representatives from the other World Showcase nations. It's a cultural exchange program on the highest level. These young men and women save the World Showcase from being merely touristy, and provide your kids with the chance to rub elbows, however briefly, with folks from other cultures.

World Showcase Attractions

O Canada!

This 20-minute Circle-Vision 360 film, starring Martin Short, is gorgeous and stirring, but difficult to view with kids under 6. To enjoy the effect of the circular screen, you must stand during the presentation, and no strollers are allowed in the theater. This means babies and toddlers must be held, and preschoolers, who can't see anything in a room full of standing adults, often clamor to be lifted up as well.

Impressions de France

What a difference a seat makes! Like all the Epcot films, *Impressions de France* is exceedingly well done, with lush music and a 200-degree wide-screen feel. It's easy to get in, even in the afternoon, and no one minds if babies take a little nap. The 20-minute film shows on the hour and half hour, and there is rarely a wait to get in.

Insider's Secret

One of the best ways to get kids involved in the World Showcase experience is by visiting the Kidcot Fun Stops. Children begin a craft project (at present it's Duffy Bear, but sometimes you can make a mask or musical instruments as well) at the first booth they visit, and as they move to the next country, they receive another element to add to their project. It's a great icebreaker, and gets them interacting with people from other countries.

The American Adventure

This multimedia presentation, combining Audio-Animatronics figures with film, is popular with all age groups. The technological highlight comes when the Ben Franklin robot walks up the stairs to visit Thomas Jefferson, but the entire 30-minute presentation is packed with elaborate sets that rise from the stage, film montages, and moving music.

It's worth noting that some guests find the patriotism of the American Adventure a little heavy-handed. There seem to be two primary reactions to the show—some people weep through it and some people sleep through it. Most of our readers rate it as one of the best attractions in Epcot.

Reflections of China

Another lovely 360-degree film. But again, it's not an easy attraction to view with young children.

Maelstrom

In this Norwegian boat ride, your Viking ship sails through fjords and storms, over waterfalls, and past a threatening three-headed troll—all within four minutes. You disembark in a North Sea coastal village, where a short film is presented. (If you want to skip the film, no biggie . . . just keep on walking through the theater. Most families do.) The adjacent Kringla Bakeri Og Kafe is one of the best places in the World Showcase for a quick snack or lunch.

Hidden Mickey

Check out the mural of Vikings in the line before you board Maelstrom. One of the guys in the ship is wearing mouse ears!

The Scare Factor

Maelstrom sounds terrifying, but the reality is much tamer than the ride description. The much-touted "backward plunge over a waterfall" is so subtle that passengers in the front of the boat are not even aware of the impending doom. The darkness and the troll put off some preschoolers, but the ride is generally fine for kids 5 and up.

Gran Fiesta Tour

This mild little boat ride stars the Three Caballeros. The story line has Donald skipping out on a singing gig and José and Panchito searching throughout Mexico for their friend. The Gran Fiesta Tour is a very simple ride, somewhat reminiscent of it's a small world on a more limited scale, but younger kids like it.

Food Choices at Epcot

Epcot is *the* food park. It has such an embarrassment of riches that it's hard to choose.

For sit-down dining, one perennial favorite is the San Angel Inn in Mexico, which is a great place to escape on a hot sunny day. A shadowy waterway gurgles by and the scene is that of an evening marketplace, romantically dark even at high noon. Another popular spot is Chefs de France in—you guessed it—

France. Here the feel is of a Parisian sidewalk café with white tablecloths and bustling waiters. Le Cellier in Canada is perhaps the most popular Epcot restaurant, due to its tasty steaks and elaborate desserts, and the Tutto Italia Ristorante in Italy serves up delicious classics. Kids enjoy the show-style teppanyaki dining at the Teppan Edo in Japan, and the food—which includes such upscale items as Kobe beef—is outstanding.

One of the greatest recent additions to Epcot dining, believe it or not, is a pizzeria. But what a pizzeria! Via Napoli is a great lunch stop.

Not up for full-service dining? For a quick casual meal in Future World, head for the Sunshine Seasons food court in the Land, where you can choose from healthy salads, hearty sandwiches, and a variety of well-prepared ethnic dishes at different counters.

In terms of World Showcase fast food, you have plenty of possibilities. If you're concerned about how the kids will react to unfamiliar cuisine, not to worry. On kiddie menus the food is a nod to the country in question—for example, skewered chicken in Morocco or fish-and-chips in the United Kingdom—but the entrées are smaller and less spicy than the adult meals and look enough like chicken nuggets and fish sticks that the kids will eat them.

The Tangierine Café in Morocco has Mediterranean wraps, hummus, salads, and platters of chicken and lamb. The food is served in a pretty patio area with a perfect view of the pavilion. Don't miss the pastry counter in the back for baklava and other honeyed delights, not to mention Turkish coffee so strong that you may set a land-speed record on your next lap around the World Showcase.

While the Tangierine Café is right in the middle of the action, the Yakitori House in Japan is tucked away in the back of the pavilion with a soothing view of the manicured gardens and koi ponds. The food—especially the broiled skewers of chicken,

Money-Saving Tip

Not on the Dining Plan but you'd still like to size up a few of Epcot's posh restaurants? To save both time and money, stick to fast-food places for meals and make reservations at a sit-down restaurant for a truly off-time, like 3 pm or 10 pm and just have dessert. You can soak up the ambience for an investment of 30 minutes and 20 bucks.

Alternatively, as the average Epcot dinner for four costs about $100 without wine or beer, you can slice that bill in half if you visit the sit-down restaurant of your choice at lunch instead of dinner.

shrimp, and beef—is tasty and a bit lighter than many of the counter-service options. Another good choice is Kringla Bakeri Og Kafe in Norway, which has wonderful open-face salmon sandwiches and delicious pastries.

The Yorkshire County Fish and Chips stand in the United Kingdom is always popular. Carry your food into the back garden and sit on a park bench while you listen to the British Invasion sing Beatles classics.

The Boulangerie Patisserie in France emits such phenomenal aromas of coffee and croissants that there's always a line, even though the café is in an out-of-the-way back alley. Drop by for sandwiches, quiche, and a wide selection of decadent pastries, which are so good that they make the Boulangerie a favorite with Disney cast members. *Bon appétit!*

Epcot Extras

The Magic Kingdom isn't the only place to see the characters, catch a show, watch fireworks, or buy souvenirs. Epcot provides a whole range of entertainment, but with an international spin.

Characters

The character meetings and shows at Epcot are rarely as crowded as those at the Magic Kingdom. A well-marked character spot to the right of the fountains in Future World is your best bet to meet Mickey and his pals, and, in the World Showcase, the backdrops for individual character appearances can't be beat. You might meet Aladdin in Morocco, for example, or Mary Poppins in the United Kingdom. Check your entertainment schedule for times.

Insider's Secret

The princess character meals at Epcot are popular but not as well known as those in the Magic Kingdom. Akershus Royal Banquet Hall in Norway is the host, and at present the princesses show up at breakfast, lunch, and dinner. They stay for only about an hour, though, so be sure to verify that you're booking your meal at the time the characters are slated to appear. Also note that you may see Belle, Snow White, Mulan, or Sleeping Beauty, but Cinderella appears only in the Magic Kingdom. Reservations are a must; call 407/WDW–DINE up to 180 days before the date you wish to attend. The earlier the better!

The princess meals aren't just for girls. Consider this note from a mother of two in Delaware: "Even though it's somewhat geared toward girls, my 7-year-old son really enjoyed the princess breakfast in the Norway pavilion. The waiter greeted him by calling him 'Prince,' which he loved, and the princesses treated him like royalty throughout the whole meal. He seemed quite smitten with them."

World Showcase Performers

Singers, dancers, jugglers, and artisans from around the globe perform throughout the World Showcase daily. Times are outlined on your entertainment schedule.

Some of these presentations are more child-oriented than others. Children especially enjoy the young acrobats in China and the balancing act in France. Older kids can enter into the raucous action of the King Arthur skit in the United Kingdom or catch the "high-energy progressive Celtic music" of Off-Kilter in Canada. This translates to rock music with bagpipes— a must-see. The British Invasion, a talented rock 'n' roll group that plays in the United Kingdom, is also popular.

The shows are set up so that you can pretty much flow from one to the other as you work your way around the World Showcase. If you're there 10 minutes before showtime you can usually get a decent spot. Be forewarned that for most of the shows you'll either be standing or sitting on the sidewalk; only the stage where Off-Kilter appears has actual seats, and even that venue is way too small for the crowds the group attracts.

A mother of two from Illinois wrote, "Please stress how great the World Showcase performers are. We got wonderful pictures of our children with the comedy performers, and the Chinese acrobats were so good that we went back for another show. You don't hear much about the live entertainment in the World Showcase, but we found it to be the highlight of our day at Epcot."

Agent P's World Showcase Adventure

Want to save the world—or at least make the World Showcase more appealing to your kids? The Kidcot Fun Stops give preschoolers a reason to explore the World Showcase, and older siblings also have an inducement: a new high-tech mission called Agent P's World Showcase Adventure.

It works like this: as you're passing through Future World, you'll see the Agent P booths (one inside of Innoventions East, the other on the bridge into the World Showcase Plaza). If you'd like to go on a mission, stop by and pick up a free ticket. You'll be directed to a second booth inside one of the World Showcase countries, and there you'll be given a secret agent device. From there kids can help the beloved platypus, Perry, alias Agent P, from the cartoon series *Phineas and Ferb,* fight the evil Dr. Doofenshmirtz in seven of the 11 countries around the World Showcase. The secret agent device prompts kids to solve clues and defeat different "Inators," helping Agent P fight the evil doctor.

We can only hope the words "Curse you, Perry the Platypus!" will soon be echoing around the World Showcase Lagoon.

IllumiNations

This display of lasers, fireworks, syncopated fountains, and stirring music is a real-life fantasia and an unsurpassed Disney World classic. Very popular, very crowded, and the perfect way to end an Epcot day, IllumiNations takes place over the World Showcase lagoon at the 9 pm closing time. If you watch from the Mexico or Canada pavilions, you'll be able to beat the crowd to the exits afterward. Guests staying at the Yacht and Beach Clubs, or the BoardWalk, Swan, or Dolphin resorts, and thus leaving via the "back-door" exit, can watch from the bridge between the United Kingdom and France pavilions.

Insider's Secret

IllumiNations produces a lot of smoke. Before you select your vantage point, note which way the wind is blowing. If you have a pleasant breeze in your face now, you can be sure you'll catch the full brunt of the smoke during the show.

Shopping

You'll see things in Epcot that aren't available anywhere else in Disney World: German wines, Chinese silk robes, Mexican piñatas, Norwegian sweaters, and English teas are all within strolling distance of each other. Once you've made your purchases, either have them sent to Package Pick-Up near the front gate and retrieve them as you exit or, if you're staying on-site, have them delivered to your hotel. Both services are free.

Epcot International Food & Wine Festival

Dining your way around the World Showcase is always a treat, but it gets even better during one of the park's premier special events, the annual Epcot International Food & Wine Festival. It runs for approximately eight weeks, from late September through November. You can get exact dates and information by calling 407/WDW–FEST.

Open-air booths serving the food, wine, and beer of more than 60 nations are set up around the World Showcase, offering everything from New Zealand lamb chops to Bavarian strudel. The sample-size servings range from $1.50 to $4.50, so you can happily nosh your way around the world, indulging in WDW's biggest buffet. If you want to learn more about what you're eating and drinking, cooking demonstrations and wine tastings are scheduled daily and are usually free.

True foodies and wine enthusiasts should consider one of the special-event dinners. The Party for the Senses, Winemaker Dinners, and Reserve Dinners are very heady events, held in secluded glamour points all around Disney property, and they sell out weeks in advance. Call 407/WDW–FEST for a list of participants, dates, prices, and reservations. Details are also posted at www.disneyworld.com.

Insider's Secret

If you're intrigued by the Segways zipping around Epcot, guests 16 and up can sign up to learn how to ride and take a lap around the World Showcase—in the morning, before the park opens to the general public. Call 407/WDW–TOUR for details; at present pricing runs at $99 per person.

Afternoon Resting Places

- @ The American Adventure
- @ Circle of Life in the Land pavilion
- @ Captain E-O
- @ Impressions de France
- @ Universe of Energy

Helpful Hint

Epcot has many shows, so if the kids need to run off a little energy between presentations, check out the play fountains. One set is near Mission: SPACE, and the others are just to the right of the bridge leading to the World Showcase. They're a great place to cool off on a hot afternoon, especially if you bring along bathing suits or waterproof diapers.

Tips for Your Last Hour at Epcot

- @ If you're staying for IllumiNations, find a spot around the World Showcase lagoon 30 minutes in advance during the off-season, 45 to 60 minutes in advance during the on-season. Have a snack to help pass the time.

@ When staking out the perfect spot to watch Illumi-Nations, remember that much of the show takes place above you. If you sit beneath a tree or awning you'll have trouble seeing the fireworks in their full glory.

@ Not staying for IllumiNations? This is the perfect chance to swing back through Future World and ride Soarin,' Mission: SPACE, or Test Track on your way out. Just be sure you're at the exit gates by the time the fireworks end and the onslaught of people begins.

@ Lights are kept low during closing time to accentuate the effects of IllumiNations. This makes it easy to get separated from your party, so hang on tight to younger kids and make plans to meet at a certain place in case you lose each other in the exiting crowd.

Disney's Hollywood Studios

Disney's Hollywood Studios

Catastrophe Canyon

12 Lights, Motor, Action!

Mama Melrose's

Toy Story Pizza Planet

14

Jedi Training Academy

Star Tours

Muppet*Vision 3-D

16 **15**

Backlot Express

STREETS OF AMERICA

11 Backlot Tour

Honey, I Shrunk the Kids

13

Sci-Fi Dine-In Theater

Pixar Avenue

Sounds Dangerous Starring Drew Carey

17

Toy Story Mania

10

American Idol

19

The Great Movie Ride

Indiana Jones Epic Stunt Spectacular

18

Echo Lake

Mickey's Sorceror Hat

1

Earffel Tower

Walt Disney: One Man's Dream

9

50s Prime Time Café

Brown Derby

Hollywood & Vine Cafeteria

Hollywood Boulevard

Studios Tip Board

Voyage of the Little Mermaid

8

Oscar's Super Service

Animation Courtyard

Guest Relations and Baby Care Center

Lockers

Disney Junior– Live on Stage!

6

Entrance Plaza

Hollywood Junction Restaurant Reservations

Sunset Boulevard

The Magic of Disney Animation

7

Main Entrance

ATM

2

Beauty and the Beast–Live on Stage!

Rock 'n' Roller Coaster

4

3

Twilight Zone Tower of Terror

5 Fantasmic!

KEY

- ✕ Restaurants
- 🚻 Restrooms
- ••• Parade Route

Getting to Disney's Hollywood Studios

Compared with the Magic Kingdom, getting to Disney's Hollywood Studios is a snap. Shuttle buses run approximately every 15–20 minutes from all on-site hotels. Guests staying at the Swan, Dolphin, and BoardWalk resorts or the Yacht and Beach Clubs are a 15-minute water taxi ride from the Hollywood gate.

If you're driving to the parks, note that the Hollywood parking lot is small. If you get there at opening time and park close to the entrance, then you can forgo the parking lot tram and walk to the front gate.

Getting Around Hollywood

Hollywood is a relatively small park with no trains, boats, or buses. In other words, you'll walk.

Tips for Your First Hour at Hollywood

- Pick up a map and entertainment schedule as you enter. If you need a stroller, rent one at Oscar's Super Service Station.

- If you're at Hollywood on an Extra Magic Hour morning, the tip board at the end of Hollywood Boulevard will let you know which attractions are operative; the whole park doesn't open early but several major rides do.

- Toy Story Mania appeals to all age groups, so visit it as early as possible. Ditto with the revamped Star Tours. Fastpasses for the day are often gone by mid-morning.

- After riding Toy Story Mania and Star Tours, ask yourself: Are your kids old and bold enough for a couple of big-deal rides? If so, turn onto Sunset Boulevard and head straight toward Rock 'n' Roller Coaster and the Twilight Zone Tower of Terror. Waits are usually minimal in the morning, but if it's a busy day, get a Fastpass for one attraction, then immediately board the other. If your kids are younger, move on to Disney Junior or Voyage of the Little Mermaid.

Hollywood Touring Tips

- In general, you should save theater-style presentations— Disney Junior; Beauty and the Beast; Voyage of the Little Mermaid; Muppet*Vision 3-D; Indiana Jones; and Lights, Motors, Action!—for the afternoon. Tour continuous-loading attractions such as the Tower of Terror, The Great Movie Ride, Toy Story Mania, Rock 'n' Roller Coaster, and Star Tours early in the day.

- The one exception to this rule is if your kids are so young that you won't be going on most of the major rides. If so,

**Disney's Hollywood Studios's
Don't-Miss List**

Beauty and the Beast—Live on Stage!

Disney Junior—Live on Stage (if your kids are under 8)

The Great Movie Ride

Lights, Motors, Action!—Extreme Stunt Show

Muppet*Vision 3-D

Star Tours

Rock 'n' Roller Coaster (if your kids are 8 and up)

Toy Story Mania

**Twilight Zone Tower of Terror
(if your kids are 8 and up)**

Voyage of the Little Mermaid

ride Toy Story Mania first and then catch one of the morning shows of Disney Junior.

ℯ No matter what the ages of your kids, save the Backlot Tour and Animation Academy for after lunch.

Attractions at Hollywood Offering Fastpasses

Rock 'n' Roller Coaster

Star Tours

Toy Story Mania

Twilight Zone Tower of Terror

Hollywood Attractions

On Sunset Boulevard

Twilight Zone Tower of Terror

The Twilight Zone Tower of Terror combines the spooky ambience of a decaying, cobweb-covered 1930s-style Hollywood hotel with sheer thrills. For the clever preshow, Imagineers spliced together clips from the old *Twilight Zone* TV series, bringing back the long-deceased Rod Serling as narrator.

The story begins on a dark and stormy night in 1939 when five people—a movie star and starlet, a child actress and her nanny, and a bellboy—board a hotel elevator. The hotel is struck by lightning, the elevator drops, and the five passengers are transported into the Twilight Zone. One of the cast members who works at the attraction reports that the most common questions people ask her are "Is this a real hotel?" and "Am I going to die?" (The answer to both is "No.")

Hidden Mickey

During the Tower of Terror preshow, take note of the child actress boarding the elevator. She's holding a Mickey Mouse toy.

Your car moves out of its elevator shaft and through a hallway with holographic images before eventually settling into a second elevator shaft. (This is all drawn out with agonizing slowness.) When the car reaches a height of 150 feet, you begin your series of free falls.

That's right. Free falls is plural. When Tower of Terror first opened, you dropped only once, but Imagineers have since introduced a random drop pattern, which means that computers controlling the ride select from several possible drop sequences. You may be hauled up and dropped as many as seven times, and the trip up is as exhilarating as the trip down.

The Scare Factor

The Tower of Terror has a 40-inch height requirement, which means that many preschoolers are tall enough to ride. Nonetheless, our suggestion is 8 and up, both because of the spooky setup and the drop. The expanded drop sequence means you're bouncing around in the shaft for a good 20 to 30 seconds, which can feel like forever to a terrified child.

Rock 'n' Roller Coaster

The Rock 'n' Roller Coaster is one of the best rides in Disney World. The sound track, featuring Aerosmith, is perfectly synchronized to the movements of the coaster, and the volume is cranked to the max.

The premise is simple. You play the part of fans that have shown up at an Aerosmith taping, but unfortunately the group is in the process of leaving for a concert. They insist you come along to the show, so you're boarded into 24-passenger stretch limos, which their

Hidden Mickey

As you walk through the rotunda area before boarding Rock 'n' Roller Coaster, check out the floors; two Hidden Mickeys are in the tiles.

manager promises are "real fast," and you're off on a rock-and-roll trip through the highways of LA.

Takeoff is amazing—0 to 60 in 2.8 seconds—and then you're quickly thrown into your first total flip. The mazelike track will make a total of three inversions, and at one point you rip through an "O" in the "Hollywood" sign. The coaster is smooth and fast and offers uneasy riders one comfort: since the whole ride takes place inside a building, you never go very high,

Quick Guide to

Attraction	Location	Height Requirement
American Idol	Hollywood Blvd.	None
Backlot Tour	Pixar Ave.	None
Beauty and the Beast—Live on Stage!	Sunset Blvd.	None
Disney Junior—Live onstage!	Animation Courtyard	None
Fantasmic!	Sunset Blvd.	None
The Great Movie Ride	Hollywood Blvd.	None
Honey, I Shrunk the Kids Movie Set	Streets of America	None
Indiana Jones Epic Stunt Spectacular	Hollywood Blvd.	None
Lights, Motors, Action! Extreme Stunt Show	Streets of America	None
The Magic of Disney Animation	Animation Courtyard	None
Muppet*Vision 3-D	Streets of America	None
Rock 'n' Roller Coaster	Sunset Blvd.	48 inches
Star Tours	Hollywood Blvd.	40 inches
Toy Story Mania	Pixar Ave.	None
Twilight Zone Tower of Terror	Sunset Blvd.	40 inches
Walt Disney: One Man's Dream	Pixar Ave.	None

Scare Factor
0 = Unlikely to scare any child of any age.
! = Has dark or loud elements; might rattle some toddlers.
!! = A couple of gotcha! moments; should be fine for school-age kids.
!!! = You need to be pretty big and pretty brave to handle this ride.

Hollywood Attractions

Speed of Line	Duration of Ride/Show	Scare Factor	Age Range
n/a	35 min.	0	7 and up
Fast	35 min.	!	5 and up
Fast	30 min.	0	All
Moderate	15 min.	0	All
Fast	25 min.	!!	3 and up
Fast	25 min.	!	5 and up
Slow	n/a	0	2 and up
Fast	30 min.	!	All
Moderate	25 min.	!!	All
Moderate	35 min.	0	All
Fast	20 min.	!	2 and up
Moderate	3 min.	!!!	8 and up
Moderate	10 min.	!!	5 and up
Moderate	12 min.	0	All
Moderate	10 min.	!!!	8 and up
Moderate	20 min.	0	8 and up

The Scare Factor

Loud, fast, and wild, especially at takeoff, Rock 'n' Roller Coaster is for older kids and teens. With a 48-inch height requirement, suffice it to say that this will be much too much for kids under 8.

so there's no plunging sensation. Rock 'n' Roller Coaster is more about speed than big drops.

Beauty and the Beast—Live on Stage!

The Theater of the Stars is modeled on the Hollywood Bowl, and it's the perfect setting for this appealing 30-minute show. The costuming, choreography, and production are first-rate. The plot is drastically compressed, but since about 99.9% of the audience has seen the movie, it's not a problem. Beauty and the Beast is a good choice for the afternoon. The theater is covered and large enough to seat 1,500, so if you show up 20 minutes before showtime you should easily get a seat.

Fantasmic!

Fantasmic! may be the best show in any Disney park. It has everything—lasers, fireworks, lighting effects, music, fountains, a 6,900-seat amphitheater, 1.9 million gallons of water, 45 cast members, and a 50-foot fire-breathing dragon. The show plays at closing every night during the on-season and twice nightly on extremely busy days. During the off-season, it may play as

The Scare Factor

In Fantasmic! every Disney villain you can think of shows up for the cartoon Armageddon, and the middle scenes of the show are emotionally wrenching for preschoolers. Mickey saves the day, of course, and most kids adore the show. The noise is enough to frighten some babies and toddlers.

Insider's Secret

One problem that arises with all Disney's theater-style attractions is especially acute in huge venues like the Hollywood Bowl, where Beauty and the Beast plays, and the Fantasmic! theater. Let's say you arrive comfortably before the stated showtime and find yourself a terrific seat. As others file into the theater, cast members encourage you to move over and make room, and this goes on all the way until the split second the show starts. Ironically, those who came earliest often end up politely sliding their way into the far corners of the theaters, while stragglers end up with the best seats. And if you try to avoid this by swooping in at the last minute, you may not get a seat at all. Try this: instead of staking out aisle seats in side sections (where you'll find yourself being pushed to the walls), arrive early and sit along one of the aisles in the center section. You'll still be asked to keep sliding, but at least you'll end up near the middle of the theater.

rarely as twice a week, so make sure to arrange your touring plan so that you'll be in Hollywood Studios on a night when Fantasmic! is scheduled.

Mickey performs in his role as the Sorcerer's Apprentice, fighting off a horde of evil Disney characters with a variety of special effects, including the projection of film images onto a screen of water. For a while it looks like the bad guys are winning, and these dark scenes are upsetting for some children. In due time,

Helpful Hint

At Fantasmic!, sit at least 15 rows back from the front to avoid being sprayed with water.

however, Mickey's imagination conjures up images of happiness, love, and friendship, and the good-guy characters show up in force. Children of all ages rate the show highly, and it's surprisingly moving, even for adults.

Insider's Secret

Fantasmic! is always packed, but one surefire way to guarantee you get in is to purchase a Fantasmic! Dinner Package. It includes a meal at one of three Hollywood restaurants (the Brown Derby, Mama Melrose, or Hollywood & Vine) plus access to a priority-seating area of the Fantasmic! theater. Prices depend on the restaurant you choose, and the dinner package is included in the Disney Dining Plan.

At the Brown Derby or Mama Melrose's you can eat either lunch or dinner; at Hollywood & Vine it has to be dinner. As you pay for your meal, you're given a voucher that lets you into the priority-seating area. Don't arrive at the last minute though—you aren't guaranteed a specific seat, just a seat within a specific area. Make reservations by calling 407/939–3463 (407/WDW–DINE).

On Hollywood Boulevard

The Great Movie Ride

Beginning in the Chinese Theater at the end of Hollywood Boulevard, The Great Movie Ride is a bona fide classic. Disney's largest ride-through attraction, it loads steadily and fairly swiftly and is best toured either mid-morning or in the last hour before the park closes.

Your tour guide provides an amusing spiel as you glide past soundstage sets from *Casablanca, Alien, The Wizard of Oz,*

The Scare Factor

On The Great Movie Ride you'll encounter the Alien from *Alien*, the Wicked Witch from *The Wizard of Oz*, and any number of no-gooders on your trip. Some of the scenes are startling for preschoolers— the pretend gunfire as well as the confrontations, however campy, can be jarring to some—but the fact that your tram driver disappears and reappears does underscore the fact that it's all "just pretend."

and other great films. The Audio-Animatronics figures of Gene Kelly, Julie Andrews, and Clint Eastwood are among Disney's best. But things suddenly turn ugly as your car stalls and the movie scenes come to life. Depending on which car you've boarded, you're about to be overrun by either a Mafia-style gangster or a Western desperado. Your tram will be taken hostage, but don't fret too much. In a later scene, drawn from *Indiana Jones and the Temple of Doom,* justice prevails. Was there ever any doubt there would be a happy ending?

Afternoon Parade

A theme parade runs every afternoon, and the exact time and route are outlined on your map. Stake out curb space 30 minutes in advance during the on-season. Because the parade route is so short, the crowds can be 8 to 10 people deep, and no vantage point is significantly less crowded than another. It's worth it though; the energy and athleticism of the performers will amaze you.

On Echo Lake

Star Tours

Motion-simulation technology and a jostling cabin combine to produce the real feel of flight in Star Tours. The ride is the best of both worlds—3-D effects so convincing that you'll clutch

The Scare Factor

Most kids love Star Tours, and the new 3-D technology has actually cut down on the problem of motion sickness, which was formerly a complaint from some riders. The height requirement is 40 inches.

your arm rails but actual rumbles so mild that only the youngest children are eliminated as passengers.

A 2011 revamp added 3-D technology and allowed for 54 possible story lines. You read that right: 54. There are three possible opening sequences, three possible closing sequences, and between them you might travel to any variety of destinations from the movies. The ride is a little different every time, so ardent fans opt to take multiple trips. Use Fastpass for wait times over 40 minutes.

Jedi Training Academy

Younglings will jump at the chance to participate in the Jedi Training Academy, held several times a day on a stage outside of Star Tours. A Jedi knight selects audience volunteers (ages 4–12) and is leading them through some basic light-saber moves when suddenly (who could have seen this coming?) Darth Vader and his Storm Troopers show up looking for trouble. Each young Jedi-in-training gets a chance to show off his or her fighting skills in defense of the Force. "My 6-year-old son loved this attraction," reported one father from Michigan. "We ended up coming back for another show."

This Academy, which started out as a simple sidewalk show, has become so popular that Padawan hopefuls need to sign up first thing in the morning. The present sign-up site is right in front of Star Tours, but this may be changing; check with Guest Relations (a.k.a. Guest Services) as you enter to confirm. It's a little extra effort, but as a mom from Florida explains, it's all worth it. "My daughter loves Star Tours. A lady in Guest Rela-

Insider's Secret

If the Jedi Training Academy washes out due to a sudden rainstorm, this can be a good time to ride Star Tours. Not only is the attraction inside and thus safe and dry, but sometimes Darth Vader and his Storm Troopers find themselves dressed up with nowhere to go and are on hand to greet guests. Or stop into the gift shop Tatooine Traders, which had fun interactive experiences such as Make a Droid or Build a Light Saber. For a fee, of course.

tions told us we'd have to rush over to get her signed up, and we barely got her on for the last show of the day. A bonus is that the PhotoPass photographer was there. He got some great up-close shots of her fighting Darth Vader. She still talks about the experience, and the photos are among her most prized possessions."

Helpful Hint

The Jedi Training Academy can be great fun to watch even if you don't have a child in training. The young Padawan are adorable and it's pretty exciting when Vader shows up. The best place to watch is from the elevated and shady patio of the nearby fast-food spot, the Backlot Express.

Indiana Jones Epic Stunt Spectacular

This stunt show is loud, lively, and full of laughs. Audience volunteers are a key part of the action, and your odds of being tapped improve if you show up early and are near the front of the line. Professional stunt people re-create daring scenes from the Indiana Jones movies, and this 30-minute show is a great chance to see how some of those difficult and dangerous stunts actually wind up on film.

The Scare Factor
The gunfire and explosions in the Indiana Jones show startle some kids, but the fact that the theater is outdoors does dilute the intensity.

It's a huge theater, so even people who show up right at showtime are still usually seated.

The American Idol Experience
Fans of the TV show will love this attraction. A sign as you enter the park directs would-be superstars on where to audition, and the most promising performers are given a quick vocal lesson, a mini-makeover, and a slot to perform during one of the day's scheduled shows. Theme-park guests—with the help of critiques by professional judges who humorously fill the shoes of the show's celebrity judges—choose a winner from each show and these singers move on to the last show of the day. Whoever wins this Finale Show gets front-of-the-line access to audition for the real Idol judges.

Even if you're too tone-deaf to audition, watching the shows and voting is a lot of fun, and the studio is an amazing mock-up of the *Idol* set. Showtimes are listed in your entertainment guide, and, needless to say, the Finale Show is the hardest to get into. Show up early to get a seat. For the sake of the understandably nervous amateur singers, kids need to be old enough to enjoy watching the "filming" of a mock TV show and sit in reasonable silence during a 35-minute presentation.

In Animation Courtyard
Voyage of the Little Mermaid
Using puppets, animation, and live actors to retell the story of Ariel and Prince Eric, Voyage of the Little Mermaid remains one of the most popular shows at Hollywood.

The special effects in this 20-minute show are among the best Disney has to offer. You'll feel as if you're really underwater, and the interplay between the animation, puppetry, and live actors is ingenious.

The Scare Factor

Voyage of the Little Mermaid does have some frightening elements. The storm scene is dark and loud, and Ursula the Sea Witch is one big ugly puppet. That said, most kids have seen the movie and know enough to expect a happy ending, so they usually make it through the dark scenes without becoming too upset.

The Magic of Disney Animation

The Magic of Disney Animation opens with a fast and funny show starring Mushu, the pint-size dragon from *Mulan* with the voice of Eddie Murphy, and a live Disney animator. The animator describes how a character evolves in the animation process, and Mushu learns, to his horror, that he originally wasn't destined to be a dragon at all.

After the show, it's on to the interactive exhibits. These are fun for all ages, and you can stay as long as you like. "You're a Character," a quiz that tells you which Disney character is most like you, will save you years of money otherwise spent on therapy. (Don't like your character? Try the test again!) Or you can insert your own voice into clips of animated classics, digitally color a cartoon, or—most exciting for youngsters—meet the stars of Pixar's latest film. While stars from the Disney flicks circulate through all the parks, Hollywood is your best bet to meet the newest stars.

The best part of the attraction for older kids is the Animation Academy, where you can learn to draw a Disney character. Your drawing becomes a great free souvenir that you can take home. Many kids like to have the character they drew autograph the picture the next time they see him or her in the park. Or you can buy a frame for your masterpiece as you exit the attraction. "Learning to draw Pooh was an unexpected highlight for our family," wrote one mom. "I think we may have discovered an unknown talent in our 8-year-old son!"

Disney Junior—Live on Stage!

Younger kids love this stage show where they sing, dance, and play along with costumed cast members from Disney Channel shows. (Characters are updated periodically to make sure they're from currently popular programs.) The performance space holds large crowds, with the children (largely preschoolers) grouped on the floor where they can participate in the show, i.e., they can stand, jump, sing, and shriek within the confines of your claimed spot on the carpeted floor. Show emcees and performers are skilled at drawing even the youngest and the shyest of children into the action.

Although the show is simple, it's a big hit with toddlers and preschoolers, and substantial lines begin forming about 30 minutes before showtime. Visit whenever your kids are at their happiest and most rested.

Oh, and there's more excitement as you exit. Characters are often on hand for meet and greets in the Animation Courtyard, and this is the only place you'll see Disney Junior stars.

On Pixar Avenue

Walt Disney: One Man's Dream

This is more of an exhibit than an attraction, but it does remind you that almost everything in Disney World sprang from the extraordinary vision of a single man. There are plenty of artifacts and memorabilia, as well as a film about Walt Disney's life.

Backlot Tour

The Backlot Tour begins with a stop at the special-effects water tank, where audience volunteers help film a naval battle scene. Then you stroll through the props department before boarding a tram that stops in Catastrophe Canyon where you're caught in an earthquake and flash flood. (If you're sitting on the left side, prepare to get wet.) After the rumbles subside, you ride behind the canyon to see how the disasters were created. Note that the Backlot Tour is frequently closed in the off-season and there are rumors that it might close for good.

Toy Story Mania

Ever fancied being one of the toys in *Toy Story*? Well, going on this ride may be the closest you ever get, and there's no doubt you'll feel—ahem—animated. Toy Story Mania combines a ride through a cartoon toy box with the challenge of playing carnival midway games. You put on 3-D glasses and suddenly you've been shrunk into a toy spinning around with Woody, Hamm, Rex, and other familiar characters. Just when you're starting to get the hang of being in a cartoon, you come across the first interactive games. Using spring-action shooters, you'll launch rings at aliens, shoot darts at balloons, and hurl eggs at barnyard targets. Best of all, the ride gauges your skill level during the practice round and then adjusts the difficulty for each rider in order to create a level playing field. So a 5-year-old can compete *mano a mano* with her 12-year-old brother.

Time-Saving Tip

Toy Story Mania is a great crowd favorite, so go early and use Fastpass. "We arrived at 10:30 am to find that all the Fastpasses for the day had already been distributed," says one mother from Philadelphia. "We ended up standing in line for 90 minutes."

Toy Story Mania is similar in concept to Buzz Lightyear's Space Ranger Spin in the Magic Kingdom, but the technology is considerably more advanced. As you play, you see the "virtual objects" you've launched from your shooters either hit or miss targets. And at times it even seems as if objects are whirling past you as they pop out of the 3-D scenes. Like any attraction with scoring, Toy Story Mania is addictive, with riders coming back time after time to try and beat their own scores. "The best ride in Hollywood," enthused one mother of three, "and maybe in all of Disney World. The kids loved it and it took me and my husband back to our childhoods."

On Streets of America

Honey, I Shrunk the Kids

This playground is based on the film of the same name. "Miniaturized" guests scramble through a world of 9-foot Cheerios and spiderwebs three stories high. It's the perfect place for kids to blow off steam and very popular with the under-10 set. The only complaint is that it needs to be about four times larger!

Muppet*Vision 3-D

The Muppets combine slapstick and high wit, so everyone from preschoolers to adults will find something to make them laugh. Kids love the 3-D glasses and the eye-popping special effects. And the preshow is nearly as clever as the 20-minute main show. This is a good choice for early afternoon, when you've ridden several rides and would like to just sit and laugh for a while. The 3-D effects are more convincing if you sit near the center toward the back of the theater.

The Scare Factor

Although Muppet*Vision 3-D tested highly among kids ages 2 to 5, some parents reported that children under 2 were unnerved by the sheer volume of the finale.

Lights, Motors, Action!—Extreme Stunt Show

Based on the popular Moteurs . . . Action! Stunt Show Spectacular at Disneyland Paris, this show features special cars, motorcycles, and Jet Skis built to blow up, split in half, and perform other high-octane stunts. When the show starts you've been transported to a movie set, where the director is filming chase scenes and other daring feats with a cast and crew of 50.

The Scare Factor

The engines and pyrotechnics in Lights, Motors, Action! may startle babies and toddlers.

"The Lights, Motors, Action! stunt show was incredible," wrote one mother of two from Massachusetts. "We saw it twice. It's an especially good show for boys, since some of the other shows at Hollywood are a little girly."

Helpful Hint

Lights, Motors, Action! shows in a large arena, but you should still try to be there 20 minutes in advance. Showtimes will be listed on your entertainment schedule and the tip board on Hollywood Boulevard.

Meeting the Characters at Hollywood

Hollywood is a great place to meet the characters. Consult your map or the tip board, which is midway down Hollywood Boulevard, for the times and places they'll appear.

- A variety of characters greet you at park opening and return to the entrances around 3 pm.
- Toy Story characters appear across from Toy Story Mania. Other Pixar characters can be found inside the Animation Studio.

@ The stars of *Cars* can be found in their own little garage to the right of the entrance into Lights, Motors, Action! Extreme Stunt Show.

@ The newest Disney stars are inside the Animation Studio, along with Mickey in his Sorcerer's outfit.

@ Disney Junior stars are in the Animation Courtyard.

@ Disney Channel stars such as Phineas and Ferb are often found in the Backlot area. Check your Entertainment Schedule or stop by Guest Relations to see who is scheduled to appear.

Food Choices at Hollywood

The Hollywood Brown Derby is one of the best restaurants inside a Disney theme park—or any theme park, for that matter. Although it has gourmet cuisine and a beautifully urbane setting, it's still casual and friendly enough to take the kids to. The menu changes seasonally and is frequently updated, but one thing that's always available is the signature Cobb salad.

Other Hollywood restaurants offer big doses of fun for kids. The '50s Prime Time Café plunks you down in the middle of a television sitcom and serves comfort food like meat loaf, milk shakes, and mac and cheese. TVs play nonstop, you're seated in replicas of baby-boomer kitchens, and the waitress pretends to be your mom. Before the meal is over, everyone gets into the act, and "Mom" is likely to inspect your hands for cleanliness before she'll feed you, or she may force the kids to finish their green beans using the dreaded airplane technique.

Equally campy is the Sci-Fi Dine-In Theater Restaurant, where you eat sandwiches, salads, and pasta in cars as if you were at a drive-in movie. Your waiters are carhops, the film clips are cheesy, and the waiters add to the fun by presenting your bill as a speeding ticket. Drinks even come with glow-in-the-dark ice cubes. The one drawback to the Sci-Fi is that the monster clips that are shown on the drive-in screen are so graphic and so huge that they alarm some children, and the creepiness is accentuated by the fact that the restaurant is extremely dark.

The stars of Disney Junior appear for breakfast and lunch at the Hollywood & Vine buffeteria. Reservations are definitely a good idea for this one.

Due to its out-of-the-way location near Muppet*Vision 3-D, Mama Melrose's is definitely the least crowded and the fastest of the sit-down places. The veal *saltimbocca* and penne *alla vodka* are excellent.

If you just want a quick nosh, the Backlot Express lives up to its name and serves burgers and salads fast. Pizza Planet gets consistently high marks from our readers for both its *Toy Story* ambience and kid-friendly plain cheese pizza. If your party can't agree on what to eat, head for the open-air food court called the Sunset Ranch Market on Sunset Boulevard. You can each go in different directions for pizza, hot dogs, turkey legs, ice cream, and fruit, then all meet back at your table.

Tips for Your Last Hour at Hollywood

@ To guarantee yourself a seat for Fantasmic!, you'll need to enter the stadium at least an hour in advance, 90 minutes during the on-season. That's quite a wait, so you may want to eat dinner while you hold your seat. The stadium sells hot dogs and such, but if you want a more elaborate meal, you can buy fast food from anywhere in the park and carry it in.

@ If you're not watching Fantasmic!, the last hour before closing is a great time to hit any attraction you missed early in the day or to revisit favorites. Just be sure to be out of the park before the show wraps up. The big fireworks salvo at the end is your cue to get moving toward the exits.

@ Although a terrific show that more than justifies any in-convenience, Fantasmic! draws virtually everyone in the park to one spot at closing. Ergo, exiting afterward is a nightmare. Try to sit near the back of the Mickey section so you'll not only have the best view but also the best shot at getting out fast and beating the crowds to the buses, trams, or water taxis. But be forewarned—this is prime real estate and fills up early. If you end up near the water or in one of the sections to the extreme right or extreme left of the stadium, you've got no choice but to deal with the crowd. One option is to sit tight and wait for the stadium to at least partially empty, then eat or shop your way through the park, allowing most of the people to exit ahead of you.

CHAPTER
8.
The
Animal
Kingdom

Disney's Animal Kingdom

Kilimanjaro
Safaris
13

12 Pangani Forest
Exploration Trail

AFRICA

Rafiki's
Planet Watch
11

Tusker
House ✕

Harambe ◆

Wildlife
Express
Train ◆

ASIA

10 Maharajah
Jungle Trek

9 Flights of
Wonder

8 Kali River
Rapids

First
Aid ◆

Discovery River

Tree of Life—
It's Tough
to Be a Bug!
1

✕ Pizzafari

DISCOVERY ISLAND

KEY
✕ Restaurants
♿ Restrooms
⋯ Parade Route

7
Expedition
Everest

Character
Greeting Area

Island
Mercantile

Disney
Outfitters

✕ Flame Tree
Barbecue

**CAMP MINNIE-
MICKEY**

Festival of the
Lion King **14**

OASIS

The Boneyard
2

Guest
Relations ◆

Garden
Gate Gifts ◆

ATM

Restaurantosaurus ✕

TriceraTop
Spin
4

Primeval
Whirl
5

Finding Nemo—the Musical

6

Theater
in the Wild

Lockers ◆

Lockers

DINOLAND

Rainforest ✕
Café

Entrance

3
Dinosaur

Africa

Kilimanjaro Safaris **13**

Pangani Forest
Exploration Trail **12**

Rafiki's Planet Watch **11**

Asia

Expedition Everest **7**

Flights of Wonder **9**

Kali River Rapids **8**

Maharajah
Jungle Trek **10**

Camp Minnie-Mickey

Festival of the
Lion King **14**

Dinoland

The Boneyard **2**

Dinosaur **3**

Finding Nemo—
the Musical **6**

Primeval Whirl **5**

TriceraTop Spin **4**

Discovery Island

Tree of Life—It's Tough
to Be a Bug! **1**

Getting to the Animal Kingdom

The Animal Kingdom parking lot is relatively small; all on-site hotels run direct shuttles, and many off-site hotels do as well. If possible, arrive by bus. If you're coming by car, try to arrive early, before the main parking lot is filled. Otherwise, you'll be directed to an auxiliary lot.

Getting Around the Animal Kingdom

With more than 500 acres, technically the Animal Kingdom is the largest of all the Disney parks, but most of the space is earmarked for animal habitats, such as the huge 100-acre savanna featured in Kilimanjaro Safaris. The walkable part of the park is relatively compact—a good thing, since the only real means of getting around is on foot. The layout is basically circular, with the 14-story Tree of Life in the center. This may sound like the Animal Kingdom is easy enough to navigate, but in the middle of the day the area around the main entrance can become so crowded that it's nearly impassable. If you're trying to move around the park, your best bet is to cut through the Asia section, essentially going behind the Tree of Life. It looks like you're going out of your way (and, to some degree, you are), but the traffic flow works more in your favor.

At Disney World it's easy to fall into the trap of thinking "the faster you go, the more you'll see," but at the Animal Kingdom, the opposite is true. Slow your pace a little, because this park is designed for savoring. There are more than 1,700 live animals representing more than 250 species in the Animal Kingdom, and the park is also a botanical marvel, showcasing more than 3,000 species of plants. So, relax and enjoy the incredible natural beauty of the park and the many small-animal habitats tucked along the way.

Tips for Your First Hour in the Animal Kingdom

- On Extra Magic Hour mornings only a few attractions will be operative during the first hour, but they will be indicated on a sign as you enter.

- The Oasis is the entry area, much like Main Street in the Magic Kingdom, and it often opens 30 minutes before the stated entry time. Characters are usually on hand to keep the kids entertained.

- The animal-habitat areas in the Oasis are charming, but don't visit them in the morning. You'll be stampeded by the people behind you hustling to get to the big rides . . . not to mention the fact that you need to hustle to the big rides yourself. It's better to visit the Oasis in the afternoon or evening, on your way out of the park. That way it's not a big deal if you stand there for 20 minutes waiting for the three-toed sloth to move.

- When the park opens, attendants are usually standing near the Tree of Life, directing you toward attractions. Because they're on walkie-talkies with the operators of the rides, these cast members can give you approximate wait times and save you from hotfooting it to a ride only to find a 40-minute wait. The tip board in front of the Tree of Life also lists upcoming showtimes and the approximate wait time for major attractions.

@ Head first to Africa and ride Kilimanjaro Safaris. Then cross to Asia and ride Expedition Everest.

Attractions at the Animal Kingdom Offering Fastpasses

Dinosaur

Expedition Everest

Kali River Rapids

Kilimanjaro Safaris

Primeval Whirl

Festival of the Lion King

Animal Kingdom Touring Tips

@ Because of the relatively small number of attractions, you can tour the Animal Kingdom in about six hours. The park is often mobbed between 10 am and 3 pm, but it usually begins to clear out by mid-afternoon. If you can't be there first thing in the morning, consider arriving after lunch.

@ Because of their proximity, consider combining a morning visit to the Animal Kingdom and an afternoon visit to Blizzard Beach. The parks are five minutes apart by car and many hotel buses stop at both.

@ The Animal Kingdom closes early (between 5 and 7 pm depending on the season) and has no closing show.

Quick Guide to

Attraction	Location	Height Requirement
The Boneyard	DinoLand	None
Character Greeting Area	Camp Minnie-Mickey	None
Dinosaur	DinoLand	40 inches
Expedition Everest	Asia	44 inches
Festival of the Lion King	Camp Minnie-Mickey	None
Finding Nemo—the Musical	DinoLand	None
Flights of Wonder	Asia	None
Kali River Rapids	Asia	38 inches
Kilimanjaro Safaris	Africa	None
Maharajah Jungle Trek	Asia	None
Pangani Forest Exploration Trail	Africa	None
Primeval Whirl	DinoLand	48 inches
Rafiki's Planet Watch	Africa	None
Tree of Life— It's Tough to Be a Bug!	Discovery Island	None
TriceraTop Spin	DinoLand	None

Scare Factor

0 = Unlikely to scare any child of any age.
! = Has dark or loud elements; might rattle some toddlers.
!! = A couple of gotcha! moments; should be fine for school-age kids.
!!! = You need to be pretty big and pretty brave to handle this ride.

Animal Kingdom Attractions

Speed of Line	Duration of Ride/Show	Scare Factor	Age Range
n/a	n/a	0	All
Moderate	n/a	0	All
Moderate	10 min.	!!!	7 and up
Moderate	10 min.	!!!	8 and up
Moderate	25 min.	0	All
Moderate	30 min.	0	All
Fast	25 min.	0	All
Moderate	7 min.	!	4 and up
Moderate	20 min.	!	6 and up
Fast	n/a	0	All
Moderate	n/a	0	All
Slow	7 min.	!!	5 and up
Fast	20 min.	0	All
Slow	10 min.	!	All
Slow	4 min.	!	All

Insider's Secret

In your dash to get to the rides and shows, don't forget that the Animal Kingdom is really all about the animals. The Maharajah Jungle Trek and Pangani Forest Exploration Trail are major attractions, as well designed as any zoo, and there are other small enclaves of animal habitats around the Tree of Life.

The Animal Kingdom Don't-Miss List

Dinosaur (if your kids are 7 or older)

Expedition Everest (if kids are 8 or older and at least 44 inches tall)

Festival of the Lion King

Kali River Rapids

Kilimanjaro Safaris

Maharajah Jungle Trek

Pangani Forest Exploration Trail

Tree of Life—It's Tough to Be a Bug!

Finding Nemo—the Musical

Animal Kingdom Attractions

The attractions may be few, but they're powerful. Most are designed for the whole family to enjoy together.

On Discovery Island

Tree of Life—It's Tough to Be a Bug!

This state-of-the-art 3-D film is a real highlight for all ages. First of all, it's shown inside the Tree of Life, which is an amazing edifice with 325 animals carved into its trunk. Perfect for pictures. The show combines visual, sensory, and tactile effects and the cast of characters, including an accurately named Stinkbug, is so funny that everyone leaves laughing. The best effect of all is at the very end of the show.

The Scare Factor

Tree of Life—It's Tough to be a Bug! is a huge hit with most kids, but there are scary scenes. At one point large spider puppets dangle over your head. Later, the theater goes dark, you hear swarming wasps, and the back of your seat might give you a small electrical zap. (Not into pain? Simply lean forward in your seat.) Most children seem to find Flik and friends to be great fun, but there's usually at least one child crying in the audience. If your kids are scared of the dark or bugs, skip the show. "My 7-year-old girl is normally a brave thing," wrote a mom from England. "She went on Tower of Terror, Space Mountain, Expedition Everest, etc., with no problem at all. But Tree of Life—It's Tough to Be a Bug! scared her so badly she was ready to leave. . . ."

In Africa

Kilimanjaro Safaris

This is the Animal Kingdom's premier attraction, a two-mile ride through the open bush that simulates an African photo safari. The animals have a great deal of open space around them, and in fact appear to be running free—although cleverly incorporated water and plant barriers ensure that the cheetahs don't meet up with the ostriches and graphically illustrate the circle of life right in front of the kids.

Your guide helps you tell the impalas from the gazelles and at times your vehicle (called a lorry) comes startlingly close to the wildlife. The story is that you're helping the game warden look for poachers who have abducted a baby elephant.

Safari drivers say that the animals are often active in the morning, but that you have a better chance of seeing cheetahs, rhinos, and warthogs later in the day. And because of the attraction's mammoth and unpredictable animal cast, Kilimanjaro is, in essence, a different adventure every time. You could go on one safari in the morning, get a Fastpass, and return in the afternoon for a whole new show.

Coming Soon

Disney has recently announced that it will partner with James Cameron to create a new section of the Animal Kingdom that will be based on the movie Avatar. All ideas are still in their planning stages and construction isn't set to begin until 2013. Be on the lookout for more information soon!

Wild Africa Trek

Really into animals? Willing to pay for a one-of-a-kind adventure? Consider this three-hour family-friendly behind-the-scenes tour for ages 8 and up. One highlight is crossing a rope bridge that sways 50 feet above a creek full of crocodiles. You're safely tethered with a bungee cord, of course, and the bridge is created only to seem precarious, but it's still exciting. You also hike through the bush, get up close to hippos, eat a stupendously good lunch from a deck in the savanna, and have access to guides who give far more info than you'd get on Kilimanjaro Safaris. In fact, the Trek is the perfect basis for a school project. Despite the $189 per-person price, tours fill up fast. Make reservations at (407) WDW–TOUR well in advance.

Pangani Forest Exploration Trail

Near the exit of Kilimanjaro Safaris is a self-guided walking trail. The highlight is seeing the jungle home of Gino, the silverback gorilla, and his harem. (The dominant male in a gorilla troop is called the silverback because he is ordinarily older than the other males and often has gray hairs mixed in with the black.) Along the trail you also pass everything from mole rats to hippos to birds in an enclosed aviary, but children seem to especially enjoy the warthogs and meerkats in the savanna exhibit. Trail Guides are on hand to answer questions and help point out the animals.

Rafiki's Planet Watch

To learn more about how Disney cares for animals in the park, this attraction will answer many of your questions.

Helpful Hint

Rafiki's Planet Watch requires time and effort for the round-trip. Save it for after the major attractions.

You board a nifty train called the Wildlife Express for a five-minute ride to Rafiki's Planet Watch. Along the way, you'll see where the animals sleep at night—a cool peek behind the scenes that older kids appreciate. You disembark at Rafiki's Planet Watch, a station in the farthest-flung section of the park. There you'll find exhibits on the subjects of conservation and animal endangerment. Kids especially enjoy touring the veterinary labs, where newborns and sick animals get a lot of attention, and the Affection Station, where they can pat and touch the friendly goats, llamas, and sheep.

Rafiki's Planet Watch is difficult to reach with small children, since getting from the train to the station is quite a hike. For kids under 5, make sure to bring your stroller with you.

The good news is that once you get there, you can park the stroller and see everything relatively easily—including great meet-and-greet opportunities with Rafiki, Pocahontas, and the rarely seen Jiminy Cricket.

In DinoLand

DinoLand is a story unto itself. The official history of this section is that a giant collection of dinosaur bones was found in Central Florida and the scientifically minded Dino Institute built its headquarters next to the dig site. The Institute attracted so many interns that separate quarters had to be built—in what is now Restaurantosaurus—and this led to the Institute's becoming a tourist attraction. A Texan couple named Chester and Hester, never ones to let a good opportunity pass them by, bought up all the land surrounding the Institute to build a roadside attraction to entertain all those tourists. And thus the part serious/part wacky "DinoLand" was born.

The Scare Factor

Dinosaur combines atmospheric scariness with a wild-moving vehicle. The height requirement is 40 inches, which means that plenty of preschoolers qualify to board; nonetheless, based on the realism of the dinosaurs, we say wait until kids are at least 7 to ride, and even then consider whether they're brave enough to handle very big, very loud dinosaurs jumping out at them while the car takes steep drops. "As much as our young son (age 7) loves dinosaurs, this ride proved to be too much for him," wrote a mom of two. "We are planning another trip to Disney this year, and he still reminds us that he is not going on the dinosaur ride again."

Dinosaur

You're strapped into "high-speed" motion vehicles and sent back in time to the Cretaceous period to save the gentle, plant-eating iguanodon from extinction.

It's a noble mission, but it ain't easy. Along the way, Disney throws everything it has at you: asteroids, meteors, incoming pterodactyls, and ticked-off people-eating dinosaurs. The dinosaurs are extremely lifelike, and in some cases extremely close. The jeeps bounce around like mad, so Dinosaur can be a bit rough—but it's also a powerfully fun ride.

Helpful Hint

A rather secluded character greeting area is located to the right just before you cross the bridge into DinoLand. Typically, this is the best place in all of Walt Disney World to see the characters from Winnie the Pooh. A sign as you enter will help you verify which characters you'll find waiting at the end of the path.

Finding Nemo—the Musical (In Theater in the Wild)

Based on the animated film, *Finding Nemo,* this kid-pleasing musical combines performances by puppets, dancers, and acrobats, all choreographed to envelop you in Nemo's big blue world. The puppets, created by the same team who brought *The Lion King* to Broadway, are especially amazing and the special effects are dazzling.

The story will be familiar to anyone who's seen the movie—Nemo and his father, Marlin, go on separate journeys that ultimately teach them how to understand each other. The catchy pop music and the multigenerational humor are designed to appeal to all age groups, and the ending may cause

Helpful Hint

Finding Nemo is a good example of why closer isn't always better. If you sit too close to the stage you'll miss some of the action, which takes place on the catwalk behind the section that is closest to the stage. The best viewing is the center section, about two-thirds of the way back.

you to shed a tear. Arrive at the theater 20 minutes ahead of showtime, 30–45 during the on-season, to guarantee good seats.

The Boneyard

A great attraction for kids 7 and under, the Boneyard is a playground designed to simulate an archaeological dig site. Kids can dig for "fossils," excavate "bones," and play on bridges and slides. The playground is visually witty—where else can you find slides made from prehistoric animal skeletons?—and has fun surprises, such as a footprint that roars when you jump on it.

Visit the Boneyard after you've toured the biggies and the kids are ready to romp for a while. The play area can get very hot on a Florida afternoon, however, so remember the sunscreen and water bottles. If it's a really roasting day, head for the woolly mammoth dig-site area, which is covered and has large fans to cut down on the heat. "My 3-year-old loved the dig

Helpful Hint

The good news is that kids can lose themselves in the Boneyard and happily play for an hour. The bad news is that parents can lose their kids as well. The Boneyard is sprawling, so keep your eyes on young children at all times, especially when they're playing on the slides. When they enter at the top, it's often hard to tell what chute they're in or where they'll emerge.

site," reported one father. "We hung out there for about an hour while my wife took the older kids on Dinosaur."

TriceraTop Spin

The kid-friendly TriceraTop Spin is a circular ride similar to Dumbo, except that you fly in dinosaurs, naturally. The beasts tilt back and forth as you climb or descend.

The Scare Factor

If they loved Dumbo, they'll love TriceraTop Spin.

Primeval Whirl

The second ride in Chester and Hester's Dino-Rama is Primeval Whirl, a crazy mouse–style coaster with spinning cars, hairpin turns, and numerous dips. Primeval Whirl is a slow-boarding, low-capacity ride and can draw lines. If you're visiting on a busy day, use Fastpass.

The Scare Factor

A bit surprisingly, Primeval Whirl has a 48-inch height requirement. The ride is faster than it looks and has many spins. Most kids over 5 (assuming they make the height requirement) love it, but if you have any doubts, watch it make a cycle or two before joining the queue. And this is not a good choice for anyone prone to motion sickness.

In Camp Minnie-Mickey

Character Greeting Area

The highlight of Camp Minnie-Mickey is meeting the characters, all adorably decked out in picnic gear. The greeting areas are especially busy just after a showing of Festival of the Lion King.

Festival of the Lion King

This is one of the best attractions in the Animal Kingdom.

Festival of the Lion King features what you might expect—singers, dancers, the characters—as well as acrobatic "monkeys" twirling fire batons, and "birds" that dramatically take flight. The costuming is incredible, the music is wonderful, and the finale is guaranteed to give you goose bumps.

The performers interact directly with the audience, and at one point small children from the crowd are invited to join in a simple circular parade. Children sitting near the front are more apt to be tapped.

Festival of the Lion King is very popular. Disney has started offering Fastpass due to this show's crowd appeal. However, due to the Festival's very out-of-the-way location, the kiosk to pick up your Fastpass is located near It's Tough to Be a Bug! It's a little confusing, but once you see where the show is located, you'll thank Disney for saving you the walk. Besides, you'll need a Fastpass only on especially crowded days. Showtimes are printed on your entertainment schedule; be there at least 30 minutes beforehand if you'd like to sit near the front.

In Asia

Kali River Rapids

For this water ride you board an eight-passenger raft for a descent down a meandering river through rapids, geysers, and waterfalls. Expect to get very wet, possibly soaked, depending on where you're sitting in the raft. (And since the rafts are circular and constantly turning throughout the ride, it's impossible to

The Scare Factor

The height requirement is only 38 inches, reflecting the fact that Kali River Rapids is a very mild ride, with only one sizable descent along the way. It's fine for anyone who isn't afraid of getting wet.

predict which seats will catch the most spray.) Stow cameras and other water-sensitive valuables in lockers before you board, and bring your trusty poncho.

It's also good to keep your feet up on the center bar. A wet fanny is an inconvenience, but wet shoes and socks can lead to blisters and ruin your whole day. Also consider bringing a change of clothes. One mom said her soaking wet child burst into tears and had to be taken back to the hotel to change.

Insider's Secret

Are some of your kids too young or too short to ride? Let them man Kali's water cannons on the bridge as you approach the ride; there they can take aim against their older siblings as they pass in the rafts below. Revenge is sweet! And to be honest, soaking strangers can be fun, too.

Maharajah Jungle Trek

Another lovely walking path, this one goes through habitats of Asia. The Bengal tigers are the undisputed stars of the show, but you'll also encounter Komodo dragons, gibbons, and, most intriguing of all, giant fruit bats. Take time along the path to appreciate the glorious landscaping and the beauty of the architecture. In fact, if you only have time to choose one animal path, the Maharajah Jungle Trek gets the nod over Pangani Forest Exploration Trail, largely because the tigers lie around more—and thus are more likely to be in viewing range—than the gorillas.

Hidden Mickey

The Maharajah Jungle Trek is Hidden Mickey city. There are several in the drawings on the ruins just as you enter the tiger habitat.

Flights of Wonder

The Caravan Stage is home to this lovely display of birds in free flight. The show's premise is a bit silly, but you can count on seeing falcons, vultures, hawks, and toucans demonstrating their unusual talents. Several members of the audience, including kids, are invited onstage to interact with the birds. Showtimes are noted on your entertainment schedule; be there 10 minutes before showtime to assure a good seat, 20 minutes during the on-season. Flights of Wonder is a good choice for the most crowded times of the afternoon.

Expedition Everest

Expedition Everest is one of the most exciting attractions in all of Disney World. The premise is that your mountain train is

Helpful Hint

Expedition Everest draws major crowds. Although the ride does board quickly and the lines do move fast, come in the morning or use Fastpass. The ride is a huge hit with our readers, with almost 80% of them listing it as their favorite attraction in the Animal Kingdom. "I expected my 11-year-old to like it," wrote one mom from Arizona, "but to my surprise my 6-year-old loved it just as much. Even my father-in-law insisted on riding twice!"

The Scare Factor

Although Expedition Everest doesn't have the corkscrews and flips that are at Rock 'n' Roller Coaster, the yeti is indeed slightly more frightening than Steven Tyler. Also, the train moves at almost twice the speed of Space Mountain, which means the ride will probably be too intense for kids under 8. The height requirement is 44 inches.

chugging up the snowy mountainside when it suddenly encounters a break in the track. Uh-oh. Wonder why? The trip back down not only involves wild plunges and even wilder speeds, but you also meet up with the yeti that lives in the mountain, and he's not in a good mood. Your train races both forward and backward as you attempt to escape his rage.

Food Choices in the Animal Kingdom

Since the Animal Kingdom closes the earliest of all the parks—usually between 5 and 7 pm, depending on the season—people rarely eat dinner there. There are three sit-down restaurants: the Rainforest Café, which is just as you enter the park, and open for breakfast, lunch, and dinner; the Tusker House Restaurant, which features a buffet for breakfast, lunch and dinner; and the Yak & Yeti, an Asian-fusion restaurant with table service, a full

Insider's Secret

The Animal Kingdom provides interactive entertainment throughout the park. Cast members are stationed with animals, and kids are welcome to ask questions and have up-close encounters with the bugs, birds, reptiles, and small mammals. At the Dawa Bar in the Africa section you'll find storytellers, music, African drumming, and acrobats.

And keep an eye out for DeVine, a moving human topiary, who can often be found literally hanging around the park. She blends in so well with the vegetation that she's been known to startle some guests.

There's also a cute 15-minute parade in the afternoon, featuring the characters "on safari," animal puppetry, and stilt walkers. Check the tip board or your entertainment schedule to confirm showtime and stake your curb space 15 minutes in advance.

bar, quick-service options, and a beer garden that is also open for lunch and dinner.

The Tusker House in Africa is the site of the Animal Kingdom's only character meals, Donald's Safari Breakfast and Donald's Safari Lunch. Reserve before you leave home by calling 407/WDW–DINE. (After the character meals are over each day, the Tusker House serves a buffet, and remains one of the few places in the Animal Kingdom where you can consistently count on finding fresh vegetables.) "The food at the Tusker House character breakfast was outstanding," said one mom of three. "We loved the Jungle Juice and the Mickey waffles. My daughter was so happy to finally meet Daisy Duck, and the characters do a little song that's really cute."

Pizzafari, near Camp Minnie-Mickey, and Flame Tree Barbecue, near the entrance to DinoLand, are also good lunch choices. Restaurantosaurus in DinoLand offers po-boys and taco salads. All the restaurants have outdoor patios, where you can take your food, find a pretty view, and really relax. These lush, shady eating areas in the Animal Kingdom help blur the line between fast food and sit-down dining.

The Dawa Bar, adjacent to the Tusker House patio, offers alcoholic beverages and entertainment in the afternoon.

Tips for Your Last Hour in the Animal Kingdom

@ Why is there no big closing show at the Animal Kingdom? Most evening shows require fireworks, lasers, and other pyrotechnics, and all that noise and light would scare the animals.

@ Since there's no closing show, midday crowds drift out of the Animal Kingdom throughout the afternoon and early evening, and leaving isn't a problem. Return to the parking lot or bus station whenever it suits your schedule.

Typhoon Lagoon

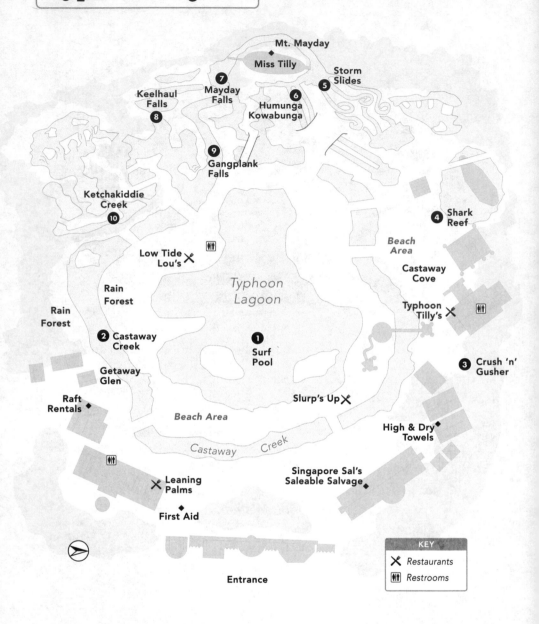

Mt. Mayday

Miss Tilly

7 Mayday Falls

Storm Slides **5**

Keelhaul Falls **8**

6 Humunga Kowabunga

9 Gangplank Falls

Ketchakiddie Creek **10**

Low Tide Lou's ✗

4 Shark Reef

Beach Area

Castaway Cove

Rain Forest

Typhoon Lagoon

Typhoon Tilly's ✗ 🚻

Rain Forest

2 Castaway Creek

1 Surf Pool

3 Crush 'n' Gusher

Getaway Glen

Raft Rentals ◆

Beach Area

Slurp's Up ✗

Castaway Creek

High & Dry Towels ◆

🚻

✗ Leaning Palms

Singapore Sal's Saleable Salvage ◆

◆ First Aid

⊛

Entrance

KEY	
✗	Restaurants
🚻	Restrooms

Getting to the Water Parks

On-site visitors can take the bus to both Typhoon Lagoon and Blizzard Beach, but expect a long commute. Getting to Typhoon Lagoon may involve sitting through the stops at Downtown Disney, and getting to Blizzard Beach often involves a stop at the Animal Kingdom. In other words, bus travel can be a headache. If you have a car, drive to the water parks.

For off-site visitors a car is definitely the best option. If you don't have one, take a cab.

Try to arrive about 20 minutes ahead of the stated opening times for the parks, particularly if you're visiting in summer or during a major holiday. During midday and afternoon hours in peak seasons the parking lots often fill to capacity.

During the most crowded days of peak season Extra Magic Hours sometimes allow on-site guests a little more time in the water parks. "Our extra magic evening at Typhoon Lagoon was the highlight of our entire week at Disney World," wrote one family from England. "It was a warm starry night and perfect for swimming in the big wave pool."

Water Parks Touring Tips

@ The water parks draw a rowdy preteen and teenage crowd, which means young kids and unsteady swimmers may get dunked and splashed more than they like. If your children are very young, stick to the kiddie sections (Ketchakiddee Creek in Typhoon Lagoon and Tike's Peak at Blizzard Beach), which are off-limits to older kids.

@ Summer afternoons in Florida often mean thunderstorms, and even a rumble of distant thunder can lead to water-park closings. If you're visiting in summer and want to make sure you have time to try everything, visit the water parks first thing in the morning.

@ You can rent towels, but they're small, so it makes more sense to bring your own. There are plenty of lockers, and the keys come on rubber bands that slip over your wrist or ankle, so you can keep them with you while you're in the water. If you arrive in the morning when a swarm of guests enters at once, getting a locker can be quite a hassle, with the rental lines sometimes 20 minutes long and the area around the lockers packed. Many families skip locker rentals altogether and keep vitals such as room keys, charge cards, and a bit of cash in one of those flat plastic holders you wear around your neck. (They sell them in the water-park gift shops for about $7.) That way they can grab the best lounge chair locations and dash straight to the rides while everyone else is still trying to get a locker.

@ Bring rubber beach shoes with nonskid bottoms if you have them. They'll protect the soles of your feet from the hot sidewalks.

@ You can borrow life vests for free at the locker-rental stand, although you have to leave your driver's license or a credit card as a deposit. Snorkeling equipment can be picked up for no charge at Hammerhead Fred's near the

The Scare Factor

Kids of any age can ride the Storm Slides, but they need to be fairly confident in the water. Although the pool you land in at the bottom isn't deep, you do hit the water with enough force to temporarily disorient a shaky swimmer. Most kids 7 to 11 love these zesty little slides, and, if they're good swimmers, some kids even younger can handle the Storm Slides.

Mayday Falls and Keelhaul Falls

A Disney employee helps you climb into your inner tube and begin your winding journey down a white-water stream. The journey is fast, giggle inducing, and has enough turns that you often feel like you're about to lose your tube.

The Scare Factor

Keelhaul Falls is slightly milder than Mayday, so let younger children try it first. Cast members can provide some smaller inner tubes with built-in bottoms. Kids as young as 4 have reported loving this ride.

Gangplank Falls

You weather these white-water rapids in four-passenger rafts. Slower and calmer (but much bumpier) than Mayday or Keelhaul, Gangplank is a good choice for families with kids who are nervous about tackling a white-water ride on their own. Gangplank Falls does load slowly, however, and the ride is short, so hit it early in the morning before the line becomes prohibitive.

Shark Reef at Typhoon Lagoon. There's no point in bringing your own fins and floats; only official Disney equipment is allowed in the pools.

- Because you're climbing uphill all day, half the time dragging a tube or mat behind you, the water parks are extremely exhausting. If you spend the day at one, plan to spend the evening in films or shows. Or take the night off.

- There are fast-food restaurants at both water parks, as well as places to picnic.

- The Lost Kids Stations at both parks are so far away from the main water areas that it's unlikely your children would find their way there. Instruct them, should they look up and find themselves separated from you, to approach the nearest person wearing a Disney name tag. A cast member will escort the kids to the Lost Kids Station, and you can meet them there. Because both of the parks are full of meandering paths with many sets of steps and slides, it's easy to get separated from your party. Set standard meeting places and times for older kids.

- Girls should wear one-piece swimsuits. More than one bathing suit top has been lost on the waterslides.

Helpful Hint

Trying to decide which Disney water park to visit? We agree with this statement from a father of two from Michigan: "Last year with our extended family we visited both water parks and concluded that Typhoon Lagoon was the favorite of the adults and the younger children because it's very pretty with nice beaches and shallow places for little ones to swim. Family members age 10 to 25 preferred Blizzard Beach because of all the big slides."

@ If you're visiting in summer, consider dropping by both Typhoon Lagoon and Blizzard Beach. They're very different experiences. Typhoon Lagoon has the better beaches and pools. Blizzard Beach is the pow! park, focusing on slides.

@ Typhoon Lagoon and Blizzard Beach are often closed for refurbishing in January and February, although it's rare for both to be closed at once unless the weather is truly cold or inclement. If you're planning a winter trip, call 407/824-4321 or visit www.disneyworld.com to see which will be open during the time you're in town.

@ Ride the slides and flumes in the morning and save the pools for the afternoon. Lines for the slides reach incredible lengths by midday.

Typhoon Lagoon

Disney calls its 56-acre Typhoon Lagoon "the world's ultimate water park," and the hyperbole is justified. Where else can you float through caves, take surfing lessons, picnic with parrots, and swim (sort of) with sharks? Typhoon Lagoon is the perfect replica of the perfect tropical isle—older kids can hit the thrill slides, younger kids can splash in the bays and dig in the sand, and parents can relax (at least in shifts) under a palm tree with a piña colada in one hand and a best-seller in the other.

For anyone with a Water Park Fun & More option, entrance to Typhoon Lagoon is included. Otherwise, admission is $52 for adults and $44 for children 3 to 9, before sales tax.

Typhoon Lagoon Attractions

Crush 'n' Gusher

This thrill ride combines flumes, spillways, and steep drops, but the real kick is that you're hit so hard with pulsating streams of water that at one point in the ride your two-person raft is actu-

The Scare Factor

The Crush 'n' Gusher is not for the nervous. The height requirement is 48 inches; even if they're tall enough, you should probably warm up younger children on Keelhaul Falls before tackling Crush 'n' Gusher.

ally propelled back uphill. The concept behind the ride is that you're lost in an abandoned fruit-processing facility. There are three paths out—the Banana Blaster, Coconut Crusher, and Pineapple Plunger—each about 420 feet long with plenty of twists and turns along the way.

Humunga Kowabunga

With three enclosed waterslides that drop you a stunning five stories in a matter of seconds, Humunga Kowabunga is definitely a thrill. Riders reach speeds of up to 30 mph!

The Scare Factor

Humunga is an intense ride that fully deserves its height requirement of 48 inches. Part of the scare factor is certainly the drop, but falling in complete darkness makes the experience even more intense. Nonetheless, once people ride it and get over that initial trepidation, they usually climb right back up to do it again.

Storm Slides

The Storm Slides are curvier and thus a little tamer than a straight plunge down the mountain. Each of the three slides offers a slightly different route, although none is necessarily wilder than the others.

Insider's Secret

The water parks are perfect for preteens and teens—and a great way to reward them for patiently waiting through a character breakfast or a morning of kiddie rides with younger siblings. The attractions at both Typhoon Lagoon and Blizzard Beach are actually more physically intense than most of the rides in the park. The surfing lessons at Typhoon Lagoon are a special treat for this age group; the cost is $160 per person, but since the pool is a controlled environment with a steady supply of perfect-sized waves and the instructors from the Craig Carroll school are top-notch, almost everyone manages to catch a wave by the end of the class.

Surf Pool

In this huge and incredible 2.5-acre lagoon, guests can ride machine-made waves up to 6 feet high. The waves come at 90-second intervals and are perfectly sized for tubing and body-surfing. A foghorn blast alerts you to when a big one is on its way; if you're bobbing around with young kids, stay in the shallow areas, where the swells won't be too overwhelming, and you can avoid the surfers.

Toddlers and preschoolers can safely splash around in two small, roped-off coves called Blustery Bay and Whitecap Cover.

The Scare Factor

The Surf Pool's waves come with a lot of force, so make sure that you keep an eye on unsteady swimmers.

Everybody's Gone Surfin' . . . at Disney's Typhoon Lagoon

At Disney's Typhoon Lagoon water park, adventurous guests

can catch a wave *and* master the rush of shooting the curls as part of **Craig Carroll's Cocoa Beach Surf School**. Guests are invited to learn from professional surfers how to cut, carve, and "hang 10" in the water park's 2.75-million-gallon wave pool. Every 90 seconds, the world's largest wave machine blasts out walls of surf that can tower up to six feet high.

The 2.5-hour program is available by reservation for $160 on select mornings prior to regular park hours. Guests (ages 8 and older) can call 407/WDW–PLAY for more information.

Castaway Creek

Castaway Creek is a meandering 2,000-foot river full of inner tubes. You simply wade out, find an empty tube, and climb aboard. It takes about 30 minutes to lazily circle the rain forest, with a bit of excitement at one point when riders drift under the waterfall. There are numerous exits along the creek, so anyone who doesn't want to get splashed can hop out before the falls. In fact, Castaway Creek serves as a means of transportation around the park; savvy guests who don't want to burn their feet on hot pavement or waste energy walking around often hop in and float their way from attraction to attraction.

The Scare Factor

Castaway Creek is a fun, relaxing ride appropriate for any age. The water is 3 feet deep throughout the ride, however, so keep a good grip on young kids or those who can't swim.

Shark Reef

An unusual attraction, Shark Reef is a saltwater pool where snorkelers swim "among" exotic marine life, including small leopard and hammerhead sharks. The sharks are behind Plexiglas and aren't too numerous, so anyone expecting the *Jaws* experience will be disappointed.

Shark Reef at Typhoon Lagoon. There's no point in bringing your own fins and floats; only official Disney equipment is allowed in the pools.

@ Because you're climbing uphill all day, half the time dragging a tube or mat behind you, the water parks are extremely exhausting. If you spend the day at one, plan to spend the evening in films or shows. Or take the night off.

@ There are fast-food restaurants at both water parks, as well as places to picnic.

@ The Lost Kids Stations at both parks are so far away from the main water areas that it's unlikely your children would find their way there. Instruct them, should they look up and find themselves separated from you, to approach the nearest person wearing a Disney name tag. A cast member will escort the kids to the Lost Kids Station, and you can meet them there. Because both of the parks are full of meandering paths with many sets of steps and slides, it's easy to get separated from your party. Set standard meeting places and times for older kids.

@ Girls should wear one-piece swimsuits. More than one bathing suit top has been lost on the waterslides.

Helpful Hint

Trying to decide which Disney water park to visit? We agree with this statement from a father of two from Michigan: "Last year with our extended family we visited both water parks and concluded that Typhoon Lagoon was the favorite of the adults and the younger children because it's very pretty with nice beaches and shallow places for little ones to swim. Family members age 10 to 25 preferred Blizzard Beach because of all the big slides."

- If you're visiting in summer, consider dropping by both Typhoon Lagoon and Blizzard Beach. They're very different experiences. Typhoon Lagoon has the better beaches and pools. Blizzard Beach is the pow! park, focusing on slides.

- Typhoon Lagoon and Blizzard Beach are often closed for refurbishing in January and February, although it's rare for both to be closed at once unless the weather is truly cold or inclement. If you're planning a winter trip, call 407/824–4321 or visit www.disneyworld.com to see which will be open during the time you're in town.

- Ride the slides and flumes in the morning and save the pools for the afternoon. Lines for the slides reach incredible lengths by midday.

Typhoon Lagoon

Disney calls its 56-acre Typhoon Lagoon "the world's ultimate water park," and the hyperbole is justified. Where else can you float through caves, take surfing lessons, picnic with parrots, and swim (sort of) with sharks? Typhoon Lagoon is the perfect replica of the perfect tropical isle—older kids can hit the thrill slides, younger kids can splash in the bays and dig in the sand, and parents can relax (at least in shifts) under a palm tree with a piña colada in one hand and a best-seller in the other.

For anyone with a Water Park Fun & More option, entrance to Typhoon Lagoon is included. Otherwise, admission is $52 for adults and $44 for children 3 to 9, before sales tax.

Typhoon Lagoon Attractions

Crush 'n' Gusher

This thrill ride combines flumes, spillways, and steep drops, but the real kick is that you're hit so hard with pulsating streams of water that at one point in the ride your two-person raft is actu-

The Scare Factor

The Crush 'n' Gusher is not for the nervous. The height requirement is 48 inches; even if they're tall enough, you should probably warm up younger children on Keelhaul Falls before tackling Crush 'n' Gusher.

ally propelled back uphill. The concept behind the ride is that you're lost in an abandoned fruit-processing facility. There are three paths out—the Banana Blaster, Coconut Crusher, and Pineapple Plunger—each about 420 feet long with plenty of twists and turns along the way.

Humunga Kowabunga

With three enclosed waterslides that drop you a stunning five stories in a matter of seconds, Humunga Kowabunga is definitely a thrill. Riders reach speeds of up to 30 mph!

The Scare Factor

Humunga is an intense ride that fully deserves its height requirement of 48 inches. Part of the scare factor is certainly the drop, but falling in complete darkness makes the experience even more intense. Nonetheless, once people ride it and get over that initial trepidation, they usually climb right back up to do it again.

Storm Slides

The Storm Slides are curvier and thus a little tamer than a straight plunge down the mountain. Each of the three slides offers a slightly different route, although none is necessarily wilder than the others.

The Scare Factor

Kids of any age can ride the Storm Slides, but they need to be fairly confident in the water. Although the pool you land in at the bottom isn't deep, you do hit the water with enough force to temporarily disorient a shaky swimmer. Most kids 7 to 11 love these zesty little slides, and, if they're good swimmers, some kids even younger can handle the Storm Slides.

Mayday Falls and Keelhaul Falls

A Disney employee helps you climb into your inner tube and begin your winding journey down a white-water stream. The journey is fast, giggle inducing, and has enough turns that you often feel like you're about to lose your tube.

The Scare Factor

Keelhaul Falls is slightly milder than Mayday, so let younger children try it first. Cast members can provide some smaller inner tubes with built-in bottoms. Kids as young as 4 have reported loving this ride.

Gangplank Falls

You weather these white-water rapids in four-passenger rafts. Slower and calmer (but much bumpier) than Mayday or Keelhaul, Gangplank is a good choice for families with kids who are nervous about tackling a white-water ride on their own. Gangplank Falls does load slowly, however, and the ride is short, so hit it early in the morning before the line becomes prohibitive.

Insider's Secret

The water parks are perfect for preteens and teens—and a great way to reward them for patiently waiting through a character breakfast or a morning of kiddie rides with younger siblings. The attractions at both Typhoon Lagoon and Blizzard Beach are actually more physically intense than most of the rides in the park. The surfing lessons at Typhoon Lagoon are a special treat for this age group; the cost is $160 per person, but since the pool is a controlled environment with a steady supply of perfect-sized waves and the instructors from the Craig Carroll school are top-notch, almost everyone manages to catch a wave by the end of the class.

Surf Pool

In this huge and incredible 2.5-acre lagoon, guests can ride machine-made waves up to 6 feet high. The waves come at 90-second intervals and are perfectly sized for tubing and body-surfing. A foghorn blast alerts you to when a big one is on its way; if you're bobbing around with young kids, stay in the shallow areas, where the swells won't be too overwhelming, and you can avoid the surfers.

Toddlers and preschoolers can safely splash around in two small, roped-off coves called Blustery Bay and Whitecap Cover.

The Scare Factor

The Surf Pool's waves come with a lot of force, so make sure that you keep an eye on unsteady swimmers.

Everybody's Gone Surfin' . . . at Disney's Typhoon Lagoon

At Disney's Typhoon Lagoon water park, adventurous guests

can catch a wave *and* master the rush of shooting the curls as part of **Craig Carroll's Cocoa Beach Surf School**. Guests are invited to learn from professional surfers how to cut, carve, and "hang 10" in the water park's 2.75-million-gallon wave pool. Every 90 seconds, the world's largest wave machine blasts out walls of surf that can tower up to six feet high.

The 2.5-hour program is available by reservation for $160 on select mornings prior to regular park hours. Guests (ages 8 and older) can call 407/WDW–PLAY for more information.

Castaway Creek

Castaway Creek is a meandering 2,000-foot river full of inner tubes. You simply wade out, find an empty tube, and climb aboard. It takes about 30 minutes to lazily circle the rain forest, with a bit of excitement at one point when riders drift under the waterfall. There are numerous exits along the creek, so anyone who doesn't want to get splashed can hop out before the falls. In fact, Castaway Creek serves as a means of transportation around the park; savvy guests who don't want to burn their feet on hot pavement or waste energy walking around often hop in and float their way from attraction to attraction.

The Scare Factor

Castaway Creek is a fun, relaxing ride appropriate for any age. The water is 3 feet deep throughout the ride, however, so keep a good grip on young kids or those who can't swim.

Shark Reef

An unusual attraction, Shark Reef is a saltwater pool where snorkelers swim "among" exotic marine life, including small leopard and hammerhead sharks. The sharks are behind Plexiglas and aren't too numerous, so anyone expecting the *Jaws* experience will be disappointed.

The Scare Factor
Shark Reef isn't scary per se, but young kids sometimes struggle with the equipment and panic when they either flood their masks or suck water through their snorkel. Swimmers need to be able to confidently cross a 60-foot pool twice, a task that might preclude the participation of some young kids who find this too physically demanding even with a floatation vest. If older kids want to suit up, younger siblings can watch from an underwater viewing area that gives you a good view of the marine life and the snorkelers.

Disney provides the snorkeling equipment and a brief orientation on how to use it. Only official Disney equipment is allowed in the pool, so don't bother packing your own masks. If you want to snorkel, it's best to visit Shark Reef in the morning. By mid-afternoon the pool can get crowded.

Ketchakiddee Creek
This is a water playground designed for toddlers and preschoolers, with geysers and waterspouts in the shapes of crocodiles and whales, as well as pint-size slides, a grotto with a waterfall, and a small white-water raft ride. No kids over 48 inches are allowed inside, which keeps the area safe for the younger kids.

Blizzard Beach

Blizzard Beach may have the cleverest theme of any Disney park. The tropical ambience of Typhoon Lagoon seems natural for a water park, but who could have predicted a melting ski lodge?

Blizzard Beach is built on the tongue-in-cheek premise that a freak snowstorm hit Orlando and a group of enterprising businesspeople built Florida's first ski resort. The sun returned in due time, and for a while it looked like all was lost—until

Blizzard Beach

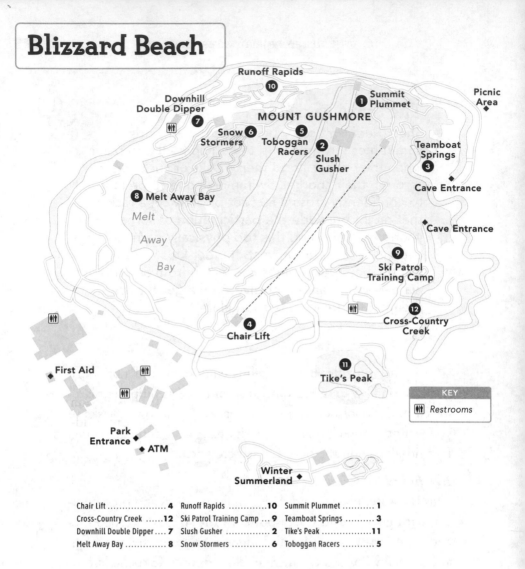

Runoff Rapids

10

Downhill
Double Dipper

7

Summit
Plummet

1

Picnic
Area

MOUNT GUSHMORE

Snow
Stormers

6

Toboggan
Racers

5

Slush
Gusher

2

Teamboat
Springs

3

Cave Entrance

8 Melt Away Bay

Melt

Away

Bay

Cave Entrance

9

Ski Patrol
Training Camp

4

Chair Lift

12

Cross-Country
Creek

First Aid

11

Tike's Peak

KEY

Restrooms

Park
Entrance

ATM

Winter
Summerland

someone spied an alligator slipping and sliding down one of the slushy slopes. Thus Blizzard Beach was born. The snow may be gone, but the jumps, sled runs, and slalom courses remain, resulting in a high-camp, high-thrill ski lodge in the palms. The motif extends into every element of the park: There are Plexiglas snowmen, a chalet-style restaurant, even ski marks running off the side of the mountain. And the original skiing alligator, Ice Gator, is the park mascot.

At the center of Blizzard Beach is "snowcapped" Mt.

Gushmore. You can get to the top via ski lift (long line, short ride) or a series of stairs (big climb, short breath), but how you get down is up to you. The bold descend via Summit Plummet or Slush Gusher, but there are medium-intensity flumes, tube rides, and white-water raft rides as well.

There are big crowds in the morning, but—at least during peak season in the summer—showing up early is the only way you can ensure you'll get in at all. Like Typhoon Lagoon, Blizzard Beach is included in Water Park Fun & More; otherwise, admission is $52 for adults and $44 for children 3 to 9, not including sales tax.

Blizzard Beach Attractions

Summit Plummet

The icon of the park, Summit Plummet is 120 feet tall, making it considerably longer than Humunga Kowabunga at Typhoon Lagoon. From the outside, it looks like Summit Plummet riders are shooting out of the side of the mountain into midair. And in reality the ride is nearly as intense, with a 60-degree, 60-mph drop that's almost twice as fast as Space Mountain—and here you're not even riding in a car.

The Scare Factor

The height requirement for Summit Plummet is 48 inches. Although it's a very short experience—less than four seconds from top to bottom—the drop feels like free fall and may be the most intense sensation in all of Disney World. In short, this flume is not for the faint of heart.

Slush Gusher

This is another monster slide, but with a couple of bumps along the way to slow you down. Akin in intensity to Humunga Kowabunga at Typhoon Lagoon, Slush Gusher is so

Insider's Secret

If you're riding either Summit Plummet or the Slush Gusher, don't forget to cross your legs as you descend. Your bathing suit will still ride up, but at least you'll have some protection against the Mother of All Wedgies. And, women and girls should wear one-piece swimsuits unless they want their tops up by their ears as they land.

The Scare Factor

Kids must be 48 inches tall to ride Slush Gusher. Try it as a plunge test before you queue up for Summit Plummet.

much fun that many kids insist on doing it more than once, despite the climb to the top and the long line.

Runoff Rapids

You take a separate set of stairs up the back of Mt. Gushmore to reach these three inner-tube rides. To start, you get to choose between tubes that seat either one or two people. Just remember, the heavier the raft the faster the descent, so don't assume that by piling both kids in one raft you're toning down the experience. The rapids are great fun, and each of the slides provides a slightly different thrill so you can try it over and over. The only downside is that each time you have to troop up the seven zillion stairs (157, to be exact); visit early in the morning before your stamina fails.

Snow Stormers

This is a mock slalom run that you descend on your belly as you clutch a foam rubber "sled." The three slides are full of twists and turns that splash water into your face, and if you'd like, you can race the sledders on the other two slides to the bottom. It's so much fun that hardly anyone does it just once.

Toboggan Racers

Eight riders on rubber mats are pitted against one another on a straight ride down the mountain. The heavier the rider, the faster the descent, so the attendant at the top of the slide will give kids a head start over adults. Not quite as wild as Snow Stormers, Toboggan Racers lets kids get used to the sensation of sliding downhill on a rubber sled.

Teamboat Springs

In one of the best rides in the park, the whole family can join forces to tackle the white water as a group. The round boats, which you board at the top of Mt. Gushmore, carry up to six people, and the ride downhill is zippy, with lots of splashes and sharp curves. Teamboat Springs draws an enthusiastic thumbs-up from all age groups, from preschoolers to grandparents. It's much longer, wilder, and more fun than Gangplank Falls, the comparable white-water ride at Typhoon Lagoon.

Downhill Double Dipper

On this individual tube ride, you race the rider in the other chute, going through water curtains and free falls during your descent. At one point in the ride you're completely airborne. The Double Dipper is fun and addictive, albeit a bit more jarring than some of the other rides at Blizzard Beach. Test the kids on nearby Runoff Rapids before you tackle it.

The Scare Factor

Downhill Double Dipper is a bit rougher than it looks, and has a 48-inch height requirement.

Ski Patrol Training Camp

This special play area is designed for kids 5 to 11 who are too old for Tike's Peak but not quite ready for the big-deal rides. They can walk across icebergs, swing from T-bars, test their mountaineering skills, and ride medium-intensity slides.

Tike's Peak

This is where the toddlers and preschoolers gather to play on small slides and flumes, in igloo-style forts, and in a wading pool that looks like a broken ice-skating rink. No kids over 48 inches tall are allowed to play.

Chair Lift

The Chair Lift offers direct transportation to the top of Mt. Gushmore where Summit Plummet, Slush Gusher, and Teamboat Springs await. It's also a fun little diversion in itself, but lines can grow unbelievably long in the afternoon. Hiking up the steps is a lot faster. And while there's nothing scary about the ride, it's tough to hold on to a squirming toddler who's been slathered with sunscreen, so there's a height requirement of 32 inches.

Melt Away Bay

Unlike the huge Surfing Lagoon at Typhoon Lagoon, this swimming area is relatively small and offers mild swells instead of big waves. Fed by "melting snow" waterfalls, the pool is perfect for young kids and unsteady swimmers. There are plenty of chairs and shady huts nearby for relaxing, but these tend to be claimed early in the day.

Cross-Country Creek

Blizzard Beach has its own version of a lazy river. There are plenty of inner tubes—just wade in, climb on, and float along on a relaxing loop of the park.

CHAPTER 10

The Rest of the World

Downtown Disney

Village Lake

◆ *Ferry Launch*

Cirque du Soleil

THE WEST SIDE

Ferry Lau

Disney Quest

House of Blues

Characters in Flight

Splittsville

Wolfgang Puck Café

Bongo's Cuban Café

SHOPS

PARKING

AMC Movie Theaters

Planet Hollywood

◆ *Bus Stop*

PARKING

Buena Vista Drive

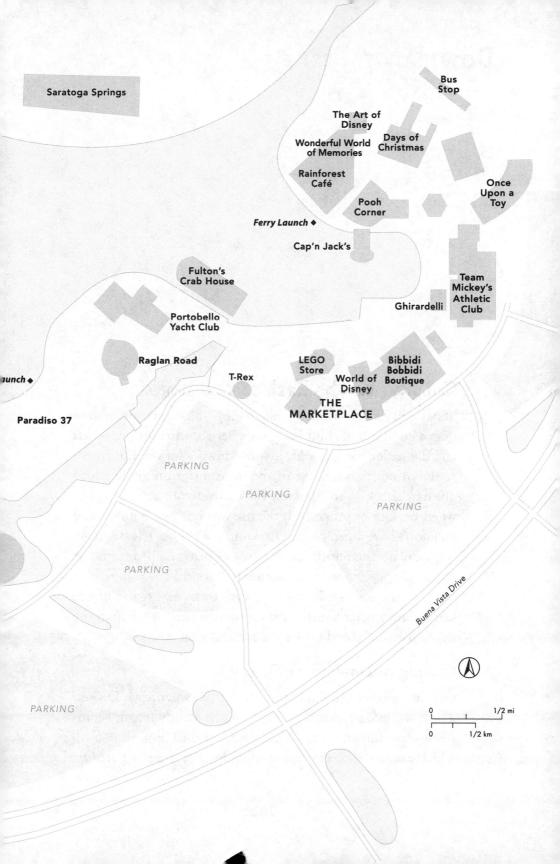

Saratoga Springs

Bus Stop

The Art of Disney

Wonderful World of Memories

Days of Christmas

Rainforest Café

Once Upon a Toy

Pooh Corner

Ferry Launch ◆

Cap'n Jack's

Fulton's Crab House

Team Mickey's Athletic Club

Ghirardelli

Portobello Yacht Club

Raglan Road

LEGO Store

Bibbidi Bobbidi Boutique

T-Rex

World of Disney

...aunch ◆

THE MARKETPLACE

Paradiso 37

PARKING

PARKING

PARKING

PARKING

PARKING

Buena Vista Drive

0   1/2 mi

0   1/2 km

Getting to the Rest of the World

Staying on-site? Although the Disney transportation system does a good job of shuttling guests between the on-site hotels and the major theme parks, it slows down a bit when it comes to the minor parks. Consult the transportation guide you're given at check-in for the best route from your resort to anywhere on Disney property. If the trip involves two transfers and you don't have a car, consider taking a cab. They're easy to get from any on-site resort, and the cost of being hauled from one end of Disney property to another is around $15–$20.

Staying off-site? If you have your own car, use it. Off-site hotels rarely offer shuttle service to anything other than the major parks. If you don't have a car, call a cab.

Getting to Downtown Disney

On-site hotels have direct bus service to Downtown Disney. The buses make two stops, which means a fairly lengthy commute, especially to get to DisneyQuest or the Cirque du Soleil, which are far from any bus stops. Those staying at Port Orleans, Saratoga Springs, or Old Key West have boat service directly to the Marketplace.

In addition, on-site and off-site guests can drive directly to Downtown Disney. There's no charge for parking.

Getting to the ESPN Wide World of Sports

The fastest route is to drive your own car. Otherwise, buses are an option, but few run to this out-of-the-way location. Check your transportation guide for the best route from your resort; if more than two transfers are involved, take a cab.

Getting from One Resort to Another

On-site guests with their own cars can simply drive to the new resort and inform the guard they're visiting for dinner or another activity. If you don't have your own car, your simplest option is to take a cab. Your cheapest option is to use the theme park that's closest to you as a transfer station. For example, if you're staying at the Grand Floridian and have dinner reservations at the BoardWalk, take the monorail to the Magic Kingdom and catch a bus to the BoardWalk from there.

Downtown Disney

The enormous entertainment, dining, and shopping complex known as Downtown Disney is packed at night. Families who'd like to visit when there are fewer crowds should show up in the afternoon and eat dinner relatively early, like at 5 pm. It's a great spot for the first afternoon or evening of your vacation. It doesn't require a ticket, but still has plenty of Disney spirit.

"We didn't want to buy a ticket for our first day, since we were landing in Orlando around noon," reported one woman who visited with her husband and 14-year-old sister. "Instead we went to Downtown Disney, and had a great meal and then

**The Don't-Miss List for the
Rest of the World**

Character Breakfasts (if you have kids under 9)

Cirque du Soleil

DisneyQuest (if you have kids over 10)

Downtown Disney

did some shopping. It was a low-key, perfect introduction to Disney World."

Off season, Downtown Disney sections open at staggered times. If you have questions about hours, check with Guest Relations (a.k.a. Guest Services) at your hotel.

Downtown Disney Marketplace

The Marketplace section of Downtown Disney, not surprisingly, is full of shops. A good place to start is the World of Disney, the largest Disney store on Earth, and the best place to find that perfect souvenir. Little girls will freak out at the sight of the Bibbidi Bobbidi Boutique (a.k.a. "the Princess Room"), where they can try on princess costumes, then have their hair, makeup, and nails done. Packages range from $50 for hairstyling and makeup to over $190 for a complete photo portfolio and costume you can keep. Kids must be 3 and older to participate, and you can make appointments 180 days in advance by calling 407/939–7895 (407/WDW–STYLE).

Warning: Once you go princess, it's hard to go back. "We were arriving in Orlando in the afternoon," wrote a mother from New York, "and as you suggested we went to Downtown Disney, so we wouldn't burn a day on our theme-park tickets. We thought it would be cute to have our 5-year-old daughter Kate outfitted at Bibbidi Bobbidi Boutique to kick off her Dis-

Helpful Hint

If you're trying to decide which boutique is best for your little princess, consider that the Magic Kingdom location—while undeniably more glamorous— requires theme-park admission. To maximize your expensive tickets, it makes more sense to spend your day in the Magic Kingdom visiting attractions, not hanging out in a hair salon. Visit the Bibbidi Bobbidi Boutique at Downtown Disney on your day off, the first evening you arrive, or any other time when you're not burning a day on your ticket.

ney vacation, but as it turns out, she was so enchanted with her new look that she refused to take down her hairdo, change clothes, or wash her face for the next seven days. In pictures we took near the end of vacation, Kate looks like Belle on crack."

Another must-see is Once Upon a Toy, the ultimate shop for Disney-theme toys. Kids also enjoy Team Mickey's Athletic Club, which sells sporting equipment and clothes, and the Days of Christmas. The LEGO Store is just amazing, with enormous LEGO sea serpents, spaceships, and life-size people scattered around the lagoon, as well as a play area where kids can build their own models. Of course, without a budget, this can get out of control very fast. "I do have to take issue with your description of Downtown Disney as 'free,'" wrote one mother from Virginia. "We ended up spending more there than we did in any of the theme parks!"

Stop by the Art of Disney, where you can view limited-edition cels and other collectibles. Scrapbook hobbyists will enjoy Disney's Wonderful World of Memories next door, which offers Disney scrapbook supplies.

The Rainforest Café is great fun because birds and fish (real) and rhinos and giraffes (fake) surround your table while you eat. Check out the bar stools with their flamingo and zebra

Hidden Mickey
Look closely at the fountains near the entrance to the Downtown Disney Marketplace. Does the shape look familiar?

legs. T-Rex with its dinosaur theme (duh) is also oriented towards families. You're greeted by a life-size T-Rex as you enter and walk through a prehistoric environment with waterfalls, geysers, and a fossil dig site.

The part of Downtown Disney known as Pleasure Island is in transition; this area will reopen in stages. Right now it looks like a ghost town, but some shops and restaurants—including the popular Irish pub Raglan Road and the restaurant Paradiso 37—are currently open and worth the walk. Also, between Pleasure Island and the West Side is a tethered hot-air balloon known as Characters In Flight as a tribute to Peter Pan, Mary Poppins, and some of Disney's other lofty stars. The balloon gently lifts 400 feet into the air for a great view of the surrounding area. Prices are $18 adult, $12 child.

Insider's Secret
A waterfront district named Hyperion Wharf is coming to Downtown Disney in late 2013—although Disney is already talking about potential delays. It will be a modern version of an amusement pier, with shopping, dining, and entertainment options for the whole family.

Downtown Disney West Side
The West Side is home to a variety of shops and restaurants, a 24-screen AMC theater, a 30-lane bowling alley called Splittsville, and two major attractions: DisneyQuest and Cirque du Soleil.

Bongos Cuban Café offers an Americanized version of Cuban dishes, a wild tropical decor, and throbbing Latin music.

The House of Blues serves up Cajun and Creole cooking along with live jazz, country, and blues music. The Gospel Brunch at 10:30 am and 1 pm on Sundays is an especially good choice for families. Prices are $36 for adults and $18 for kids 3 to 9. Call 407/934–2583 (407/934–BLUE) to buy tickets.

Wolfgang Puck Café serves terrific pizzas and sushi downstairs. Request the upstairs dining room for tonier adult dining. The giant blue globe of Planet Hollywood holds movie props, and even the menus—printed with high school graduation pictures of stars—are entertaining. Film clips run constantly on giant screens and the atmosphere is loud and cheerful.

Splittsville, in addition to its 30 bowling lanes, features billiards, live entertainment, and its own restaurant, which serves pizza, sushi, and sliders. Be warned: after 8 pm Splittsville caters to an adult crowd. Visit in the afternoon or early evening.

DisneyQuest

Most people call DisneyQuest an arcade—and within its five levels you will, indeed, find classic arcade games. But you'll also find high-tech interactive experiences that almost defy description.

Favorite games include Pirates of the Caribbean, where you take the deck to battle phantom buccaneers, and Virtual Jungle Cruise, an exhausting river-raft ride in which you paddle through the rapids of a prehistoric world. During your stay you can also battle comic-book villains, shoot foam balls at

Helpful Hint
DisneyQuest is large and loud, and each play zone has steps leading to other levels. In other words, it's easy to lose your kids. If you're going to let older kids and teens explore on their own, pick a designated time and place to regroup.

Time-Saving Tip

DisneyQuest gets crowded in the evening, on weekends, and on rainy days. To make sure you have the
chance to try out everything, visit at opening time
on a weekday, which is usually around 11:30 am.

your competitors in a bumper-car war, and become a human
joystick in a hockey-style pinball game.

The centerpiece attraction of DisneyQuest is CyberSpace
Mountain, in which you design your own virtual roller coaster.
You can build in as many flips, spirals, and hills as time and distance allow; program in the speed of the car; and even get to
name the sucker. When you're finished, your coaster is given a
scariness rating from 1 to 5, meaning that you can either design
a gentle, rolling grade-1 coaster suitable for kids or a flip-you-
over, slam-you-down grade-5 coaster. (If your coaster gets a rating that's too mild or too wild, you can always redesign it.)
Then you enter a booth where you're strapped into a capsule,
and you ride a virtual re-
creation of your design.

Helpful Hint

No strollers are allowed
inside DisneyQuest, and
there are a lot of stairs.
Plan accordingly.

Needless to say, pre-
teens and teens can get
hooked on this stuff very
fast, and DisneyQuest is
primarily designed for the
age 10–20 set. But there's
entertainment for younger siblings as well, and any age can
enjoy the arcade games or the Create Zone where you can design your own toy or learn to draw a Disney character.

DisneyQuest usually opens at 11:30 am although hours
may vary during the on-season. A single entry price ($43 for
adults, $37 for kids 3 to 9) lets you play as long and as much as

you like—an alarming thought for the parents of a 12-year-old boy. Admission is also included with the Water Park Fun & More option and, if you're willing to buy in advance, online discounts are often available as well.

Cirque du Soleil

After a week at Disney World, probably the last thing you're itching to do is to buy an expensive ticket to watch an acrobatic show. But the Cirque du Soleil show *La Nouba* positively wowed the families we surveyed.

Although the athleticism and agility of the troupe will amaze you, it's their ability to use props, sets, costumes, and their bodies to set a mood and tell a story that makes Cirque du Soleil so unique. Don't expect any elephants or people being shot out of cannons—Cirque performances are more like theater than traditional circuses. Cirque du Soleil can best be appreciated by kids ages 8 and up.

Cirque du Soleil has a multitiered pricing structure. Depending on where you sit and when you visit, general tickets range from $78 to $136 for adults and $62 to $109 for kids ages 3 to 9. The 90-minute show normally runs Tuesday through Saturday, twice daily at 6 and 9 pm. For reservations,

Helpful Hint

It can take quite a long bus ride to get to Downtown Disney West Side (where Cirque du Soleil is located), even from an on-site hotel. Buses will drop you off at Pleasure Island and you then walk. Since the resorts often share buses to Downtown Disney, you'll have to sit through several stops before you arrive. The moral? Drive if you can, but if you're taking a bus to Cirque du Soleil, leave your hotel an hour and a half before showtime.

details, and specific pricing for the dates you'll be visiting, visit www.cirquedusoleil.com or call 407/939–7600.

BoardWalk and the ESPN Club

Not up for the sprawl of Downtown Disney? At night, the shops, restaurants, and nightclubs in front of the BoardWalk Resort take on a whole new glitter. You can find plenty of low-key entertainment—face painting, hair braiding, midway games, and sometimes comics and magic acts—along the waterfront. Eat dinner at the Flying Fish Café if you're feeling fancy, then rent a surrey bike ($20 to $28 for 30 minutes, depending upon bike size) for a lap around the lagoon.

The ESPN Club contains a broadcast and production facility (meaning celebrity athletes are sometimes on hand) and serves up—and I quote—"the best ballpark cuisine from around the country." This bold claim translates into sandwiches, salads, and burgers, all sized for hearty appetites.

Two BoardWalk clubs are open strictly to adults 21 and older. The Atlantic Dance Club changes format frequently, but is presently offering DJ-spun Top 40 dance music without a cover charge. Jellyrolls is a sing-along piano bar with lots of audience participation.

The fact that the BoardWalk isn't as vast and crowded as Downtown Disney appeals to many visitors; you can have a good meal and some entertainment without getting back into the mouse race. And at night, with the glowing Yacht and Beach Clubs visible across the water and the fireworks of Epcot in the distance, the BoardWalk ranks as one of the most beautiful spots in Disney World. Pull up a rocker and let the world go by.

On-site guests can take monorails or buses to any theme park and then transfer to the BoardWalk bus. If you're staying at the Yacht and Beach Clubs, the Swan, or the Dolphin, just walk. Off-site guests can either park in the BoardWalk lot or pay for the $12 valet parking, which is worth it on weekend evenings when the regular lot is crowded.

Disney Extras

Dinner Shows and Character Breakfasts

Book any dinner shows you would like to attend before you leave home by calling 407/939–3463 (407/WDW–DINE). Reservations are accepted up to 180 days in advance, and range in price depending upon the time of year you're visiting. The on-site dinner shows include the following:

- *The Hoop-Dee-Doo Musical Revue* plays three times nightly (at 5, 7:15, and 9:30 pm) at Pioneer Hall in Fort Wilderness campground. You can dine on ribs, fried chicken, and strawberry shortcake while watching a lovably hokey show that includes lots of audience participation. The cost is $54–$68 for adults, $27–$35 for children 3 to 9.

- *The Spirit of Aloha* is presented seasonally at 5:15 and 8 pm in the open-air theater in Luau Cove at the Polynesian Resort. The luau features hula dancing, music, and a "Polynesian feast," which translates as fruit, chicken, pork ribs, and pineapple bread. The cost is $58–$72 for adults and $30–$37 for children 3 to 9. "The Polynesian is a beautiful setting," wrote one family from Connecticut, "but we expected more of a traditional luau. Just be aware that this show has a modern story line."

- *Mickey's Backyard Barbecue* is presented on select nights (usually Thursday and Saturday) at Fort Wilderness and features a country band, line dancing with the characters, and picnic food such as barbecued ribs, roast chicken, and corn on the cob. Prices are $51–$55 for adults, $28–$32 for children 3 to 9. The barbecue is decidedly rowdier than other Disney dinner events. A mother of four from

New York wrote, "The closest we came to a never-again moment was Mickey's Backyard Barbecue. It was a free-for-all with characters and kids running loose on the dance floor. On the other hand, the Polynesian luau was a delight, with plenty of entertainment for the kids but a much calmer atmosphere."

Allow plenty of time to get to your character meal. If you're relying on Disney transportation, your journey begins at the Magic Kingdom. For the luau, take the resort monorail from the Magic Kingdom to the Polynesian and follow the signs to the beach. For the Hoop-Dee-Doo or the barbecue, take the ferry from the Magic Kingdom to Fort Wilderness. Either way, you're in for a lot of walking. "It takes too much Hoop-Dee-Doo just to get there," wrote one reader from California who is still steaming over missing her appetizer. If you have a car, obviously driving is easier. Or take a cab.

Character Dining

The character meals are time-consuming and expensive, but families with young kids give them very high marks. It's not about the food, which is usually fine; it's about the chance to have the characters actually visit your table so that there's plenty of time for pictures, hugs, and autographs. Reservations can (and should) be arranged 180 days in advance by calling 407/

Helpful Hint

Kids under 3 get into the parks for free, but what's the deal with character meals? Historically the buffets are more liberal than the sit-down venues about comping the under-3 set, but don't assume: Anytime you book a character meal, ask the restaurant to spell out its policy about who, if anyone, eats for free.

Money-Saving Tip

Unlike regular restaurant reservations, which can be canceled at the last minute or simply ignored, making reservations for dinner shows and character meals requires a credit-card guarantee. If your plans change, and you fail to cancel your reservation at least 48 hours in advance, you're charged in full.

939–3463 (407/WDW–DINE). Any character meal that takes place inside a theme park requires theme-park admission.

The character meal that gets the most attention is Cinderella's Royal Table, which is always booked up months in advance—despite being by far the most expensive. Granted there are some little extras (like a photo) included in the cost, but the drastic price jump is a clue to the popularity of this venue; people are willing to pay almost twice as much as the typical character meal just to get their daughters inside the castle. During the on-season it is often sold out within minutes of the reservation line opening. Your best bet is to call 407/939–3463 (407/WDW–DINE) EXACTLY 180 days in advance and PRECISELY at 7 am. And if you still can't get in, be prepared with a backup plan in the form of either the Princess Storybook Dining at Akershus in the Norway pavilion at Epcot, which features almost every Disney princess except Cinderella, or 1900 Park Fare at the Grand Floridian, which offers a specialty dinner called Cinderella's Feast.

And don't forget: If you're going to dine with royalty, it's only fitting that little girls dress for the occasion. If you think the full princess outfit is a little too much for a day in the parks, change your girl back into casual clothes after the meal.

Character-meal times, places, prices, and the characters featured change often, so call to confirm the information before you book the meal. If your child has his heart set on meeting a particular character, be sure to verify that the character will actually be there when you visit. And confirm pricing when calling—meals are often cheaper in the off-season.

Since dining will take about two hours, try to book the first character breakfast of the day. Families who have scheduled character breakfasts on the last day of their visits have also noted that a long breakfast coincides well with the usual 11 am check-out time at most Orlando hotels.

In the Resorts

- @ Cape May Café, Beach Club Resort—Seaside picnic breakfast buffet with Goofy, Donald, and Minnie. Breakfast only: adults, $27–$30, children (3–9) $14–$17.

- @ Chef Mickey's, Contemporary Resort—Party with Mickey, Minnie, Donald, Pluto, and Goofy. Breakfast: adults, $30, children $17. Dinner: adults, $41–$47, children $20–$23.

- @ My Disney Girl's Perfectly Princess Tea Party—For the ultimate princess experience, pull out your wallet, take a deep gulp, and head to the Grand Floridian for the Perfectly Princess Tea Party. The tea party includes a meet and greet with Princess Aurora from *Sleeping Beauty*, plus storytelling, sing-alongs, and a princess parade. (Needless to say, all little girls suit up in princess gear for this one.) Tea-party guests receive a special My Disney Girl doll dressed like Aurora, a ribbon tiara, bracelet, and princess scrapbook. The cost is $250 for one adult and one child aged 3–11. Additional adults are $100 each, and an additional child is $150. The tea party is offered from 10:30 to noon every day but Tuesday and Saturday. Lunch is served, but with all the excitement, don't be surprised if no one eats it. Reservations can be made at 407/939–3463 (407/WDW–DINE).

- @ 1900 Park Fare, Grand Floridian—Breakfast with Mary Poppins, Alice in Wonderland, the Mad Hatter, and Pooh and dinner with Cinderella, Prince Charming, the Evil Stepmother, and the Stepsisters. Several of our readers have given a special shout-out to Lady Tremaine and her daughters. "The evil stepmother is the only person in Disney who isn't constantly smiling," a dad from New York noted approvingly while a mom from Virginia added, "The stepsisters were loud, obnoxious, graceless, and a lot of fun." Breakfast: adults $23–$27, children $13–$15. Dinner: adults $38–$42, children $19–$22.

@ 'Ohana, Polynesian Resort—Luau breakfast with Lilo and Stitch, as well as Mickey and Pluto. Breakfast: adults $25, children $14.

Insider's Secret

The fact that the 'Ohana breakfast is the only character meal featuring that prankster Stitch makes it especially lively—and an especially good choice for boys who may have seen one princess too many. "Stitch took my brother's Buzz Lightyear gun and engaged Pluto in a stickup," one boy happily reported. "It's a memory my family will cherish forever."

In the Magic Kingdom

@ Cinderella's Royal Table in Cinderella Castle—Medieval banquet meals in the perfect setting. Cinderella greets you downstairs and poses with you for a portrait, which is included in the price, along with wands for girls and swords for boys. After the royal greeting, you're escorted upstairs to meet the Fairy Godmother and at least two other princesses. Disney rotates them, but Snow White, Belle, Aurora, and Jasmine are often featured. Be sure to confirm all this when you book because of the insane popularity of Cinderella's Royal Table. Disney has changed this character meal more frequently than most, trying to figure out how to move people through more efficiently. If it's any consolation, most of the families surveyed think this is worth the trouble, using terms like "magnificient" and "unsurpassed." Breakfast: adults $52–$57, children (3–9) $35. Lunch: adults $55–$60, children $34–$39. Dinner: adults $65–$70, children $39–$42.

@ Crystal Palace—Breakfast, lunch, and dinner buffets with Pooh and friends. "The food was OK," says one mother from New Jersey. "Nothing special, but they did have a separate buffet for the kids filled with things they would eat. What really made our character meal worth it is that the Pooh characters came around to our tables and our 3- and 5-year-olds didn't have to fight for their attention. The servers did a good job of keeping things orderly. When Tigger was visiting our table, a child from another family got so excited he ran up to join in. The server gently steered him back to his own seat, explaining Tigger would be there next." Breakfast: adults $25–$28, children $14–$16. Lunch: adults $27–$31, children $15–$17. Dinner: adults $40–$44, children $20–$22.

In Epcot

@ Akershus Royal Banquet Hall in Norway—Breakfast, lunch, and dinner buffets in a castle setting. At present Snow White, Mulan, Mary Poppins, Belle, Aurora, and Jasmine show up at breakfast. At lunch and dinner you'll meet Belle, Jasmine, Aurora, Alice in Wonderland, Pocahontas, and Ariel—who, we're happy to report, is walking just fine in a ball gown. The princesses are sometimes reshuffled, so if your child has a preference, confirm who's expected to appear. Breakfast: adults $40–$47, children (3–9) $25–$28. Lunch: adults $41–$50, children $25–$29. Dinner: adults $47–$56, children $25–$30.

Money-Saving Tip

When you enter a character meal, you'll probably be ushered into a line where families are waiting to have their pictures taken with the characters by a professional photographer. These shots can be added to your PhotoPass or, if you want to save a few bucks (not to mention the wait in line), ask to be shown directly to your seats. There will be plenty of time later for you to take your own pictures with the characters as they visit your table.

@ Garden Grill in the Land—This rotating restaurant offers Epcot's only evening character dinner, this one with Mickey, Pluto, Chip, and Dale. They're dressed in cute farmer clothing in a nod to the agricultural theme of the Land pavilion. Dinner: adults $37–$42, children $18–$21.

In Hollywood Studios

@ Hollywood & Vine—Stars from Disney Junior television shows meet and greet guests during breakfast and lunch, so it's a good choice for the 2-to-5 set. Breakfast: adults $27–$30, children (3–9) $15–$17. Lunch: adults $31–$36, children $17–$19.

In the Animal Kingdom

@ Tusker House—Mickey, Donald, Daisy, and Goofy appear at a safari-themed breakfast. This one gets high marks from our readers for both the food and the general cuteness of the presentation. Breakfast: adults $26–$31, children (3–9) $15–$16. Lunch: adults $27–$30, children (3–9) $15–$18.

Special Holiday Parties and Events

Disney World is at its most magical during the holidays. Hours are extended, special parades and shows debut, and the parks and hotels are beautifully decorated.

The week between Christmas and New Year's is the absolute busiest of the year at WDW, but it's possible to celebrate the holidays at Disney without being caught in the crush. Decorations go up just before Thanksgiving, and the special shows and parades debut shortly thereafter. The first two weeks of December are among the least crowded of the year—perfect for celebrating Christmas at Disney (assuming that your child's school schedule can accommodate the trip).

Each resort puts up its own theme decorations as well—a nautical tree for the Yacht Club, seashell ornaments at the Beach Club, Native American tepees at the Wilderness Lodge, an enormous Victorian dazzler at the Grand Floridian. These decorations, in fact, are so gorgeous that holiday tours of the Disney hotels are popular among Orlando locals.

Mickey's Very Merry Christmas Party

Christmas at Disney World is lovely all on its own, but Disney also offers a special ticketed party event on select evenings in the Magic Kingdom with holiday-themed shows and parades. Tickets for Mickey's Very Merry Christmas Party ($59–$65 adults, $54–$60 kids 3–9) should be purchased well in advance, either online at www.disneyworld.com or by calling 407/934–7639 (407/W–DISNEY).

Insider's Secret

If you have preteens and teens who are up for a gorier scene, check out the super-scary Halloween Horror Nights event at Universal Studios.

Mickey's Not-So-Scary Halloween Party

On selected evenings during September and October the Magic Kingdom hosts Mickey's Not-So-Scary Halloween Party. As the name implies, this celebration is geared toward younger kids, with fortune-tellers, face painters, and trick-or-treating throughout the park; parades featuring the characters in costume; and a special fireworks finale. Be sure to bring along everyone's Halloween costumes.

Advance tickets for Mickey's Not-So-Scary Halloween Party are a must, so visit www.disneyworld.com or call 407/ 934–7639 (407/W–DISNEY) before you leave home. The party is offered on up to 20 dates throughout September and October, but the October 31 party always sells out first. Tickets cost $55–$65 for adults and $49–$59 for kids 3–9.

Tours for Kids and Families

Most of Disney's behind-the-scenes tours require that guests be 16 and up to participate, but there are two programs at the Grand Floridian that are created specifically for kids and one tour in the Magic Kingdom that was designed for families.

Pirate Adventure

This rollicking two-hour boat tour takes kids on a treasure hunt across the Seven Seas Lagoon with stops at all the Magic Kingdom resort marinas. Counselors help kids collect clues and complete a map that leads them to buried treasure. It's a good choice for active kids in the 4-to-12-age range. A snack is served on the pontoon boat after the last stop, and everyone leaves with a bag of treasure. "My 6-year-old son loved the Pirate Adventure at the Grand Floridian," reported one mom from New York. "It's very reasonably priced, and since I'm a single parent, I have to confess it was wonderful to just have a couple of hours to lie by the pool while he was on tour."

The Adventure currently departs the Grand Floridian marina at 9:30 am daily. Kids ages 4 to 12 may participate in this child-only event that costs $34. Reservations are a must, because this program fills up fast; call 407/939–3463 (407/ WDW–DINE) 90 days in advance.

Wonderland Tea Party

Kids join Alice in Wonderland and the Mad Hatter for a tea party held at 1900 Park Fare in the Grand Floridian. The table is festively appointed, and kids decorate their own cupcakes. Since this is pretty much all they eat, expect an afternoon sugar high. Afterward, the characters lead them in a variety of games, and each child leaves with a souvenir photo of him- or herself with the characters.

The Wonderland Tea Party is served weekdays from 2 to 3 pm for kids ages 4 to 10 (no moms!), and the cost is $40. For reservations, call 407/939–3463 (407/WDW–DINE) 90 days in advance.

Insider's Secret

Looking for a way to kill an hour or two while the kids participate in one of the Grand Floridian programs? The spa is just around the corner.

Family Magic Tour in the Magic Kingdom

Everyone gets into the act on this tour; although the activities are geared to kids ages 3 to 10, parents and both younger and older siblings can come along. The only rule is that you have to be willing to act silly.

Your tour guide meets you at Guest Relations in the Magic Kingdom and sets up the premise of the tour. Perhaps Peter Pan has stolen Captain Hook's favorite hook, and the captain is so furious that his band of buccaneers is threatening to take over the whole Magic Kingdom. To stop him, you must follow a map that takes you around the park—hopping, skipping, hiding, and keeping an eye out for each new clue.

At the final stop of the tour, you meet up with a character

or two for a closing surprise. The tour is a great option for families who have been to the Magic Kingdom several times and are looking for a new spin. It's less appealing for first-time visitors who are itching to get on the rides.

The Family Magic Tour is held daily from 10 to noon, and the cost is $34 per person, regardless of age. Call 407/ 939–8687(407/WDW–TOUR).

Wild Africa Trek in the Animal Kingdom

Kids 8 and up who are really into animals (or who need to do a serious project to make up for the school days they're missing on this trip!) will enjoy the Wild Animal Trek, which is offered daily in the Animal Kingdom. This three-hour tour takes you behind the scenes of the park, then on a special safari through the savanna led by knowledgeable guides. Unlike the Kilimanjaro Safari, which must keep moving, the Wild Animal Trek vehicles stop at several points along the journey to allow plenty of time for animal viewing and pictures.

The behind-the-scenes part of the Trek is really a blast, and one of the reasons why this tour, despite the cost, has become so popular they're upping the number of trips per day. The highlight is a shaky walk across a "broken down" bridge extended high in the air above a river full of dozing crocodiles. You're carefully tethered in, of course, but it's still enough to get the pulse racing. And they serve you a truly terrific lunch on a viewing platform right in the middle of the savanna.

The cost is $189, and owing to the construction of some of the transportation vehicles and bridges, participants must weigh between 45 and 310 pounds. Call 407/939–8687 (407/ WDW–TOUR) for details or reservations.

Water Sports

Most on-site hotels have lovely marinas with a variety of watercraft for rent, but the major water-recreation area of WDW is the Seven Seas Lagoon in front of the Magic Kingdom. Marinas at the Grand Floridian, Polynesian, Contemporary, Fort Wilderness, and Wilderness Lodge all service the lagoon, and you don't have to be a guest of the resort to rent watercraft. (Although you'll need to show either a driver's license or a resort ID.)

Reservations are a good idea, especially in the on-season, and it also never hurts to confirm prices before you go. Call 407/939–0754 for more information.

Water-sport options include the following:

Boat Rental

The Disney fleet includes mini-speedboats called Sea Raycers, canopy boats, sailboats, pontoons, pedal boats, and kayaks. The marina staff can help you decide which watercraft best fits your needs; pontoon boats are a good option for younger kids, and the whole family can take a 30-minute ride for $37.

The best place to rent the Sea Raycer mini-speedboats is the Seven Seas Lagoon. You have plenty of room to explore and can really pick up speed. The boats are for rent at the marinas in the Contemporary, Polynesian, and Grand Floridian resorts or Wilderness Lodge. At present prices are $32 for 30 minutes. Drivers must be at least 14 years old and 5 feet tall, although kids of any age will enjoy riding along with Mom or Dad.

Fishing

Fishing equipment for an afternoon of catch-and-release is for rent at all on-site hotels with access to lakes or ponds: Fort Wilderness, Contemporary, Polynesian, Grand Floridian, Wilderness Lodge, BoardWalk, Yacht and Beach Clubs, Port Orleans, Caribbean Beach, Coronado Springs, Saratoga Springs, and Old Key West. If you'd like more action than simply dropping a line, fishing tours depart from water locations throughout WDW. The one-hour fishing tour for ages 6 to 12 starts at $28; parties of five or more should book the more elaborate two-hour tour for $230. Reservations can be made up to 180 days in advance; call 407/939–2277 (407/WDW–BASS) for exact times, locations, and prices.

Parasailing and Waterskiing

Another high-thrill activity is parasailing. Excursions leave daily from the Contemporary Resort marina, and the regular flights cost $95 for one person or $175 for two riders in tandem. That's enough for most people, but the truly adventurous can fly longer on the deluxe flight, which costs $130 for a single rider and $195 in tandem. At your top height of 600 feet above the lake you'll see all four parks. The Sammy Duvall Watersports Center also offers waterskiing, wakeboarding, kneeboarding, and tubing. For reservations and more information call 407/939–0754.

Specialty Cruises

Two of the greatest ways to spend an evening in Disney World are watching the Magic Kingdom fireworks or the pyrotechnics of IllumiNations at Epcot. And there's no classier viewing spot than aboard your private boat. "We called before we left home and rented a pontoon boat to see the Epcot fireworks," wrote one father. "What a treat. We had a great captain who drove us around then 'parked' under the bridge so we could see the show. It was great floating there, sipping a drink, while others were jam-packed in the park waiting for the show, and probably trying to figure out how they were going to exit along with thousands of others."

The fleet includes yachts and pontoons that can accommodate groups of 7 to 14 people. Factoring in the size of your party and where you'll be sailing from, the prices vary. But to give you an idea, an hour-long cruise in a simple pontoon boat holding up to 8 people is $275; in an elegant yacht that accommodates up to 12, it's $520. When you factor in how many people can participate in the experience, the specialty cruises are actually a (somewhat) cost-effective way to create a memorable evening for the whole family. Just be sure to reserve 90 days in advance by calling 407/939–7529 (407/WDW–PLAY).

Surfing

Surfing lessons are offered at Typhoon Lagoon on select mornings before the park opens. Participants must be at least 8 years old and strong swimmers. For those up to the challenge, this clinic ($160 per person) is one of the most fun things to do in all of WDW. Because the waves are controllable and the instructors are top-notch, almost everyone can ride a wave by the end of the class. Call 407/939–7529 (407/WDW–PLAY) for details. Always confirm prices when booking.

Sports on Land

Biking

Bikes are for rent at most on-site hotels at a cost of $9 an hour or $22 a day; helmets are included.

Golf

There are six courses on WDW grounds with twilight fees starting at $59 on weekdays for Disney World resort guests. The rates go straight up from there, topping out as high as $169. If you're beginning golfers who just want to give it a try, the Oak Trail, a nine-hole walking course, costs $38 for adults and $20 for kids 3–9. Visit disneyworld.disney.go.com or call 407/939–4653 (407/WDW–GOLF) to reserve tee times and confirm rates.

Health Clubs and Spas

The Contemporary, Grand Floridian, Swan, Dolphin, Yacht and Beach Clubs, BoardWalk, Animal Kingdom Lodge, Coronado Springs, Old Key West, and Saratoga Springs resorts all have health clubs. The rates average about $18 a day for guests of the resort, with reduced family or length-of-stay rates. The most complete workout facility is at Saratoga Springs.

There are full-service spas at the Grand Floridian, Saratoga Springs, and Animal Kingdom Lodge. "My 7-year-old daughter had her first manicure at the Grand Floridian spa and was in heaven," a mom from New York wrote. "She felt very grown-up, and the manicurist was the sweetest cast member I've ever met—even at Disney World, where everybody is nice!"

Horseback Riding

Guided 45-minute rides circle the wooded trails of the Fort Wilderness daily. Children must be at least 9 to ride; the horses are gentle and the pace is slow. Trail rides start at $23.

Younger kids can ride around the stables at the Fort Wilderness Petting Farm while older siblings are on the trail ride. Children 2 and over and up to 80 pounds are welcome. Fort Wilderness also offers horse-drawn wagon rides departing from Pioneer Hall nightly.

During the holidays the options are jazzed up a bit. Nightly 25-minute "haunted carriage rides" are available during the month of October, and "sleigh rides"—sans snow, of course, are offered in December. Call 407/WDW–PLAY for details.

Miniature Golf

Fantasia Gardens, just across from Disney's Hollywood Studios, is real eye candy—an 18-hole mini-golf tribute to the movie

Helpful Hint

Fantasia Fairways is too tough for golfers under 10, and even Fantasia Gardens is a fairly difficult course. Winter Summerland is a better choice for the pre-school and grade-school set.

Fantasia with dancing hippos, orchestrated fountains, and the Sorcerer's Apprentice running the whole show. A second course, Fantasia Fairways, is a miniature version of a real golf course, with sand traps, water hazards, and roughs. Although you play with a putter, the holes are 100 feet long and difficult enough to drive a veteran golfer to curses.

The second miniature golf complex at Disney World is Winter Summerland (beside Blizzard Beach), where you're greeted with the question "Would you like to play in snow or sand?" Your first clue that there's strange weather ahead is that Santa, his sleigh pulled by flamingos, has crash-landed on the roof and skidded through a snowbank–sandbank into the wackiest campground on earth. You can opt to play either the icy white "greens" of the winter course, where you can find a hockey rink, a snow castle, and slalom ski runs, or the sandy shores of the summer course, where the Beach Boys serenade you amid pools, waves, and barbecue pits. While both of the Winter Summerland courses are child-friendly, the summer course is the harder of the two. Must be all those sand traps.

Rates at Fantasia Gardens, Fantasia Fairways, and Winter Summerland are $12 for adults and $10 for kids ages 3 to 9. Reservations aren't necessary.

Running

Trails cut through the grounds of nearly every Disney resort. Consult Guest Relations for ideas on the best route around your particular hotel. Wilderness Lodge, with its invitingly shady trails, is an especially good choice if you're visiting in summer when even morning runs can be steamy.

Tennis

Several on-site resorts (the Contemporary, the Grand Floridian, the Yacht and Beach Clubs, BoardWalk, Old Key West, Saratoga Springs, the Swan, and the Dolphin) have tennis courts, and the Contemporary also offers clinics for guests 10 and older. There's considerable variation in rental rates and reservation policies, so call 407/939–7529 (407/WDW–PLAY) for details.

ESPN Wide World of Sports Complex

This multimillion-dollar sports complex hosts competitions and tournaments, with facilities to accommodate 25 different kinds of sports, including the ever-growing number of Disney-sponsored race events. It's also the spring training camp of the Atlanta Braves. You can have lunch or dinner at the ESPN Wide World of Sports Grille, a sports bar with multiple screens and interactive games.

Activities at the Wide World of Sports vary widely, so call 407/939–4263 or visit www.disneyworldsports.com before you leave home to find out what will be going on during your visit. Admission varies with the event, but averages $14 for adults, $10 for kids ages 3 to 9.

CHAPTER

11

Dining at Disney

Full-Service Restaurants at Disney

You've come to ride, but you also need to eat. The good news is that the variety and quality of the on-site restaurants have vastly improved in the 24 years I've been doing this guide. The bad news is that the size of the crowds has also increased, making it more of a hassle to get into the restaurants.

The biggest change in the Disney restaurant system in the past few years has been the Dining Plan, which allows guests to include meals and snacks in their vacation package and thus create the equivalent of an all-inclusive resort stay. The Dining Plan makes more sense for some families than others, but it has an effect on every family that visits Walt Disney World, even those who opt not to include it with their tickets. Why? Because it means that more restaurant reservations are being made and that they're being made earlier than ever. Unless you book your dinners and character meals well in advance, you may find yourself unable to get into the most popular restaurants, simply because families on the Dining Plan have beaten you to the punch. Sure, there's still a chance you can get a last-minute reservation if you're not picky about when and where you eat,

Insider's Secret

The Disney Dining Plan has been a runaway success—so much so that it's more important than ever to make advance reservations for character meals. The reason is this: All families on the plan will be eating at least one full-service meal each day, which in itself means more general dining demand, since in the past many budget-conscious families stuck to counter-service meals. More families are also going for character meals under the plan; many of the character meals only count as one full-service credit, and others, such as those in Cinderella castle, require you to combine two credits. Either way, it means that since character dining is more affordable under the plan, there are more people than ever trying to book those seats.

The fact that the system allows guests to combine meals if they want to try a signature dining venue means that people who otherwise wouldn't have considered the California Grill or other upscale spots are trying to get in. The result? Guests on the Disney Dining Plan are flooding the full-service restaurants in such great numbers that all guests—including those who aren't on the plan or who aren't staying at Disney hotels—are feeling the squeeze.

Consider the experience of this grandmother from Rhode Island. "We have visited Disney World many times and have certain restaurants we know we enjoy. For our upcoming visit we decided against the dining plan but imagine my surprise when I called for reservations two months in advance and found that we could not get into eight of our 10 favorites. Some of them were giving us ridiculous times like 10 pm for dinner, and others were simply saying there was nothing available at all. We were crushed!"

but your selection will be curtailed. So even families opting not to participate in the Dining Plan still need to make their restaurant reservations as early as possible.

We'll go into this in more detail later, but just so you understand the basics: The standard Disney Dining Plan includes one table-service meal, one quick-service meal, and one snack per person per day. If you plan carefully, you can have plenty of culinary adventures by using two of your table-service credits to experience (a) princess character dining; (b) a dinner show; or (c) one of Disney's signature restaurants, such as Citricos, Flying Fish, or the California Grill. When you purchase the Dining Plan, you'll receive a brochure outlining all of your options.

And here's the other side of that coin. "We were all about the credit combining," says a dad from Texas. "On a couple of days we ate fast food all three meals, so each member of our family had two table-service credits left over. We combined those for our breakfast in Cinderella Castle, which turned out to be a major cost savings. I almost passed out when I ran the numbers for how much that breakfast would have cost us otherwise."

The basic Dining Plan is by far the most popular, but there are other options. It's certainly possible to upgrade to the deluxe or wine-and-dine plans, but if your kids are young it's unlikely you'll want to spend that much time in restaurants. "In order to make sure our investment in the deluxe plan paid off, we scheduled lots of table-service meals," wrote one mother. "By the second day my husband was complaining that he felt like a slave to all of our reservations and we ended up canceling quite a few, which was disappointing. But we decided as first-time visitors we'd be better off spending that time in the parks."

At the other end of the spectrum is the quick-service plan, which includes two quick-service meals and two snacks per person per day. This plan is about 30% cheaper than the standard one, and some families prefer it, especially those with preschoolers who like to snack at regular intervals and who quickly grow impatient at full-service restaurants.

Once you're in Orlando, your Dining Plan info is loaded into your ticket/resort ID card, and the system keeps track of how you're doing—in fact, each time you use the card your server will give you a receipt showing the remaining balance. Remember that your number of meals is tied to the number of nights you're staying. If you remain all day on your last day, you'll probably run out of meals.

Making Reservations

The system works like this: a reservation doesn't hold the restaurant to a specific time for seating you, but rather guarantees you the next available table after you arrive. Let's say you made advance reservations for four people at 7 pm. When you show up at 7, your table won't be waiting with your name on it, but you will be given the next available table for four. Waits average between 10 and 30 minutes, but it's still far better than walking in with no prior arrangement.

A mom from New Jersey offers this council: "Get to your reservation a few minutes early. They'll seat you in the order

Helpful Hint

Families not sure of exactly of where they would be each night were making multiple reservations for each evening, resulting in a 30% no-show rate for many restaurants. Since the restaurants, thinking they were full, were turning away people and thus losing money, it didn't take Disney long to amend the situation. Now there's a new cancellation policy at the upscale restaurants and character meals. A credit card is required to make the reservation and a $10 fee is charged for no-shows. If you cancel the reservation in advance, the fee is waived.

Helpful Hint
Disney restaurant hours are sometimes changed or shortened during the off-season, but signature restaurants are always open.

that you arrive and check in, so someone arriving at 5:50 for a 6 pm reservation gets the jump on the other six people who have reservations for the same time."

So how do you make reservations? You can either call 407/939–3463 (407/WDW–DINE) or make them online up to 180 days in advance of the day for which you want reservations. Admittedly, this requires some planning. Ideally, you'll sketch out a general schedule for each day and evening of your vacation, so you'll know that on Tuesday you're having dinner at Epcot and on Saturday you're having a character breakfast.

If you've arrived at Disney without dining reservations, you can try to get last-minute slots by calling 407/WDW–DINE as soon as you know where you want to eat. Call with your cell phone while you're in line for a ride, or, if you're staying at an on-site hotel, you can also press the dining button on your hotel room phone. You won't get Saturday-night seating at California Grill by waiting until you get there, but if you're flexible about where and when you eat, finding last-minute reservations is possible.

You can also try to reserve in person at the restaurants or at Guest Relations (a.k.a. Guest Services) on arrival. There's no guarantee, but you might get lucky.

A mom from Virginia has this to add: "If the dining-reservations phone line or Guest Relations tells you there's no availability, you can always just show up at the restaurant and talk to the hostess. What the dining line and Guest Relations can't know is if there are going to be any no-shows that night, but the hostess certainly knows and sometimes they can work you in. Using this method on a recent trip, we were seated at two restaurants that the reservations guide had assured us were totally booked."

There are quite a few buffets at Disney World and, for families, they solve certain problems, i.e., you get the food fast (as in, immediately) and there are plenty of options for picky eaters. But consider working some full-service venues into your week as well. As one mother from Oregon wrote, "The fast-food and buffet venues have the same hectic atmosphere as the parks—you still have to stand in a line, carry things, and try to keep an eye on the kids in the meantime. And they're so loud, especially the character meals! We had an elegant, wonderfully relaxing lunch at the Brown Derby one day, and my husband said it was the perfect getaway from theme-park chaos—almost as if we'd gone back to our hotel room for a break."

And if you're worried that the kids will get antsy during a full-service dinner, rest assured that Disney is all about getting the food out fast. The kiddie menus have games and puzzles, and waiters will bring out crayons, crackers, and drinks with lids to keep the kids busy while you wait.

Finding Healthy Food

Disney has removed trans fats from all of its meals, making it easier to feel good about grabbing snacks. You'll also find health-conscious choices in the kids' meals—fruit instead of chips and milk or water instead of soda, for instance. To find your best bets at each venue, stop by Guest Relations in each park for a healthy dining guide. There will be at least one low-fat and one vegetarian entrée at every full-service restaurant.

And guests give Disney chefs major (trans-fat-free) brownie points for their willingness to address specific dietary needs. The chefs at full-service restaurants prefer advance warning (you can note any special dietary requests when you make your reservations) but are also pretty adept at meeting guests' needs with shorter notice, as evidenced by this New Jersey

Best Fast-Food Options for Families

IN THE MAGIC KINGDOM: COSMIC RAY'S STARLIGHT CAFÉ

Okay, admittedly, this is not fine dining, but remember that the Magic Kingdom is pretty much about getting basic food as fast as you can without being stampeded in the process. There's plenty of seating at Cosmic Ray's, the line moves fast, and they have sandwiches and salads in addition to the usual hamburgers and chicken fingers. (Cosmic Ray's is also one of the few counter-service restaurants to offer kosher alternatives.)

AT EPCOT: TAQUERIA DE LAGO

This relatively new quick-service spot in Mexico is getting high marks from readers for its taquitos and quesadillas. If you can't get seating, check next door at the Cantina de San Angel, which only serves snacks but has a pretty outdoor dining area.

AT DISNEY'S HOLLYWOOD STUDIOS: TOY STORY PIZZA PLANET

Good standard pizza, fast service, and an arcade combine to keep the kids happy.

IN THE ANIMAL KINGDOM: FLAME TREE BARBECUE

Smoked ribs, chicken, and sandwiches and a shady patio to boot.

mother's story. "I've been on a weight-loss plan for several months and am happy to have lost 50 pounds. But the very thought of going to Disney World terrified me. I pictured nothing but grease and sugar. Our very first meal was at the Brown Derby restaurant in Hollywood, and when I asked the server a question about how something was prepared she said 'Just a minute.' Almost immediately the chef came out and he practically created a new entrée for me on the spot. After that,

I asked to speak to the chef every time we sat down for a meal. My son started calling me 'The Dining Room Diva.'"

Another mother wrote, "Both of my sons, ages 4 and 7, are allergic to dairy, eggs, and nuts, and dining out is usually a challenge for us. We had reserved a character dinner at the Crystal Palace, and after I spoke to the chef about our dietary restrictions, he couldn't have been more wonderful. He walked me through the buffet pointing out which foods would be safe and which were risky, and he made a special batch of pasta just for our boys. For dessert he brought them banana splits using the same soy ice cream we buy at home. They were in their glory!"

Rating the Disney Restaurants

The restaurant descriptions that make up the bulk of this chapter cover only full-service sit-down restaurants. Let's face it, most fast-food places are pretty similar, and there's only so much you can say about burgers, fries, and soft-serve ice cream. Therefore, we decided not to overwhelm you with full descriptions of all of the 100-plus food-service venues throughout Walt Disney World and to focus on restaurants where you're apt to be spending more time and more money and will thus have higher expectations.

Definition of Quick-Guide Ratings

Food Quality

★★★ Exceptionally good
  ★★ Tasty food
  ★ Okay in a pinch

Price for an Adult Meal Comprising a Main Course and an Appetizer

$$$ Expensive; about $30 and up
 $$ Moderate; about $15–$30
  $ Inexpensive; about $15

Reservations

Not Offered: This restaurant doesn't accept reservations unless you have a party of 10 or more. You can show up at an off-time and get a beeper, then shop nearby while you wait for your table.

Recommended: This restaurant draws average-size crowds. In high season it will fill to capacity, so you should make reservations. If you're touring in the off-season or dining at off-hours, you should be able to make reservations at the last minute or be seated as a walk-in.

Necessary: This is a popular restaurant. If you haven't made reservations, you'll probably be closed out.

Suitability for Kids

High: The restaurant is informal, with food choices designed to appeal to kids. There may be some sort of entertainment going on, or perhaps the setting itself is interesting.

Moderate: This restaurant is casual and family-oriented.

Low: This is one of WDW's more adult restaurants with sophisticated menu choices and leisurely service.

Meals Served

B is for breakfast, L is for lunch, and D is for dinner.

Magic Kingdom Restaurants

Cinderella's Royal Table   ★★★

High amid the spires of Cinderella Castle in Fantasyland, this restaurant is the most glamorous in the Magic Kingdom. The food is expensive and admittedly elegantly presented—although the three-star rating is more the result of the overall experience than the cuisine. Cinderella's Royal Table is the home of the princess character meals, the toughest ticket in all of Disney World. A mother of two from Virginia reported, "It took us three days to get through the phone line for the princess breakfast in the Magic Kingdom, but it was well worth it! My 4-year-old daughter wore her Cinderella dress, and she loved all the special attention she received. It was a year ago and she still talks about it." "Too magical for words," agrees the mom of a 5-year-old in Maine.

The Crystal Palace

Winnie the Pooh and friends circulate among diners . . . and everybody agrees that that's cool, but there's a real split of opinion on the quality of the food. Consider this report from a Texas mother of two: "In general I dislike buffets, but the food here was far better than I expected and our children absolutely loved the ice-cream sundae bar. (Even though things got so messy that we did have to change their shirts after lunch!) The Crystal Palace would be a good choice even if it didn't have the Pooh characters." But a mother from Florida was less pleased, writing, "You might want to reevaluate your rating on this one. We showed up starving but hardly anyone, including the children, found anything on the buffet they were willing to eat."

Liberty Tree Tavern

In Liberty Square and decorated in a style reminiscent of colonial Williamsburg, the Tavern serves salads, sandwiches, and New England clam chowder at lunch. The evening menu is an all-you-can-eat Thanksgiving-style feast with turkey and stuffing, flank steak, mac and cheese, and other family favorites.

The Plaza Restaurant ★

The salads, sandwiches, and burgers here are very filling—but also very bland. The restaurant has a wide selection of ice-cream treats, which come from the Ice Cream Parlor next door.

Quick Guide to Full-in the Magic

Restaurant	Description	Location
Cinderella's Royal Table	Dine in the castle with the princess characters	Fantasyland
The Crystal Palace	Buffet dining with Winnie the Pooh and friends	Main Street
Liberty Tree Tavern	Thanksgiving-style feast	Liberty Square
The Plaza Restaurant	Don't miss the sundaes	Main Street
Tony's Town Square Restaurant	*Lady and the Tramp* theme and Italian classics	Main Street

Tony's Town Square Restaurant ★★

Located in the Main Street Hub, this thoroughly enjoyable restaurant is dedicated to *Lady and the Tramp*, with scenes from the film dotting the walls and a statue of the canine romantics in the center. The cuisine, like that of the café where Tramp wooed Lady, is classic Italian, and the portions are generous.

Epcot Restaurants

Akershus

The Norwegian buffet at Akershus (which one parent described as "all the herring you can eat") never really caught on, so this

Service Restaurants Kingdom

Rating	Price	Advance Reservations	Suitability for Kids	Meals Served
★★★	$$$	Necessary	High	B, L, D
★★	$$	Necessary	High	B, L, D
★★	$$	Recommended	Moderate	L, D
★	$$	Recommended	Moderate	L, D
★★	$$	Recommended	High	L, D

lovely castlelike restaurant in the Norway pavilion has shifted its buffet menu to include more American staples. Even better, Akershus has princess-theme character dining at breakfast, lunch, and dinner. This takes some of the pressure off the popular Cinderella Castle breakfast in the Magic Kingdom, but you'll still need to make reservations 180 days in advance.

Biergarten ★★

There's plenty of room to move about in this German beer hall where yodelers and an oompah-pah band get the whole crowd involved in singing and dancing. The all-you-can-eat buffet features traditional Bavarian dishes: bratwurst, spaetzle, and salads.

Bistro de Paris

The Bistro is quieter, calmer, and more elegant than its sister, Les Chefs de France, located below it. It's also a tad too civilized for kids under 12. Expect classic French cuisine, a wonderful wine selection, and continental service.

Coral Reef

One whole wall of this restaurant is glass, giving you a remarkable view of the Living Seas tank. Watching the fish keeps the kids entertained while parents browse the menu, which features, naturally, upscale seafood dishes.

Garden Grill Restaurant

Easily recognizable American dishes make this a good choice for younger children. The restaurant is on a revolving platform, allowing you to observe scenes from the Living with the Land boat ride below. There's character dining in the evening.

Le Cellier

Le Cellier is one of the most popular restaurants in Epcot, perhaps because there are relatively few steak houses in Disney World. The steaks here are excellent, as is the salmon, and the desserts are as big as the prairies of Alberta.

Les Chefs de France

Modeled after the sidewalk cafés of Paris, this restaurant bustles pleasantly. The classical French menu is a bit hit-or-miss in quality, but the waiters are charming, and you can gaze out at the World Showcase action. With any luck, you might even spot the elusive Remy from *Ratatouille*, one of the less frequently seen characters in the park.

Marrakesh   ★★

Ready for exotic surroundings and unusual entertainment? Kids enjoy the belly dancers, and the ladies sometimes invite them to enter into the act. The unfamiliarity of the food may pose a problem, but if the kids can be persuaded to give it a try, they can find that roasted chicken tastes pretty much the same the world over.

Nine Dragons   ★★

Nine Dragons has taken the concept of an exhibition kitchen to new levels. Easily recognizable Chinese dishes are on the menu, along with more exotic offerings from five different cooking stations.

Rose & Crown Pub & Dining Room   ★★

This charming bar and restaurant has live entertainment, friendly service, and upscale pub grub such as fish-and-chips and meat pies. If you eat on the patio, you have a great view of the World Showcase Lagoon.

San Angel Inn   ★★

A beautiful location inside the Mayan pyramid of the Mexico pavilion, with the Rio del Tiempo murmuring in the background, makes this restaurant a charming choice. The service is swift and friendly, and older kids can browse among the market stalls of the pavilion or even ride the Gran Fiesta Tour while waiting for their food.

Teppan Edo   ★★★

In the Japan pavilion, the revamped Teppan Edo offers grilled specialties at large tables, in front of which the chefs slice and

Quick Guide to Full-

Restaurant	Description	Location
Akershus	Authentic Norwegian cuisine and princess-character buffets	Norway
Biergarten	Rousing, noisy atmosphere, and live entertainment	Germany
Bistro de Paris	Classic French cuisine—very elegant, very adult	France
Coral Reef	Great views of the Living Seas tank	Living Seas pavilion
Garden Grill Restaurant	American dishes and the Disney characters	Land pavilion
Le Cellier	Great steaks, excellent salmon, huge desserts	Canada
Les Chefs de France	Like a Paris sidewalk café	France
Marrakesh	Exotic food and surroundings, belly dancers	Morocco
Nine Dragons	Cuisine representing every region in China	China
Rose & Crown Pub & Dining Room	Pub atmosphere and live entertainment	United Kingdom
San Angel Inn	Beautiful, romantic setting	Mexico
Teppan Edo	Dining room chefs slice and dice before your eyes	Japan
Tokyo Dining	Casual with sushi and batter-fried entrees	Japan
Tutto Italia	Upscale Italian, lively service	Italy
Via Napoli	Best pizza in park; charming setting with equally charming service	Italy

Service Restaurants at Epcot

Rating	Price	Advance Reservations	Suitability for Kids	Meals Served
★★	$$	Necessary	High	B, L, D
★★	$$	Recommended	High	L, D
★★★	$$$	Necessary	Low	D
★★	$$$	Necessary	High	L, D
★★	$$	Recommended	Moderate	D
★★★	$$$	Recommended	Low	L, D
★★	$$$	Necessary	Moderate	L, D
★★	$$	Recommended	Moderate	L, D
★★	$$	Recommended	Low	L, D
★★	$$	Recommended	Moderate	L, D
★★	$$	Recommended	Moderate	L, D
★★★	$$$	Necessary	High	L, D
★★	$$	Recommended	Moderate	L, D
★★★	$$$	Necessary	Moderate	L, D
★★★	$$	Necessary	High	L, D

dice in the best Benihana tradition. Upscale options such as wagyu and Kobe beef are available. It's terrifically entertaining for the kids—the chefs often jazz up the presentation even more in their honor—and the stir-fried, simply prepared food is a hit with all ages. A father of four from Ohio wrote a rave review: "Japan is a good choice if you want to eat out in Epcot with kids. The chefs toss food and catch it in their hats, make silly jokes like throwing the butter and saying 'butterfly.' And one time when we were in, they had a lady making origami animals for the children. Plus, since they cook at the table, you get your food really fast."

Toyko Dining

Connected to Teppan Edo is a delightful sushi bar called Toyko Dining, where you'll find great Japanese food without the fun but admittedly time-consuming ceremony of the full-fledged restaurant. Grilled steak and chicken are available for any sushi-shy members of the party.

Tutto Italia

Expect authentic Italian food, equally authentic waiters, and a lovely setting, which, since it's tucked away in the far reaches of the Italy pavilion, actually feels a little secluded, at least by Disney World standards. The food is top-notch, especially the calamari, and the bustling ambience works well for families.

Via Napoli

I'd give this lunch and dinner place four stars if I could. It's certainly not your neighborhood pizza place—unless you live in Naples, that is. The pizzas emerge from giant wood-burning ovens—each oven named after a volcano—and they're incredibly tasty. The truffle-oil pizza alone is enough to induce a swoon. You sit at large tables, and the waiters bustle, so Via Napoli isn't exactly fine dining or a break from the stress of the theme parks, but the food is excellent, reasonably priced, and the servers are adorable.

Restaurants at Disney's Hollywood Studios

'50s Prime Time Café

With its kitschy decor and ditzy waitresses dressed like June Cleaver, this restaurant is almost an attraction in itself. Meat loaf, macaroni, milk shakes, and other comfort foods are served in a 1950s-style kitchen, while dozens of TVs blare clips from classic shows in the background.

"Hi kids," says your waitress, pulling up a chair to the Formica-top table. "You didn't leave your bikes in the driveway, did you? Let me see those hands." Assuming you pass her clean-fingernails inspection, "Mom" will go on to advise you on your food choices. "I'll bring peas with that. Vegetables are good for you." The camp is lost on young kids, but they nonetheless love the no-frills food and the fact that Mom brings around crayons and coloring books, then hangs their artwork on the front of a refrigerator with magnets. But it's the baby-boomer parents, raised on the sitcoms that the restaurant spoofs, who really adore this restaurant. "You just have to get in the mood of the place," advised a mother of one from Illinois. "The whole routine about being on a TV show is very corny and very funny and the servers are great. We liked the food (chicken, pot roast, steak, salads, the basics), but when we left, my 8-year-old daughter said 'That was a good show,' and I think that's exactly the way you need to think of it."

Quick Guide to Full-at Disney's

Restaurant	Description
'50s Prime Time Café	Want to star in a 1950s sitcom?
The Hollywood Brown Derby	Elegant and lovely with upscale cuisine
Hollywood & Vine	Large, attractive buffeteria, character meals with Playhouse Disney gang
Mama Melrose's Ristorante Italiano	Good food, good service, rarely too crowded
Sci-Fi Dine-In Theater	Campy; you eat in cars at a drive-in theater

The Hollywood Brown Derby ★★★

A signature Cobb salad as well as veal, pasta, and fresh seafood are served at the Derby, where, just as you'd expect, caricatures of movie stars line the walls. The food is quite sophisticated considering that you're inside a theme park, and the restaurant itself is elegant and lovely, like stepping back into Hollywood in its heyday. The wine program, which offers suggested pairings by the glass with each entrée, is one of the best in Disney World.

Hollywood & Vine ★★

This large, attractive, art deco "buffeteria" offers classic American dishes at breakfast, lunch, and dinner. Lines move quickly,

Service Restaurants Hollywood Studios

Rating	Price	Advance Reservations	Suitability for Kids	Meals Served
★★★	$$	Recommended	High	L, D
★★★	$$$	Recommended	Low	L, D
★★	$	Recommended	High	B, L, D
★★	$$	Recommended	Moderate	L, D
★★	$$	Recommended	High	L, D

and the variety makes this a good choice for families. This is the only character-dining venue in Disney World to feature characters from the popular Disney Junior television shows. That alone guarantees that you'll find plenty of toddlers and preschoolers at every meal.

Mama Melrose's Ristorante Italiano ★★

This restaurant is tucked away near the Muppet*Vision 3-D plaza, and the out-of-the-way location means that you can sometimes squeeze in without advance reservations. Expect a casual New York feel and quick service. The restaurant serves gourmet flatbreads from a wood-burning oven and a wide variety of pasta dishes; the penne *alla vodka* is a favorite.

Sci-Fi Dine-In Theater

At least as campy as the '50s Prime Time Café, the Sci-Fi seats
you in vintage cars while hokey movie clips run on a giant
screen. Offerings range from drive-in staples like milk shakes
and popcorn all the way to seafood and St. Louis–style ribs.
Older kids adore the setting and the funny waiters; in fact they
often get so absorbed in the old movie clips that they sit quietly
while parents relax in the backseat. Younger kids, in contrast,
might be spooked. "Only okay food but really very fun," said
one mom, while another wrote, "My 4-year-old was so freaked
out by the atmosphere we had to leave early."

Animal Kingdom Restaurants

Rainforest Café

The jungle motif and large aquariums make the Rainforest Café
great fun for kids. The food is nothing special, but tasty enough,
with an emphasis on appetizers and other simple meals, like
burgers, sandwiches, and huge salads. There are locations at
both the Animal Kingdom and Downtown Disney.

Tusker House

The Tusker House is a favorite with families, offering buffets
with a lot of variety and a popular character breakfast in the
morning. "We tried this character breakfast when we got closed
out of the ones at the Magic Kingdom," said one dad, "But it
turned out to be a real treat. Good food, cute character presentation, and it moved fast—everything we needed."

Yak and Yeti ★★

This Asian-fusion restaurant in the Asia section offers full-
service dining, casual outdoor dining, a full bar, and a beer gar-

den. The food is quite good, and the setting is the most adult and relaxing of all the Animal Kingdom restaurants.

Restaurants in the WDW Hotels

Artist Point ★★

The most upscale of the Wilderness Lodge eateries, Artist Point offers Pacific Northwest–theme food in a casual, almost rustic, setting. The salmon is the house specialty, and the wine list highlights excellent selections from the Pacific Northwest.

Big River Grille & Brewing Works ★

WDW's only on-site brewpub is a good place to sample new beers and a couple of specialty ales. The food—mostly sandwiches and salads—is pedestrian, but the pleasant patio allows you to take in the action of the BoardWalk while you sip your beer.

bluezoo ★★

Famed chef Todd English brought this sleek, contemporary seafood restaurant to the Dolphin. Although it's far too tony in atmosphere and eclectic in menu for most kids, bluezoo is a good spot for drinks or a parents' night out. The menu changes regularly but tends to feature unusual seafood dishes, such as the butter-poached Maine lobster with truffle-potato ravioli.

Boatwright's Dining Hall ★★

An upgraded menu has brought significant improvements to Boatwright's, which is the only full-service restaurant in Port Orleans and located in the Riverside section. The food is still a mixture of Cajun specialties and American classics, but the Cajun dishes have been literally spiced up, and there are some

Quick Guide to Full-in the Animal

Restaurant	Description
Rainforest Café	Large and lively
Tusker House	Buffet with great variety, character breakfast and lunch
Yak & Yeti	Asian fusion, complete with bar and beer garden

interesting additions, such as a selection of microbrews from New Orleans. The Southern-inspired dessert menu—which includes an excellent pecan pie—rounds out the meal. One word of warning: Since the restaurant is adjacent to the food court and has an open-wall design, it's always loud. The designation "dining hall" is accurate.

Boma ★★★

This large family restaurant in the Animal Kingdom Lodge offers one of the best breakfast buffets in all of WDW. You can find the usual American classics, like eggs and pancakes, plus excellent grilled sausage and an outstanding selection of breads and pastries. The dinner buffet features African-inspired dishes, including wonderful grilled meats and a variety of wholesome grain dishes and salads. "The food was fresh and

Service Restaurants Kingdom

Rating	Price	Advance Reservations	Suitability for Kids	Meals Served
★★	$$	Not accepted	High	B, L, D
★★	$$	Necessary for character meals; otherwise suggested	High	B, L, D
★★	$$	Suggested	Moderate	L, D

beautifully prepared," said a mom from Georgia. "Both the kids and the adults loved it."

California Grill

Widely acknowledged to be the best restaurant in all of Disney World, the California Grill is very popular and always crowded. (One clue to the quality: Disney executives dine here.) "We used two Dining Plan table-service credits," reported one mother of three from Alabama, "but it was totally worth it. The only problem is we ate our first meal there and it set the bar so high that nothing else compared. We spent the rest of the vacation saying 'It's okay, but it's not the California Grill.'" Not only is the food excellent and stylishly presented, but the views from the top of the Contemporary are unparalleled, especially during the Magic Kingdom fireworks.

Quick Guide to Full-
in the

Restaurant	Description	Location
Artist Point	Fine dining in a rustic setting	Wilderness Lodge
Big River Grille & Brewing Works	Casual restaurant and brewpub	BoardWalk
bluezoo	Fine seafood in a sleek, upscale setting	Dolphin
Boatwright's Dining Hall	Southern dishes and Cajun food	Port Orleans, Riverside
Boma	African-inspired buffet and great breakfasts	Animal Kingdom Lodge
California Grill	The best of all	Contemporary
Cape May Café	Character dining at breakfast, clambakes in the evening	Beach Club
Captain's Grille	Cheery and bright—a cut above a coffee shop	Yacht Club
Chef Mickey's	Character dining while the monorail zooms by	Contemporary
Citricos	Gourmet cuisine and an outstanding wine list	Grand Floridian
Coral Café	Buffets in the evening	Dolphin
ESPN Club	The perfect place to watch the big game	BoardWalk
Flying Fish Café	Excellent seafood and steaks	BoardWalk
Grand Floridian Café	Great variety, Southern classics	Grand Floridian
Gulliver's Grill at Garden Grove	Whimsical decor, basic food	Swan

Service Restaurants
WDW Hotels

Rating	Price	Advance Reservations	Suitability for Kids	Meals Served
★★	$$$	Recommended	Low	D
★	$$	Not accepted	Moderate	L, D
★★	$$$	Necessary	Low	D
★★	$$	Recommended	Moderate	B, D
★★★	$$$	Recommended	Moderate	B, D
★★★	$$$	Necessary	High	D
★★	$$	Recommended	High	B, D
★★	$$	Recommended	Moderate	B, L, D
★★	$$	Necessary	High	B, D
★★★	$$$	Necessary	Low	D
★	$$	For large parties only, recommended	Low	B, L, D
★	$	Not accepted	Moderate	L, D
★★★	$$$	Necessary	Low	D
★★	$$	Recommended	Moderate	B, L, D
★	$$	Recommended	Moderate	B, L, D

(continued)

Quick Guide to Full-
in the

Restaurant	Description	Location
Jiko	African-influenced cuisine, South African wines	Animal Kingdom Lodge
Kimonos	Sushi in an elegant setting	Swan
Kona Café	Pacific Rim food with a tropical emphasis	Polynesian
Kouzzina	Iron Chef Cat Cora's contribution to upscale family dining	Boardwalk
Maya Grill	Latin American–inspired cuisine	Coronado Springs
Narcoossee's	Great fresh seafood; view of MK fireworks	Grand Floridian
1900 Park Fare	Buffet-style character dining	Grand Floridian
'Ohana	Family-friendly, with island entertainment	Polynesian
Palio	Gourmet Italian in a colorful setting	Swan
Sanaa	Indian food in a colorful setting with a view of the Savanna	Animal Kingdom Lodge
Shula's	Linebacker-size steaks in a dignified atmosphere	Dolphin
Shutters	Casual island fare	Caribbean Beach
Victoria & Albert's	The most elegant restaurant on Disney property	Grand Floridian

Service Restaurants
WDW Hotels

Rating	Price	Advance Reservations	Suitability for Kids	Meals Served
★★★	$$$	Recommended	Moderate	D
★★	$$	For large parties only, recommended	Low	D
★★	$$	Recommended	Moderate	B, L, D
★★	$$	Recommended	Moderate	B, D
★	$$	Recommended	Low	B, D
★★	$$$	Recommended	Low	D
★★	$$$	Necessary	High	B, D
★★	$$	Recommended	High	B, D
★★	$$$	Recommended	Moderate	D
★★	$$$	Necessary	Moderate	D
★★★	$$$	Recommended	Low	D
★	$$	Recommended	Moderate	D
★★★	$$$	Necessary	Low	D

(continued)

Quick Guide to Full-
in the

Restaurant	Description	Location
The Wave . . . of American Flavors	Innovative regional cuisine	Contemporary
Whispering Canyon Café	Comfort food, family-style service	Wilderness Lodge
Yachtsman Steakhouse	One of the premier steak houses in Disney World	Yacht Club

Cape May Café

Our readers give high marks to this bright and airy eatery in the heart of the Beach Club. It has an excellent seafood buffet at dinner, featuring shrimp, clams, mussels, and a couple of land-lubber choices. The breakfast buffet, during which the characters, dressed in adorable old-fashioned bathing attire, circulate among the diners, is very popular. Consider this report from a grandmother of four from Ohio: "We wouldn't consider it a trip to Walt Disney World without a stop at the Beach Club's Cape May Café. It's a family tradition, and the food is wonderful. We always leave the theme parks in the afternoon to take a nap, and Cape May is the perfect place to eat dinner before you go back into Epcot to see IllumiNations."

Service Restaurants WDW Hotels

Rating	Price	Advance Reservations	Suitability for Kids	Meals Served
★★	$$	Recommended	Low	B, L, D
★★	$$	Recommended	High	B, L, D
★★	$$$	Recommended	Low	D

Captain's Grille

This restaurant, off the main drag in the Yacht Club Resort, serves fish, chicken, and beef in a pleasant nautical-theme room. The enormous breakfasts offer hearty eaters the chance to load up for a day of touring.

Chef Mickey's

The Contemporary Resort is one of the best places in Disney World for a character breakfast or dinner. As Mickey and the crew wander among the diners, the monorail whisks by overhead. The buffet has classic American breakfast food in the morning and family-pleasing standards like pasta, chicken, and roast beef in the evening, plus a sundae bar for the kids. A father of three from New Jersey echoed the reports of many of our readers: "Chef Mickey's is definitely the way to go if you want to see the basic old-fashioned Disney characters like Mickey and Goofy. The buffet was great, and the characters spent plenty of time with our sons."

Citricos   ★★★

Citricos offers Mediterranean cuisine in the Grand Floridian, and the restaurant is known for its outstanding wine list. Up to 20 labels are available by the glass, with a specific wine paired with each appetizer and entrée on the menu. A beautiful setting with consistently delightful cuisine, Citricos is a real treat for a parents' night out.

Coral Café   ★

With breakfast and dinner buffets as well as an à la carte menu, the Coral Café is the largest restaurant in the Dolphin Resort. Picture an upscale coffee shop with long hours and casual food and you have the idea.

ESPN Club   ★

Anchoring one end of the BoardWalk, the ESPN Club is better known for broadcasting sports events than for its food. "Our teenaged sons loved going to the ESPN Club on a Sunday during football season," wrote one mom of three from Pennsylvania. "The place was packed with people from all over the country, all wearing jerseys and screaming for their teams. We should have packed our Eagles jerseys—next time we'll know!" Menu choices include buffalo wings, burgers, nachos, and, of course, plenty of beer. There's an arcade next door to entertain the kids.

Flying Fish Café

The zany art deco decor is by Martin Dorf, who also designed the California Grill and Citricos. The menu is updated frequently, but generally includes wonderful seafood, delicious steaks, and excellent risottos. If you haven't made reservations, you can always dine at the bar and watch the chefs at work.

Grand Floridian Café

If you'd like a good solid meal of traditional favorites, simply served, with a pretty view of the Grand Floridian grounds, this café is for you. The menu tilts to the South—fried chicken, local fish, and key lime pie.

Gulliver's Grill at Garden Grove

This is the largest restaurant in the Swan, and it has a bit of a split identity. In the morning and at lunch it's an upscale coffee shop. In the evening it becomes Gulliver's Grill, with more elaborate dining. Weekend character breakfasts are also available, but they don't get very high marks from our readers. "Overpriced, with so-so food, and even the characters seemed bored," wrote one mom from Georgia. "Our other character meal was at Chef Mickey, and there was no comparison."

Jiko

Jiko (Swahili for "cooking place") is the flagship restaurant of the Animal Kingdom Lodge, and the menu features contemporary African cuisine with an emphasis on fresh vegetables, grains, and game. Two wood-burning stoves simulate the effect of cooking in the open bush. "Very exotic with wonderful food and a lovely setting," reported a father of two from New York. "Our server was extremely knowledgeable about the South African wines. We'll be back!"

Kimonos ★★

If you love sushi and sashimi, you'll adore this elegant restaurant in the Swan Resort.

Kona Café ★★

The Kona Café offers Pacific Rim food with a tropical emphasis. The crab cakes are delicious, and the desserts alone make the Kona worth the trip. Situated in the Polynesian, this is also one of the best places among all the Magic Kingdom resorts for breakfast.

Kouzzina ★★

"Kouzzina" is Greek for "kitchen" and this lively restaurant in the BoardWalk resort offered by Iron Chef Cat Cora does indeed feature a large exhibition kitchen and the ambience of a family celebration. In terms of food, stick with the classics such as moussaka and don't miss the potatoes, which are tasty beyond belief.

Maya Grill ★

The Maya Grill, located in Disney's Coronado Springs Resort, serves steak, pork, chicken, and seafood with a nuevo Latin touch. Many of the entrées are grilled over an open fire. Sadly, the quality doesn't match the variety.

Narcoossee's

Inside the white octagonal building on the water at the Grand Floridian, Narcoossee's offers pretty views as well as fresh seafood. As a bonus, you can see the Magic Kingdom fireworks.

1900 Park Fare

This large, pleasant Grand Floridian restaurant is appealing to families because it offers character dining and large buffets with kid-pleasing food. Be forewarned—this place is always loud, even when the characters aren't in attendance.

'Ohana

A fun, family-friendly place—the name, in fact, means "family" in Hawaiian—in the Polynesian Resort, 'Ohana specializes in skewered meats, teriyaki- and citrus-based sauces, and tropical fruits and vegetables. The food is prepared in a large, open-fire pit, and there's often some sort of activity, such as limbo contests, to keep the kids entertained. "This place is a blast," a mom from North Carolina wrote. "The food is good, and they get it out fast, but the really nice thing is all the activities for the kids, like crazy relay races and hula lessons. We sat down at the table, ordered some of those big tropical umbrella drinks, and just relaxed and watched the kids have a ball." A mom from Massachusetts confirms, "The service here is excellent. Our waiter was so busy trying to keep our 1-year-old entertained it was almost like having a babysitter."

Palio ★★

The Swan is home to this trattoria, which serves wonderful pasta in a pleasant, open setting. Palio is Italian for "flag," and, indeed, many brightly colored flags hang from the rafters.

Sanaa ★★

Sanaa, which stands for "artwork" in Swahili, is indeed one of the most beautifully decorated resturants at Disney World. Located at Kidani Village, the Vacation Club side of the Animal Kingdom Lodge, it also offers diners a view of the animals on the savanna. The food here is African with a strong Indian influence, a nod to the large number of Indians who have emigrated to South Africa, bringing their delicious cuisine with them. A great choice for adventurous guests, it can be less popular with young children or picky eaters.

Shula's ★★★

The Dolphin's swankiest steak house is owned by former Miami Dolphin coach Don Shula. (Nice tie-in!) The restaurant is quite dignified, despite the football theme, and you'll need an NFL-size appetite to finish the 48-ounce porterhouse or 4-pound lobster. Note: This is not, repeat not, a family restaurant. The menu pointedly states, "No children's menu available."

Shutters ★

Shutters, in the Caribbean Beach Resort, is a casual island-theme restaurant serving prime rib, lamb chops, and jerk chicken. The food is nothing special, but if you just can't go to Florida without sampling a big, fruity rum drink, this is your kind of place.

Victoria & Albert's ★★★

Extraordinarily elegant cuisine and special attention to details, such as personalized menus, harp music, and roses for the ladies, are the hallmarks of this lovely restaurant in the Grand Floridian. The only AAA five-diamond restaurant in WDW (and the most expensive), V&A is the ultimate spot for a parents' night out.

The Wave . . . of American Flavors

Located in the Contemporary Resort, The Wave's seasonal menu features local and regional products as well as organic beers, trendy cocktails, and an international wine list that literally offers a twist. All of the wines have screw tops instead of corks. Breakfast here is terrific, but the other meals don't quite live up to the hype.

Whispering Canyon Café

Kids can saddle up and ride stick ponies to their table at this family-style eatery in the Wilderness Lodge. All-you-can-eat barbecue dinners are brought to the table in cast-iron buckets, or you can order à la carte. If you like home cooking in a casual atmosphere where the kids can get a bit rowdy, Whispering Canyon is a good bet.

Yachtsman Steakhouse ★★

We're not sure how a yachtsman gets his hands on so much good beef, but this restaurant is one of the premier steak houses in Disney World. Hand-cut steaks and chops with your choice of sauces are served in a clubby dining room.

Restaurants in the Rest of the World

Except for the grill restaurant in ESPN Wild World of Sports, all these restaurants can be found in Downtown Disney.

Bongos Cuban Café

Founded by singer Gloria Estefan, Bongos delivers an Americanized version of Cuban dishes (e.g., black bean soup and grilled pork), a wildly tropical decor, and loud Latin music.

Quick Guide to Full-
in the Rest

Restaurant	Description	Location
Bongos Cuban Café	Americanized versions of Cuban dishes	Downtown Disney West Side
ESPN Wide World of Sports Grill	Ultimate sports bar with cool games for the kids	ESPN's Wide World of Sports Complex
Fulton's Crab House	Fine dining on a riverboat	Downtown Disney
House of Blues	Cajun and Creole cooking with live music	Downtown Disney West Side
Paradiso 37	Food from 37 different countries across the Americas, terrific tequila bar	Downtown Disney
Planet Hollywood	Always fun; film clips run constantly	Downtown Disney West Side
Portobello Yacht Club	Northern Italian cuisine	Downtown Disney
Raglan Road	Upmarket Irish pub with music and dance	Downtown Disney
Rainforest Café	Fun and funky atmosphere	Downtown Disney Marketplace
T-Rex	Casual dining with a dinosaur theme	Dowtown Disney Marketplace
Wolfgang Puck Café	Terrific salads, pizza, and sushi	Downtown Disney West Side

Service Restaurants of the World

Rating	Price	Advance Reservations	Suitability for Kids	Meals Served
★	$$	Not accepted	Moderate	L, D
★★	$$	Not accepted	Moderate	L, D
★★★	$$$	Recommended	Low	L, D
★★	$$	Not accepted	Moderate	Sunday brunch, L, D
★★★	$$	Recommended	Low	L, D
★★	$$	Recommended	High	L, D
★★	$$	Recommended	Low	D
★★	$$	Recommended	Low	L, D
★	$$	Not accepted	High	B, L, D
★	$$	Not accepted	High	L, D
★★★	$$$	Only upstairs, recommended	Moderate	L, D

ESPN Wide World of Sports Grill

This sports bar is the only full-service restaurant at the ESPN complex. Televisions broadcast events from every wall. Expect pasta, pizza, sandwiches, and burgers.

Fulton's Crab House

Fulton's, on the Empress Lilly riverboat, offers seafood flown in daily from all over the world. Try the raw oysters.

House of Blues

The House of Blues serves up Cajun and Creole cooking while a nightclub attached to the restaurant serves up jazz, country, rock and roll, and, yes, blues music. The Gospel brunch on Sunday is an especially good choice for families. To find out who's playing or to purchase tickets call 407/934–2583 (407/934–BLUE).

Paradiso 37 ★★★

The "37" in the restaurant name refers to the fact that the menu features cuisine from 37 different countries in North and South America. The "paradiso" no doubt refers to the tequila bar, which offers plenty of variety too. The food here is ethnic-lite, hearty, and generally very good. The appetizers are designed for sharing tapas-style and this can be a fun way to sample several things. And because Paradiso 37 is located in the perpetually-under-refurbishment section of Downtown Disney that was formerly known as Pleasure Island, it doesn't yet draw the crowds that are common at some other Downtown Disney restaurants.

Planet Hollywood

Planet Hollywood's giant blue globe holds numerous movie props, including the bus from *Speed*, which hovers menacingly overhead. Film clips run constantly and even the menus, which are printed with the high school graduation pictures of stars, are entertaining. The food is just what you'd expect.

Portobello Yacht Club

A recent revamp transformed the Portobello Yacht Club into a Tuscan country trattoria with an attractive interior and a wide variety of authentic Italian dishes. It's a bit quieter and more adult than many of the Downtown Disney restaurants. The patio is especially pleasant in spring and fall.

Raglan Road

A life-size bronze statue of Irish poet Patrick Kavanaugh sitting lost in thought on a bench greets you outside this Downtown Disney Irish pub. Inside are four huge wooden bars that were crafted in Ireland in the 19th century. There's often live music and, although there's no cost to get into the bar, the music and dancing bring a lot of excitement into the pub. As for the food, the classics go upscale, with Angus-beef shepherd's pie and Colorado lamb in a sophisticated port-wine sauce.

Rainforest Café

This sister restaurant to the Animal Kingdom location serves casual food in a jungle-theme atmosphere. Most kids love the Rainforest Café, but the music can get very loud, which may bother babies and toddlers. Waits can be long in the evening and advance reservations are not presently available, so take a buzzer and shop around the Marketplace while you wait.

T-Rex ★

Managed by the same company that runs the Rainforest Café, T-Rex offers casual, family-friendly dining in the form of pasta, pizzas, seafood, and salads, plus giant Audio-Animatronic dinosaurs, geysers, waterfalls, and a fossil dig site. "A little wild," reports one father from Kansas. "We sat in the ice room, which was as cold as its name, and every fifteen minutes there was a meteor shower with all these loud special effects. The kids loved it, but after a while my wife and I were ready to escape back into the hot Florida night."

Wolfgang Puck Café ★★★

There are three parts to this restaurant: the ultracasual Express, which offers salads, sandwiches, and such; the inside restaurant, which provides Puck's signature pastas and pizzas, as well as outstanding sushi; and, upstairs, the formal dining room, serving the best Puck has to offer. Needless to say, the first two locations work best for families, and the latter is best reserved for a parents' night out. "The best meal we had during our entire time in Orlando was downstairs at Wolfgang Puck," said one father of two. "The kiddie food was a cut above average, and the adults thought the sushi was great." A father of three concurs that the inside restaurant is the perfect middle ground between the express and formal options and that, "the hoisin BBQ ribs are worth coming back for."

CHAPTER

12

Disney After Dark

Disney World After Dark with the Kids

Is there life in Disney World after 8 pm? Sure there is. The crowds thin, the temperature drops, and many attractions are especially dazzling in the dark. During peak seasons the major theme parks run extra-long hours, so it's easy to have fun at night. But, needless to say, the particular kind of fun you'll have depends on whether the kids are with you.

Evening Activities for the Whole Family

The Evening Parade in the Magic Kingdom

Disney's ever-popular evening parades blend lasers, lights, and fireworks for a dazzling display. Tinker Bell's Flight is an especially exciting part of the presentation, so when she's announced, be sure to look to the castle to watch her descent.

The parade runs every night during the on-season and twice a night on holidays and especially crowded days. In the off-season it runs only on selected evenings, so plan your schedule to ensure you'll be in the Magic Kingdom on one of the nights it's slated to run. If you miss the parade, you can still get to see the Wishes fireworks since it always closes the evening. Times and dates are listed on your entertainment schedule; you can get this information in advance by calling Guest Relations (a.k.a. Guest Services) at your hotel or visiting www.disneyworld.com.

The Electrical Water Pageant

If you're staying on-site, the Electrical Water Pageant may actually float by your hotel window, because it's staged on the Seven Seas Lagoon, which connects the Polynesian, Contemporary, Grand Floridian, and Wilderness Lodge resorts. A much shorter and simpler production than the closing shows within the parks, the Electrical Water Pageant is a charming progression of moving multicolor sea images whose sparkling lights are reflected in the dark water.

Electrical Water Pageant times vary with the season, so contact Guest Relations for the exact time the parade is scheduled to float by your resort. If you're not staying at a Magic Kingdom resort but would like to see the pageant, plan to have dinner at one of the resorts in question, then wander out to the beach area at showtime.

IllumiNations

IllumiNations is Epcot's musical, laser, special effects, and fireworks extravaganza that appeals to all ages. It can be viewed nightly from anywhere around the World Showcase Lagoon at 9 pm.

Fantasmic!

This nightly closing show at Hollywood is a must-see. The combination of fantastic music, live actors performing cool stunts, lasers, fireworks, water screens, and favorite Disney characters makes for one spine-tingling show. Showtimes vary, so check your entertainment schedule.

Downtown Disney

Downtown Disney keeps hopping long after the theme parks shut down. Some families wait to shop and eat until late at night.

BoardWalk

Lively and gorgeous after dark, the BoardWalk is a hub of family-style activity. Eat dinner, then rent a surrey bike for a quick lap around the lagoon. There are also two clubs here, but they're strictly for adults 21 and over.

Miniature Golf

Evening is often the most comfortable time to check out Fantasia Gardens or Winter Summerland, especially in summer.

Night Swimming

Blizzard Beach and Typhoon Lagoon run extended hours in summer, and evening swimming can be a delight during the hottest weeks of the year. You don't have to worry about sunburn and the crowds are much lighter. Hotel pools stay open late as well, many until after midnight.

Disney World After Dark Without the Kids: Finding a Sitter

Why would any decent parent seek a sitter while on a family vacation? Consider this scenario: Meaghan's sucking the inside of her mouth. Loud. Mom keeps making everyone stop while she readjusts the strap of her shoe to accommodate the blister she picked up halfway around the World Showcase Lagoon. You spent $212 to get through the Magic Kingdom gates—and Devin spends two hours feeding quarters into the same arcade game that's in the mall back home. Dad has been singing the first line—and only the first line—of "Zip-a-Dee-Doo-Dah" since Thursday. You've asked to see the kiddie menus from nine different restaurants in nine different Epcot countries, and you end up at the American pavilion fast-food joint because Kristy won't eat anything but a hot dog. It's 108 degrees, this trip is costing $108 an hour, and that infernal sucking sound is getting on your last nerve.

Although it may seem un-American to suggest building time apart into the middle of a family vacation, the truth is that everyone will have more fun if you occasionally break up the group for a while. Even the most devoted of families aren't accustomed to being together 24 hours a day—for every meal, every ride, every potty stop. Every minute.

Some of the hotels in Orlando have responded with programs designed to get the kids involved with other children while parents have a night on the town. The idea is that everyone returns refreshed and recharged, with some happy stories to tell, and you can start the next day actually glad to be together again.

Quite a few off-site hotels have their own kids' clubs. Visit and tour the club before you drop your children off and make sure that the place seems clean, safe, and has an appropriate child-to-caregiver ratio.

On-Site Kids' Clubs

To get current pricing or make reservations at a kids' club, dial 407/WDW–DINE (407/939–3463). The following on-site hotels have kids' clubs:

Animal Kingdom Lodge	407/938–3000
BoardWalk	407/939–5100
Contemporary	407/824–1000
Dolphin	407/934–4000
Grand Floridian	407/824–3000
Polynesian	407/824–2000
Wilderness Lodge	407/824–3200
Yacht & Beach Clubs	407/934–8000

The clubs generally run in the evening for kids ages 3 to 12, but they're most interesting for the 3 to 8 set. The older the child, the more likely he or she is to be bored. The clubhouses are well stocked with toys, computers, video games, and large-screen TVs. Make reservations by calling Guest Relations at the appropriate hotel; on-site guests get first crack at the available slots, but if the clubs don't fill up, space is available to off-site visitors. Note that children must be toilet trained.

Prices, policy, and planned entertainment change quickly at the kids' clubs, so confirm everything when you make your reservations.

The clubs usually open at 4 or 4:30 pm and close at midnight. Obviously, if you'll be dining at a Disney resort, it makes sense to try to book your kids into that hotel's child-care program so that you can just drop them off, go on to your restaurant, and return to pick them up later. Parents are given pagers in case of emergencies, so you can truly relax while you enjoy your time alone. Rates are usually $11.50 per hour per child with a two-hour minimum, and a credit card guarantee is required when you make your reservation; if plans change, be sure to cancel or you'll be charged.

Insider's Secret

The Polynesian offers the most elaborate kids' program: the Never Land Club, with buffet food and entertainment for the youngsters.

In-Room Sitters

Kids' clubs aren't always the way to go. You'll need to arrange for an in-room sitter if any of the following conditions apply:

- You have a child under the age of 3. That's the cutoff point for most group programs.

- You plan to be out after midnight. Most kids' clubs close down before then, some as early as 10 pm.

- Your kids are exhausted. If you know in advance that you plan to employ an all-out touring schedule or your kids fall apart after 8 pm, hire an in-room sitter who can make sure they're in bed by their usual time. Most of the kids' clubs try to put preschoolers down in sleeping bags by 9 pm, but this involves moving them, and probably waking them, when parents return.

- You have a big family. Even with the add-on per-child rate, you can come out cheaper with an in-room sitter than you will if you book four kids into a group program.

For those staying on-site, Kids' Nite Out (407/828–0920) provides trained sitters for all the Disney hotels; the service suggests calling two weeks in advance, but can sometimes accommodate more last-minute requests. And prepare for sticker shock. The rate is $16 an hour for one child, plus $2.50 per hour for each additional child, with a four-hour minimum. A $10 transportation fee is also common, meaning that in-room sitting for two kids for four hours runs about $85. Not cheap, but for many parents it's well worth the cost.

If you're staying off-site, you can also call either Kids Nite Out or Fairy Godmothers (407/277–3724), another service that has received consistent praise from readers. Or simply contact your hotel for help with in-room sitting. Most Orlando properties have relationships with reputable services. Not only does this save you a bit of hassle, but the person at the Guest

Insider's Secret

No matter what child-care option you choose, the key point is to make your plans in advance. If you suddenly get an urge for fine dining at 4 pm on a Saturday in July, it will be hard to find a sitter or get into a kids' club.

Relations desk is also apt to know a lot more about whom to call than you do; if former guests haven't been pleased with a sitter, the hotel was undoubtedly the first to hear about it, so most family-oriented hotels use the same services over and over.

Dining Without the Kids

The following five restaurants are especially adult-oriented and a good choice when the kids aren't along.

Bistro de Paris

The Bistro, upstairs from Les Chefs de France and accessible by a back staircase, is so lovely and secluded that you might forget you're in a theme park. The wine list is one of the best in Epcot, and the classic French fare is fabulous.

California Grill

Not only does the California Grill offer marvelous cuisine with stylish preparation, but the views from the top of the Contemporary are unparalleled. In terms of the quality and variety of the food, it's superb. A mom from New York agreed: "I'm a

Insider's Secret

Disney World has some world-class restaurants, but it pains me to report that the Dining Plan has indeed taken a teensy bit of the shine out of the experience of visiting them. The reason? Parents work and strategize all week to save up credits for a splurge at one of the restaurants listed here, which makes sense—and then they bring the kids, which doesn't. It's still worth planning a parents' night out and taking some time to really relax and savor a special meal served at a leisurely pace; just be prepared for the possibility that you may be seated beside a table with exhausted children and overstressed parents.

caterer so I know food, and I consider the California Grill to be by far the best restaurant in Disney World."

Citricos

Citricos, in the Grand Floridian, is excellent, but because of its proximity to Victoria & Albert's, the restaurant can be sometimes overlooked and is thus easier to get into. The menu features Mediterranean cuisine and is updated frequently. The wine selection is noteworthy.

Jiko

The "cooking place," as the name means in Swahili, serves truly innovative, sophisticated, well-spiced food based on African cuisine. A collection of the unusual and tasty appetizers can make a meal, or your server will help you pair your main course (maize-crusted halibut, for example) with a superb South African wine. Jiko has roomy booths and a cooking island whose seats afford views of the busy chefs.

Insider's Secret

Couples who are dining late may find themselves leaving a resort restaurant after the transportation system has closed down. You can either drive your own car or use Downtown Disney (whose buses run until 2 am) as a transfer station. Your best bet, especially if you've had wine with dinner, is to let the valets at your resort or restaurant call you a cab.

Victoria & Albert's

Where Disney has built a reputation on providing entertainment to the masses, this 60-seat, AAA five-diamond restaurant in the Grand Floridian proves that there's also room in Disney World for highly individual service. At Victoria & Albert's, harp

Insider's Secret

What's more special than an evening at Victoria & Albert's? An evening at the chef's table. You're seated inside the kitchen where the chef treats you as his private guests and provides a customized meal. This is the proverbial "once-in-a-lifetime" gourmet experience, and you must reserve months in advance. The prices are $200 per person, $295 with wine pairings. Call 407/939–3463 (407/WDW–DINE) for details.

Also offered is Queen Victoria's room, which offers a 10-course tasting menu that is prepared with ingredients selected by the chef that day. Pricing is also $200 per person, $295 with wine pairings. Seating for this event is only at 5 pm.

music plays, candles flicker, menus are personalized, ladies are presented with roses, and people still dress up for dinner.

The regular six-course prix-fixe dinner costs $125 per person or $185 if you have wine paired with each course, but it's an experience so elaborate that you'll be talking about it for years afterward. For example, on the evening we visited, the salad was a floral arrangement in a crouton vase—until our server, who called herself Victoria in keeping with the theme, tapped the side of the crouton with a spoon. It then broke, releasing the greens into a fan-shaped pattern on the plate. We were nearly hypnotized by the ceremony and the tremendous attention to detail in everything from the *amuse-bouche* to the coffee service. This is by far the most elegant and refined restaurant you'll find on Disney property.

The Disney Cruise Line

The Cruise Vacation Options

Disney is now entering its 15th year in the cruise-line business, and its family-oriented cruises are more popular than ever.

Disney has four ships. The original two, the *Magic* and the *Wonder*, handle the longer sailings, which at present include Hawaii, Alaska, Mexico, and Canada. The even bigger and better *Dream* and *Fantasy* make the popular three-, four-, and seven-night sailings to the Bahamas and Disney's own island, Castaway Cay. With a fleet of four at its disposal, Disney has a wide variety of itineraries and ports of call. Check out all the offerings at www.disneycruise.com.

But no matter where you sail, the key thing about the Disney cruises is that the activities and the attitude are decidedly geared toward families. There are no casinos on board, entertainment is wholesome, drinking and carousing are de-emphasized, shore excursions tend toward kid-friendly pursuits like snorkeling and dolphin swims, and there are excellent (in fact, award-winning) child-care centers. Disney cruises are perfect for the family that needs a bit of everything in the course of a

Helpful Hint

Not sure what kind of cruise is right for you? The website www.disneycruise.com has a wealth of information. Start by going to the section marked "Search for a Cruise," then click on "Find a Cruise." You can plug in the month you wish to travel, the amount of time you wish to spend, your ideal port of departure, and your dream destination. A list of cruises fitting your particular criteria will pop up, but if none of them suits your needs you can slightly adjust the criteria—maybe travel in July instead of June or cruise for four days instead of three, for example—and find more options.

vacation: time for the adults to relax alone and time with everyone together. Families whose kids vary in ages are especially sold on the cruises. Because there are so many kids on board and the age categories in the youth programs are tight, it's equally likely that your 3-year-old and 13-year-old will each have found a friend by the end of the first day. Let's face it—nothing beats a vacation where everyone is happy.

Insider's Secret

Not surprisingly, Disney does a lot of research in the area of travel trends and family dynamics, and, again not surprisingly, these studies show that 83% of kids love the idea of a theme-park vacation. But the big news is that their interest in cruising is almost equal—and rising. Of the children surveyed, 77% said they would like to take a cruise vacation in the next year, a stat perhaps fostered by the cruise-ship ads Disney has been running prior to their movie releases. Whatever the reason, kids are getting increasingly hip to cruising.

Insider's Secret

The most popular cruises are the short runs to the Bahamas on the Disney *Dream* and Disney *Fantasy*. The three-day cruise goes only to Nassau and Castaway Cay. The four-day cruise adds a day at sea, and the five-day cruise has a day at sea and two stops at Castaway Cay. These cruises can be combined with a stay at Walt Disney World.

The Pre- and Post- Cruise "Package"

Many Disney visitors combine a stay at Walt Disney World with a three-, four-, or five-day cruise. To call this a "package" is a bit of a misnomer, since Disney allows families to totally customize their vacation. In other words, you treat the Orlando segment as an add-on before or after your cruise, choosing any resort you like and staying as long as you decide. It's a good way to get the best of both worlds.

Although it's possible to reverse the order, most families like touring first and cruising last. That way the relaxing cruise segment follows the more exhausting theme-park segment of the week.

You're met at the Orlando airport and escorted directly to your resort, where you can find all the documentation you need for the entire week. After the theme-park segment of the trip is over, you're transported by a special Disney Cruise Line (DCL) bus to the ship, which waits in Port Canaveral harbor, approximately an hour from Orlando.

Disney does everything possible to make the transition "seamless"; the key to your Orlando hotel room is also the key to your stateroom on the ship, and you can use it as a charge card both at Disney World and onboard the ship. Your bags are picked up from your hotel room and transferred directly to your room on the ship. In short, the logistics of checking in and checking out, arranging transportation, and lugging baggage are all handled for you.

Families leaving from California or Europe on their cruises also have hotel options, which are detailed in the website.

Approximate Costs

Calculating the exact cost of your cruise depends on several factors: the time of year, the size of your family, the itinerary, and the level of cabin or stateroom you choose. It's probably a little too late to do anything about the size of your family, but the other three factors are within your control.

Time of year has a huge impact on price. If you're going in the middle of summer, spring break, or Christmas week, you'll pay top dollar. If you're traveling during the off-season, say something like the third week of October, the rates will automatically drop about 30%. Most of the specials and discounts you'll find through AAA and independent websites like www. mousesavers.com are also for the off-season.

Lodging also affects the bottom line. All staterooms are nicely appointed, designed for families, and therefore 25% larger than standard cruise-ship cabins, so it's really just a matter of how much space you're willing to pay for.

And then there's the issue of itinerary. Obviously it costs considerably more to cruise to Hawaii for 14 nights than it does to take a three-day run to the Bahamas.

Insider's Secret

When shopping for discounts, leave no stone unturned—and make no assumptions. Although some families report that travel agents found them the best deals, others say that agents quoted higher rates than those given when they called Disney directly.

Let's see how all this shakes out with some examples. For example, a family of four taking the basic four-day Bahamas cruise on the *Disney Dream* in July will pay about $6,000. If that makes you gulp, consider that the same trip in February is $3,000. The type of stateroom is also a factor. If you want a private veranda and full stateroom for your seven-day cruise to Alaska in July, the cost for a family of four is $8,000. Swap to an inside stateroom, and the cost drops to $5,000. The length of the cruise and distance covered is the other big variable. The 14-day cruise from Los Angeles to Hawaii in April will cost that same family of four about $10,000. (Note: These quoted prices do not include airfare. Adding it on is always an option, and the price rises accordingly, depending on where your flight originates.)

Get the picture? Costs can vary dramatically. To estimate the price of your cruise, start by going to www.disneycruise.com and typing in the destination you wish to visit, the month you wish to travel, the preferred length of the cruise, and the number of people in your party. This will direct you to a page that shows all of your options, from highest to lowest. You can fine-tune from there, and once you have a ballpark price you can more intelligently comparison shop with a travel agent or on other Web pages. The website is also a great source of infor-

Money-Saving Tip
The ship is going to sail no matter how many people are aboard, so cruise lines offer significant discounts as the time of departure approaches and staterooms remain unbooked. Disney is no exception to this rule, but be aware that the cheaper stateroom levels sell out first, so discounts are more likely to be available on the unsold concierge-level (premium) staterooms. So last-minute travelers might not find lower prices, but they might well find more bang for their buck.

mation on ports of call, shore excursions, and the layout of staterooms.

Other Expenses

One of the beauties of cruising is that most of your expenses are included in your package price. Here's a list of what isn't included.

Alcoholic beverages

Arcade games

Child care for children under 3

Medical services

Merchandise bought on board or at ports of call

Palo, the adults-only restaurant on all four ships, which charges a $20 per person cover; Remy, the even more upscale adults-only restaurant on the *Dream* and *Fantasy*, has an upcharge of $75 per person.

Photography

Ship-to-shore phone calls

Shore excursions

Spa treatments

Tipping (Based on industry suggestions, this will be about $12–$15 per person per day. This cost, along with any other purchases made aboard the ship, can be added to your general bill, so don't worry about bringing a lot of cash.)

Cabins

The Disney Cruise Line website contains renderings of all the staterooms, from the basic inside stateroom designed for three to a two-bedroom suite that can sleep as many as seven. Most staterooms are in the deluxe ocean-view category, many of them with verandas, and most about 200–250 square feet. (Most of the cabins are outside staterooms, so if you're planning to save a few bucks by booking an inside stateroom, call early.)

"The general rule is, the longer you'll be on the ship, the more important the size of your stateroom is," reports a mom of three from Florida, who describes herself as a "grizzled cruise veteran." She adds: "For a three-day cruise we're okay with being piled on top of each other, and we go for the cheapest option we can find. On these short runs, you're hardly ever in the cabin anyway. But if you're on a longer cruise that includes multiple days at sea, the size and comfort of your stateroom matters a lot more."

One other innovation to note: The *Dream* and *Fantasy* alleviate cabin fever by putting "virtual portholes" in the inside staterooms. High-definition cameras placed on the exterior of the ship feed live video to your screen. Keep an eye out . . . sometimes a character pops by as well. These portholes have been such a hit that Disney reports quite a few families prefer the inside cabins simply because of them. "We booked late and were initially disappointed we didn't have a veranda," reports one mom. "But our 3- and 4-year-old were so entranced by the portholes that it didn't matter. They kept screaming out the name of whatever character was drifting by."

Dining

Disney makes onboard dining very special. For starters you don't dine in the same restaurant every night. "We figured that a family on vacation wouldn't ordinarily eat at the same restaurant three nights in a row," says Amy Foley of the DCL. "So why would a family on a cruise ship want to eat in the same dining room every night?"

Instead, you experience "rotation dining," trying a different onboard restaurant each evening of your cruise. (Your server and tablemates rotate right along with you.) On the *Magic*, there's Lumiere's, with a theme based on *Beauty and the Beast*. On the *Wonder*, your fine-dining option is Triton's, named for the Little Mermaid's father. On the *Dream* and the *Fantasy* it's the Royal Palace, home to Cinderella and her princess pals.

Other nights are more casual. On both the *Magic* and the *Wonder* there's Parrot Cay, where the mood and the food is Bahamian. On the *Dream* and the *Fantasy* there's the Enchanted Garden, inspired by the gardens of Versailles and featuring an environment that changes from day to night in the course of your meal.

But Animator's Palate—which is available on all ships—is the real showstopper, an interactive dining experience in which the restaurant transforms into a brilliant palette of color as you dine. The meal begins in a room that is utterly black and white, right down to the framed animation sketches on the wall and the servers' somber attire. With each course, more color is added to the artwork, the walls, the table settings, and the servers' costumes. By dessert the whole room is glowing. On the *Dream* and the *Fantasy,* the restaurant has one more wonderful touch. Crush, the surfer-dude turtle from *Finding Nemo,* appears and interacts with diners, using the same type of technology found in the popular Turtle Talk with Crush attraction at Epcot. "Having Crush greet him by name and interact with him was the highlight of the whole cruise for my 4-year-old son," says one father. "When he found out about the restaurant rotation—in other words that we wouldn't be going back to Animator's Palate the next night— he was, excuse the expression, completely crushed."

On all four ships, adults have a fourth dining option, Palo, an Italian restaurant perched high atop the ship, offering a sweeping view of the ocean. Palo serves wonderful food and is very popular. It's so popular, in fact, that if you want to book a table, you need to do so either before you leave home or immediately upon boarding the ship. There's a well-worth-it $20 surcharge for dinner or brunch and $10 for High Tea, which is available only on longer sailings. Excellent wine-tasting classes are held there as well.

On the *Dream* and the *Fantasy* you'll find a second adults-only option called Remy's, with an opulent setting and a French-inspired menu that's a nod to the film *Ratatouille*. Scott Hummel, the executive chef at Victoria & Albert's at the Grand Floridian, is one of the consulting chefs, and many of his dishes are on the menu; in other words, while a meal at Palo's is on par with California Grill, Citricos, Flying Fish, or Jiko's, Remy's takes it a step farther, offering cuisine and service more like you'd find at Victoria & Albert's. Ergo, there's a $75 per person upcharge for dining at Remy's. If you go with the six-course tasting menu and add a wine pairing with each course, the price goes up an additional $99. Certainly not a cheap night out, but it's a meal to remember, with many little surprise touches designed to elevate your experience.

When you book your cruise, you'll have to choose your meal times: either early or late. The main seating means you

Helpful Hint

So where do the kids eat on the night Mom and Dad dine at Palo or Remy's? First of all, make sure you don't plan your date night on the evening when you're scheduled for Animator's Palate. It's a thrill for kids and adults. Once you do choose a night and make a reservation at Palo, you have two options for the kids: sign them up for one of the kids' programs that includes dinner, or escort them to the buffet or one of the fast-food restaurants for an early meal. Afterward, drop them off at the kids' center and head upstairs to Palo or Remy's.

have dinner as early as 6, depending on the ship, while the second seating is often as late as 8:30. If you have young kids the early seating works best, although it does mean a crack-of-dawn breakfast time. But I've seen preschoolers literally fall asleep at the table at late seatings—active days bring about early bedtimes. Besides, if you want to sleep in, you can always skip the full breakfast and grab something light at the buffet.

Not all the dining is formal. A breakfast buffet is available daily on the pool level for families that want to get an early start. You can also find a casual buffet lunch daily, and, in case you don't want to take even a minute out of your fun, pizza, burgers, salad, sandwiches, and ice cream are served all afternoon out by the pools.

Is Bigger Better?

The *Dream* and *Fantasy*, which cover the shorter Bahamian cruises, are Disney's latest and largest addition to the fleet and have some real bonus features. First of all, they're 40% larger than the *Magic* or the *Wonder,* and they've used that extra space for expanded adult and child entertainment areas. Innovations include the aforementioned virtual portholes for inside cabins, art that comes "to life," a ship-wide detective game for kids, and separate areas for teens and tweens. But the star of the bigger ships, hands down, is the AquaDuck, a full-fledged water coaster. The AquaDuck is essentially a 765-foot Plexiglass tube stretching high above the ship's highest deck. Jets propel you along, and the track features a "swing out" loop that shoots you over the side of the ship. The ocean—if you dare to look—is 150 feet below. The minimum ride-height requirement is 48 inches, and the rafts allow two family members to ride together.

Ports of Call

The three- and four-day cruises spend one day in Nassau, giving you a chance to shop, sightsee, or visit a casino. There are shore excursions designed for families (and kids of all ages are apt to enjoy a horse-drawn carriage ride), but, frankly, the Nassau stop exists mostly to placate the adults on board who miss the presence of a casino. If you do want to try your luck at the slots, or if your children are too young to comfortably take along on a shopping trip to the straw market, you can always leave them on board in the kids' programs.

Helpful Hint

The older ships, the *Magic* and the *Wonder*, will sail from a variety of ports of embarkation and explore a variety of ports of call. For details on upcoming voyages, visit www.disneycruise.com.

The seven-day cruises offer family-friendly shore excursions at every stop such as sailing lessons, snorkeling, and submarine trips. The Alaskan, Hawaiian, and longer Caribbean/Mexican cruises also offer shore excursions at every port of call, and the list of possibilities is staggering. A complete list of all shore excursions for every port of call can be found at www.disneycruise.com.

Time-Saving Tip

Once you book your cruise, reserve shore excursions via www.disneycruise.com or your travel agent. This guarantees you can get everything you want and also saves you from having to stand in line at the shore-excursion desk on the first day of your cruise.

Castaway Cay

All the Caribbean and Bahamas cruises stop at Castaway Cay, Disney's own private island, and a true little piece of paradise. You disembark at the pier (cutting out the time-consuming tendering process often required when a large ship stops at a small island) and stroll or take a shuttle to a beautiful beach. Once there you can hike, bike, play volleyball, take a Jet Ski ride, rent sailboats or sea kayaks, or simply sun yourself. Organized excursions for families include a stingray swim and snorkeling tours. Lunch is cooked right on the island, and there are small shops in case you find yourself in need of beach toys, towels, or sunscreen.

The children's programs go full force on the island, so after you've played a while as a family, you can drop the kids off and have a little adult time. Counselors lead youngsters on scavenger hunts, "whale excavations," and sand castle–building contests; older kids participate in boat races or bike trips around the island with the counselors; teens have their own beach Olympics and *Survivor*-style games.

Insider's Secret

Disney has planted a few cute "shipwrecks" and a hidden Mickey or two along the snorkeling paths of Castaway Cay, but the water there is sometimes cloudy, and there are so many people in a small space it can be overwhelming to kids. Most kids 8 and older, assuming they're reasonably capable swimmers, can master the mask and tube. Everyone wears life jackets so you can periodically bob and rest.

Meanwhile, adults can escape to the separate mile-long quiet beach called Serenity Bay, where they can sip a piña colada or have an open-air massage in a private cabana.

Castaway Cay is so popular that some itineraries stop there twice. If you'd like a lot of beach time on your cruise, consider one of those sailings.

Kids' Programs Onboard

Flounder's Reef is the nursery on the *Wonder* and *Magic,* while on the *Dream* and *Fantasy* you'll find it's a small world. No matter what it's called, the baby center has plenty of cribs, high chairs, swings, and changing tables, along with play areas for children between 3 months and 3 years of age. The nurseries don't run the extensive hours of the other children's programs, but are open daily to give the parents of infants and toddlers time to relax together or play with their older kids. This is the only child-care option on the ship that charges a fee, and prices vary, so check when you book.

Disney's Oceaneer Club for kids ages 3 to 7 occupies a huge play area complete with a re-creation of Captain Hook's pirate ship. The well-trained and upbeat counselors lead the kids in games and crafts. On the first evening aboard the ship counselors meet with the parents to explain the program and help ease the kids in.

Kids ages 8 to 11 hang out in the Oceaneer Lab, where they have their own crafts and games such as learning how to make flubber, draw animation cels, or carve race cars from soap. There's also plenty of outdoor action, from games on the sports deck to water activities in the sports pool.

The activities at Oceaneer's Club and Oceaneer's Lab run throughout the day and night. Whenever you drop your kids off, a pager ensures you can be reached in case of an emergency. But the most likely "emergency" is that your kids are having so much fun they refuse to leave.

As you're probably already only too aware, the 11–13 "tween" years are tough, with these "neither here nor there" kids

Insider's Secret

Young children, already overwhelmed by the size and newness of the ship, often suffer a bit of separation anxiety the first time they're dropped off at one of the programs. Try to persuade them to join the activities that first evening, when everyone is new and fast friendships are made. The counselors are trained to look out for shy or nervous children and help them make a smooth transition into the group activities.

often nearly impossible to entertain. Not to worry. At least on the larger ships, Disney breaks this age group out and gives them their own spaces. Edge, the appropriately named lounge for tweens, on the *Dream* and *Fantasy*, offers high-tech entertainment such as video karaoke and separate sporting events. It works well, since they're neither forced into kiddie activities nor given as much freedom as the teenagers.

Teens ages 13 to 17 have their own spaces: a private haven called Aloft aboard the *Wonder*, Vive aboard the *Dream* and *Fantasy*, and The Stack aboard the *Magic*. The spaces look like a combination coffeehouse–dorm room. Teens are pretty much given the run of the ship—counselors lead them in ship-wide scavenger hunts, video-game tournaments, and pool parties.

Onboard Entertainment

There are three pools on board: one, shaped like Mickey, with a pint-size tube slide for little kids; a second "sports pool" for games and the rowdier activities of older children; and a third "quiet pool" for adults, complete with large, elevated hot tubs. In addition, the ship has a sports deck, a full-service spa, an exercise room, and several shops. The *Dream* and *Fantasy* have the AquaDuck water coaster.

The cornerstone of onboard entertainment is the 975-seat Walt Disney Theater, one of the most technologically advanced theaters in the world and certainly the most remarkable on any cruise ship. Here DCL showcases Broadway-style shows, some of them new and some based on Disney classics. All the productions are great, but the finale show is the stunning *Believe,* which always seems to bring half the audience to tears.

A family lounge—Studio Sea on the *Magic* and *Wonder* and Studio D on the *Dream* and *Fantasy*—provides dance music, parties, and participatory game shows starring the audience. The Mickey Mania trivia game is a real blast. The Buena Vista Theater shows a variety of Disney movies daily, and, come nightfall, a jumbo screen allows you to watch movies outdoors on the deck, a good way to coax wound-up kids to calm down and give way to sleep.

Of course the characters are sailing right along with you. They turn out for deck parties—including the welcome-aboard and farewell bashes—and also appear around the ship. Check your daily onboard newsletter, the Personal Navigator, for times and locations.

One of the definite highlights is the Pirates IN the Caribbean party. Passengers dress like buccaneers and convene

Insider's Secret

The onboard spa offers a range of services, including some designed exclusively for couples. Just hanging out in the beautiful sauna and steam area is a great way to kill an afternoon. If you want to book a massage or facial, especially on a day when the ship is at sea, go immediately to the spa after boarding the ship to make an appointment. The best times get snatched up early. The *Dream* and *Fantasy* offer Chill, a separate spa area for tweens and teens.

for a rollicking deck party with the characters. Smee and Captain Hook show up and try to cause trouble, but not to worry, Captain Mickey prevails, and a good time is had by all. The evening rounds out with fireworks, music, and dancing.

Insider's Secret

More and more, large families are meeting up on cruises, where everyone can be together but still go off and do their own thing. Consider this report from a mother of three from Michigan: "My sisters and I have a family reunion at Disney World every other year. When we get all the kids and spouses together, there are 14 of us, with a wide range of ages. Last year for the first time we took the cruise and found that worked great. Those with babies could go back to their cabins whenever someone got cranky or tired, those with school-age kids could just keep going, and those with older kids could let them go to the pools and arcades on their own."

After the shows wind down, adults can congregate in the entertainment districts, dubbed Beat Street on the *Magic* and Route 66 on the *Wonder*. Expect a dance club, a sports pub, and a piano bar. The District is the expanded adult area on the *Dream* and *Fantasy*. It has five clubs—a live-music venue; a dance club; a sports bar; an upscale champagne lounge and the Skyline Bar, where the sun sets over a different city every night and there are globally themed drinks to match. What will these people think of next?

CHAPTER
14
Universal Orlando

Universal Studios

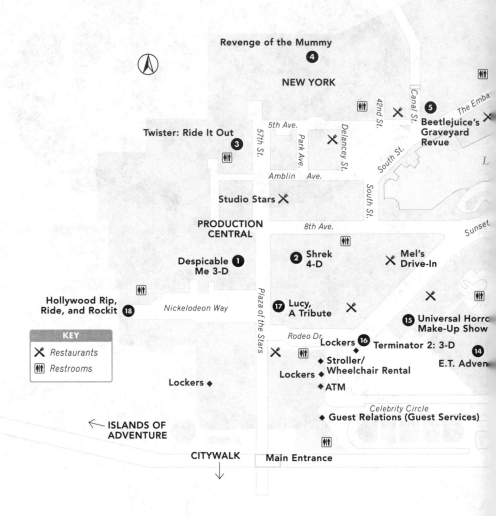

Revenge of the Mummy
4

NEW YORK

Beetlejuice's
Graveyard
Revue
5

Twister: Ride It Out
3

5th Ave.
42nd St.
Canal St.
The Emba
Delancey St.
Park Ave.
57th St.
South St.

Amblin Ave.

Studio Stars

PRODUCTION
CENTRAL

8th Ave.

South St.
Sunset

Despicable
Me 3-D   1

2 Shrek
4-D

Mel's
Drive-In

Hollywood Rip,
Ride, and Rockit   18

Nickelodeon Way

17 Lucy,
A Tribute

15 Universal Horr
Make-Up Show

KEY

✗ Restaurants
♟ Restrooms

Plaza of the Stars

Rodeo Dr.

Lockers 16

Terminator 2: 3-D

14

E.T. Adven

Lockers ♦

♦ Stroller/
Wheelchair Rental

Lockers

♦ ATM

Celebrity Circle

♦ Guest Relations (Guest Services)

← ISLANDS OF
ADVENTURE

CITYWALK   Main Entrance

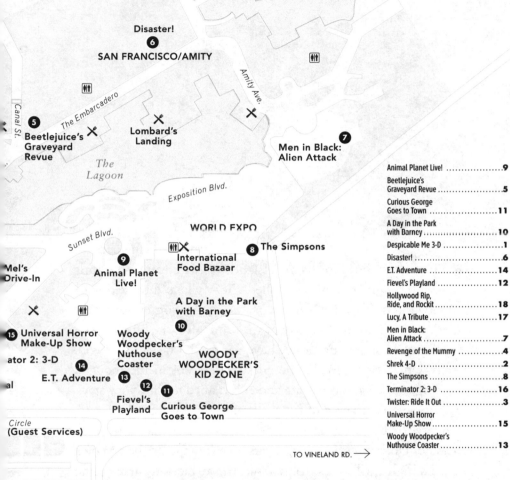

Disaster!
6
SAN FRANCISCO/AMITY

The Embarcadero

Canal St.

5
Beetlejuice's
Graveyard
Revue

Lombard's
Landing

Amity Ave.

Men in Black:
Alien Attack
7

*The
Lagoon*

Exposition Blvd.

WORLD EXPO

Sunset Blvd.

Mel's
Drive-In

9
Animal Planet
Live!

International
Food Bazaar

8 The Simpsons

A Day in the Park
with Barney
10

15 Universal Horror
Make-Up Show

ator 2: 3-D

14
E.T. Adventure

Woody
Woodpecker's
Nuthouse
Coaster

13

**WOODY
WOODPECKER'S
KID ZONE**

12
Fievel's
Playland

11
Curious George
Goes to Town

al

Circle
(Guest Services)

TO VINELAND RD. →

With two full theme parks—Universal Studios Florida and Islands of Adventure—a dining and entertainment complex called CityWalk, and three on-site resort hotels, Universal Orlando is no longer content to be the park you visit on the last day of vacation, after the bulk of your time and most of your money have gone to Disney. On the contrary, Universal is poised to be a destination, not an afterthought, aiming to keep guests on-site and entertained for multiday stays.

As you prepare a touring plan for Universal, make sure to choose the best rides and shows for your particular family. Although Universal offers attractions for every age, it's best known for its high-thrill rides. In general, the attractions here are far more intense than those at Disney, so it's important to know that the shows and rides you choose are age appropriate. A mother of one from Missouri agrees: "The first time we went to Universal Studios our daughter was 4, and there wasn't too much she could ride or enjoy at such a young age. The next time we went back she was 8, and she loved it. Kids have to be a bit older to really get into the Universal Studios style of ride."

On the other hand, if you have teenagers, you may want to spend more time at Universal than at Disney. Consider this report from a father of three: "My children love roller coasters (the wilder the better) and prefer Universal to Disney. So we do the opposite of most families, staying at Universal and driving over for a day at Disney."

Universal Orlando is off Interstate 4 at Exits 74B and 75A. Road signs to the complex are well marked. All three of the Universal resorts are within walking distance of the Universal parks, about a 20-minute drive from Walt Disney World, and about a 10-minute drive from SeaWorld. For more information, visit www.universalorlando.com or call 407/363–8000.

Helpful Hint

Just as many people confuse Walt Disney World and the Magic Kingdom, Universal suffers some confusion regarding the names of its parks. Universal Studios Florida refers to the original theme park, which has attractions based on the movies that Universal Pictures has produced over the years. The entire complex, consisting of two theme parks (Universal Studios Florida, Islands of Adventure), three hotels (Hard Rock, Portofino Bay, and Royal Pacific) and CityWalk, is called Universal Orlando.

Should We Stay On-Site?

Whether you decide to stay at one of Universal Orlando's three on-site resorts—the Portofino Bay Hotel, the Hard Rock Hotel, and the Royal Pacific Resort—depends on how much you're willing to spend for certain conveniences and privileges extended only to on-site guests. The on-site resorts are all luxurious, with the ultimate in amenities and price tags to match. Depending on the resort and the season, rates average $220–$350 a night.

There are plenty of resorts on International Drive and other roads that flank the park, but Universal draws high-spending visitors by offering lots of perks for on-site guests.

Advantages of Staying On-Site

- By far the biggest advantage is that resort guests can use the Express system on an unlimited basis. Just show your resort ID, that is, your room key card, and you'll be admitted into the Express ticket line on any ride you choose at any time you choose. This virtually eliminates having to wait in line, and it's a huge, huge perk. Depending upon when you're traveling, it's also a $30–$87 per person value—the cost of an Express pass.

- It gets better. At present, resort guests can enter The Wizarding World of Harry Potter a full hour ahead of day guests. Since the Harry Potter section of Islands of Adventure can become insanely crowded, the chance to ride and explore ahead of the bulk of the theme-park guests is an immeasurable advantage. Be sure to check to make sure this perk is still in place when you book your room.

- Resort guests get priority seating in restaurants and can make reservations in advance.

- Complimentary water taxi and bus transportation between your resort and the theme parks is included. (All three of the on-site hotels are linked to the two theme parks and CityWalk by a series of scenic waterways.) Not only does the transportation system make it easier for you to return to your room for a midday break, but it saves you the time, effort, and expense of driving to the theme parks.

- Complimentary package delivery of in-park purchases to guest rooms.

℮ Resort IDs allow you to charge merchandise, food, and tickets to your hotel room.

℮ Seasonal packages and periodic specials provide significant perks during the off-season, such as discounts on rooms, "kids eat free" deals, upgrades to suites, or complimentary breakfasts.

On-Site Hotels

Hard Rock Hotel   407/363–8000

Fun, flashy, and funky, the 650-room Hard Rock Hotel has a broad and eclectic collection of rock memorabilia. If you like the idea of a 7 am serenade from Elvis, you can even ask for a rock star wake-up call in the morning. Music plays continually throughout the beautifully landscaped grounds and sophisticated lounges. The dramatic pool area has a 260-foot waterslide, plus a 12-speaker underwater sound system, so you can get your aural fix even while taking a swim. There are three bars and two restaurants, including an Orlando version of the well-known Palm Restaurant, and a gym. The children's program center called Camp Lil Rock is open year-round in the evening with extended daytime hours during the on-season.

The Hard Rock Hotel is the perfect choice for families with older kids and teens who can appreciate the hipper-than-thou ambience. Rates range from $239 to $404 per night, and some of the pricier rooms have kids' suites. If money isn't an object, you can live like the King in the $2,000-per-night Graceland Suite, whose flamboyant amenities include a piano.

Portofino Bay Hotel   407/363–8000

The Portofino Bay is modeled after the Italian seaside village of Portofino. From the outside you see quaint, colorful row houses that are actually all connected on the inside. The 750 elegant rooms include 18 children's suites. Portofino Bay has eight restaurants and lounges; a full-service spa; three swimming pools; and Campo Portofino, a supervised children's activity center, which is open in the evenings year-round with extended daytime hours during the on-season.

Like the others at Universal, this is a Loews resort, so the service is top-notch. Of the three resorts, Portofino Bay is the most posh, with the most amenities geared to adults who want to relax in a beautiful environment. Rates for regular rooms range from $274 to $439 a night, while suites, including the roomy kids' suites, are higher, averaging about $700.

Royal Pacific Resort   407/503–3000

The Royal Pacific is the largest of the three Universal resorts, with 1,000 guest rooms on 53 acres. The lush grounds, thickly planted with tropical plants and trees, have a distinct South Pacific flair, and they're connected to CityWalk and the theme parks via water taxi and a series of winding, well-manicured pathways. There are two restaurants and two lounges, plus a luau party area, a fitness center, a children's activity center, and a massive pool area.

Perhaps most significant, the Royal Pacific is Universal's convention hotel, with 80,000 square feet of meeting space. This doesn't mean the resort won't be comfortable for families—the enormous pool and the children's center indicate that the resort is family-friendly—but you may find a lot of businesspeople mixed in with the vacationing crowd.

Rates range from $219 to $349 a night, making the Royal Pacific the most affordable of the three on-site resorts.

What Kind of Tickets Do We Need?

Universal offers several ticket options. It's smart to purchase them online at www.universalorlando.com; they go up anywhere from $8 to $20 if you wait to buy them at the gate.

One-Day, One-Park Ticket

Admits holders to either Universal Studios or Islands of Adventure for one day.

- @ Adults and children over 9: $88.
- @ Children ages 3 to 9: $82.

One-Day, Two-Park Ticket

Admits holders to Universal Studios and Islands of Adventure for one day.

- @ Adults and children over 9: $123.
- @ Children ages 3 to 9: $117.

Two-Day, Two-Park Ticket

Admits holders to both Universal Studios and Islands of Adventure for two days.

- @ Adults and children over 9: $140.
- @ Children ages 3 to 9: $130.

Two-Day, One-Park-Per-Day Ticket

Admits holders to Universal Studios one day and Islands of Adventure the other.

- @ Adults and children over 9: $120.
- @ Children ages 3 to 9: $110.

Flex Ticket

Admits holders to Universal Studios, Islands of Adventure, Wet 'n Wild, Aquatica, and SeaWorld for 14 consecutive days.

- @ Adults and children over 9: $279.
- @ Children ages 3 to 9: $259.

Money-Saving Tip

If you buy your Universal tickets online (www.
universalorlando.com), the savings can be significant.
Specials vary with the season, but there's nearly
always a reward for buying early.

You can also save money with the Universal Meal
Deal, especially if you have big eaters in the party.
The Meal Deal basically offers you all the food you'd
like from three counter-service restaurants in Universal Studios and three more in Islands of Adventure
for a base price of $21 for adults, $10 for kids 3–9. If
you're visiting both parks, the one-day price is $25
for adults and $12 for kids. And the add-on drink
option of unlimited soft drinks for $9 a person can
be a bargain for adults, considering the price of
theme-park beverages.

Tips for Your First Hour at
Universal Studios

- The parking garage is in New Jersey (it seems that way, anyhow), so arrive at least 30 minutes before the main gate opens. Parking costs $15 per car, $20 if you opt for the closer, preferred parking.

- If you arrive before the main turnstiles open, you'll have time to pose for pictures with and get the autographs of some of the Hanna-Barbera and Nickelodeon characters. This is your chance to meet SpongeBob SquarePants.

- Strollers are $15 for a single, $25 for a double. Wheelchair rental is $12, and ECVs are $50 and both require a re-fundable $50 deposit. Lockers are available for $8–$10.

- You're generally allowed through the main turnstiles and partway down Plaza of the Stars and Rodeo Drive about

Helpful Hint

Want to sleep in? Visit in the off-season, when crowds are light and lines are short. You can arrive at Universal at 10 am and still comfortably do everything.

20 minutes before the official opening time. If you want to ride the Simpsons, Men in Black, or E.T. Adventure first, go down Rodeo Drive as far as you're allowed. If you'd rather see Shrek 4-D, Twister, Revenge of the Mummy, or Disaster! first, go down Plaza of the Stars until the ropes stop you. Families who haven't had breakfast may have time for a pastry at the Beverly Hills Boulangerie before the ropes drop.

@ In the off-season, some attractions open at 9, some at 10, and some (mainly the shows) start even later. Adjust your touring plan to take in the rides as they open. Times are all marked on your touring map.

@ If the kids are up to it, start with the Simpsons; Revenge of the Mummy; and the Hollywood Rip, Ride, and Rockit. All of these attractions can draw major lines later in the day.

Do You Need an Express Pass?

You can avoid waiting in lines with the Universal Express Pass (formerly, the Express PLUS Pass). The price to upgrade a one-day ticket into an Express Pass ranges from $20 to $60, depending on the season, and upgrading a two-day ticket ranges from $26 to $65. While the goal is the same—giving guests ways to reduce the time they spend waiting in line—Universal runs its pass program a bit differently from the Disney Fastpass system. At Disney the Fastpasses are free, but you can only get one at a time. At Universal, an Express Pass is unlimited, meaning that you use it on any ride you choose at any time, but you do pay a significant surcharge for the privilege. (Unless, that is, you're staying on-site. Guests of Universal resorts get Express Pass benefits for free.)

The key thing about the Express Pass is that it's not accepted at Harry Potter and the Forbidden Journey, the centerpiece ride at the Wizarding World of Harry Potter and by far the attraction at which you're most likely to need it. Bottom line on the Express Pass? If you're staying at a Universal Resort and it's free, then great. Use it. If you're visiting on a holiday or peak time in the summer when the crowds are bad, consider it. But most of the time it's simply not worth paying the extra money for the pass.

Universal Studios Touring Tips

- If you're not an on-site resort guest and you didn't opt for the Express Pass, try to visit the major attractions— Revenge of the Mummy; Men in Black; the Simpsons; Twister; Shrek; E.T. Adventure; Disaster!; and Hollywood Rip, Ride, and Rockit—in the morning or in the evening. Take in the theater-style attractions in the afternoon.

- If you miss one of the major continuously loading attractions in the morning, hold off on it until two hours before the park closes. Midday waits of up to 60 minutes are common at popular attractions such as Men in Black and Revenge of the Mummy, but the crowds ease off a bit during the dinner hour.

- If you plan to see Universal Studios in one day, it's unlikely you'll have time for an afternoon break. However, numerous theater-style attractions offer plenty of chances to rest up and let small kids nap. A lot of shows open around noon and begin a second performance around 2 pm. Ride in the morning and then catch a midday show, have lunch, and see a second show.

@ Most of the kiddie attractions—the Woody Woodpecker Nuthouse Coaster, A Day in the Park with Barney, Curious George Goes to Town, Fievel's Playland, E.T. Adventure, and Animal Planet Live!—are in the same general area of the park. This means that you can park the strollers once and then walk from attraction to attraction.

@ The theaters that hold the Universal Horror Make-Up Show, and Terminator 2: 3-D are high capacity, so even if the lines look discouraging, odds are you'll still be seated. Consult your entertainment schedule or check the board.

Helpful Hint

Few rides at Universal have height restrictions. You must be 48 inches tall to ride Revenge of the Mummy; between 51 and 79 inches tall for Rip, Ride, and Rockit; 40 inches tall for the Simpsons; 36 inches tall for the Woody Woodpecker Nuthouse Coaster; and 42 inches tall for Men in Black. Just because your kids are tall enough to qualify, however, doesn't mean it's a good idea to let them into the attractions. Consult the ride descriptions for information about the scare factors.

Some attractions, such as E.T. Adventure, provide separate stationary seating for kids less than 40 inches, thus allowing families to go through the attraction as a group.

@ Headed to the Simpsons; Rip, Ride, and Rockit; Men in Black; or another intense attraction? Universal employees will help families traveling with a baby or toddler do a Baby Swap.

@ Universal's Superstar Parade, featuring characters from Nickelodeon, Despicable Me, and other Universal characters, currently runs at 5 pm most days. If your kids are under 8, make time for this interactive parade.

The Scare Factor at Universal Studios

Some of the shows and tours are family-oriented and fine for everyone, but several of the big-name attractions are too frightening for preschoolers. The motion-simulation rides may induce queasiness, and rides and shows are generally very loud. The volume level at Twister and Terminator can practically jolt the fillings from your teeth.

Universal seems to set its age rules based on how physically wild the motion of a ride is and, except for Revenge of the Mummy and Hollywood Rip, Ride and Rockit, none of the rides at the Studios bounces you around too much. They're psychologically scary, however, and a few minutes inside Twister may lead to more bad dreams than the wildest of roller coasters. Indeed, Twister, Terminator 2: 3-D, Beetlejuice's Graveyard Revue, and the Universal Horror Make-Up Show have parental-advisory ratings, indicating that they may be too violent, loud, or intense for younger children.

Because the rides are based on movies, how your child reacted to the movie is a good predictor of how well your child will handle the ride. If *The Mummy* movie scared him, it's a safe bet he's not going to like the ride any better. Likewise a movie

Helpful Hint

In some ways Universal is showing its age, since many attractions are based on movies of 20 to 30 years ago, which aren't familiar to contemporary kids. If your children are of an age when it's appropriate for them to watch movies such as *Men in Black*, *The Mummy*, *Twister*, or even the *Terminator* series, schedule a family movie night before you leave for Orlando. They'll enjoy the rides a lot more if they can identify the characters and have an idea of what's going on.

that was relatively tame in the theater will probably yield a mild ride. Read the ride descriptions and scare factor ratings to help you decide what's right for your child.

Universal Studios Attractions

Despicable Me 3-D

Gru, the world's most lovable villain, is bringing his three adopted daughters to Universal Studios Orlando for a brand-new mission. The 3-D experience, which replaces Jimmy Neutron's Nicktoon Blast, takes you deep into Gru's secret lab and ends with an interactive dance party. It seems like a fun way for kids of all ages to work off a little steam and a great way to give them a laugh-based, not-too-scary introduction to the 3-D experience.

The Scare Factor

Despicable Me 3-D isn't up, running, and ready for a full review at this writing, which makes giving Scare Factor advice hard. However, based on Universal's descriptions (e.g., "a hysterical mix of chaos and family fun"), the ride sounds designed to be more lively than scary. It should be fine for all ages, especially kids who saw and loved the movie.

Shrek 4-D

In the preshow you learn that vile little Lord Farquaad has plans to destroy Shrek from the great beyond. (Note the clever digs at Disney in the preshow area.) As you enter the main theater, you'll be given 3-D glasses, but what makes this show really special and different from the other 3-D attractions around town is that you're seated in special chairs that will make the experience tactile as well as visual. What does that mean? You'll not only see and hear the action happening on the screen, you'll feel

Quick Guide to

Attraction	Height Requirement
Animal Planet Live!	None
Beetlejuice's Graveyard Revue	None
Curious George Goes to Town	None
A Day in the Park with Barney	None
Despicable Me 3-D	None
Disaster!	None
E.T. Adventure	Separate seating for kids under 40 inches
Fievel's Playland	None
Hollywood Rip, Ride, and Rockit	51 inches
Lucy, A Tribute	None
Men in Black: Alien Attack	42 inches
Revenge of the Mummy	48 inches
Shrek 4-D	None
The Simpsons	40 inches
Terminator 2: 3-D	None
Twister: Ride It Out	None
Universal Horror Make-Up Show	None
Woody Woodpecker's Nuthouse Coaster	36 inches

Scare Factor
0 = Unlikely to scare any child of any age.
! = Has dark or loud elements; might rattle some toddlers.
!! = A couple of gotcha! moments; should be fine for school-age kids.
!!! = You need to be pretty big and pretty brave to handle this ride.

Universal Studios Attractions

Speed of Line	Duration of Ride/Show	Scare Factor	Age Range
Fast	20 min.	0	All
Fast	25 min.	!	5 and up
n/a	n/a	0	All
Fast	15 min.	0	All
Moderate	15 min.	!	All
Moderate	20 min.	!	5 and up
Slow	15 min.	!	All
Moderate	n/a	0	All
Moderate	7 min.	!!!	8 and up
Fast	n/a	0	All
Fast	25 min.	!!	7 and up
Moderate	15 min.	!!!	7 and up
Moderate	30 min.	!!	4 and up
Moderate	7 min.	!!	7 and up
Slow	25 min.	!!!	7 and up
Moderate	15 min.	!!	7 and up
Fast	20 min.	!!	7 and up
Moderate	1½ min.	!	4 and up

The Universal Studios Don't-Miss List

A Day in the Park with Barney (for kids under 6)

Curious George Goes to Town (for kids under 8)

Despicable Me 3-D

E.T. Adventure

Hollywood Rip, Ride, and Rockit (for kids 8 and up)

Men in Black: Alien Attack

Revenge of the Mummy

Shrek 4-D

The Simpsons

and smell some of it, too. (Mercifully, taste is the one sense not engaged in the show.) And the adventures of Shrek and Donkey are predictably hilarious as they rescue the hapless Fiona.

The Scare Factor

While Lord Farquaad isn't the most intimidating movie villain, Shrek 4-D's special effects are extremely convincing, and the whole show is very loud, which may be too much for preschoolers. Kids ages 8 and older should do fine.

Helpful Hint

Shrek is often on hand for autographs and hugs as you exit Shrek 4-D. Check your entertainment schedule for times he's due to appear.

Revenge of the Mummy

Revenge of the Mummy combines a high-speed roller coaster with the latest technology in robotics and pyrotechnic effects—no wonder it's billed as a "psychological thrill ride."

As the story begins, you walk through shadowy Egyptian catacombs on a tour of the on-location set of the next Mummy movie. Once you're in the coaster, the ride's magnetic-propulsion launch system thrusts you forward, backward, and forward again as you dodge vengeful ghosts, mummies, and other monsters. In the final scene the ceiling above you catches on fire. Yowza!

The Scare Factor

Revenge of the Mummy scares the willies out of preschoolers and some school-age kids as well. Your child must be 48 inches tall to ride.

Men in Black: Alien Attack

Remember the scene in *Men in Black* when Will Smith tries out for the force? Think you could do better?

The premise is that guests are rookie agents riding through the streets of New York and armed with laser guns called "alien-

The Scare Factor

Most kids take the aliens in Men in Black in stride—especially if they've seen the movies and know what to expect. There's a fair amount of spinning in the cars, so motion sickness is a possibility, although the spinning is sporadic and not continuous, so few people have reported having a problem. There are lockers outside Men in Black and Revenge of the Mummy where you can store purses and packages while you ride.

Insider's Secret

Want to max your Men in Black score? Near the end of the ride (when you face the mega-alien in Times Square), you will hear Zed instructing you to push the red button on your control panel "now!" Whoever hits the button at this crucial point gets a whopping 100,000 bonus points. Take that, space aliens!

ators." As in Disney's Buzz Lightyear ride, you're supposed to shoot the aliens, but unlike in the Buzz ride, these aliens can strike back, sending your vehicle into an out-of-control spin.

As you shoot at the 120 animatronics aliens, the ride keeps track of your individual score and the collective score of the six people in your vehicle. You're not only fighting off aliens, but also competing against the team of rookies in the car beside you. Here's where it gets cute. Depending on how well you and your vehicle-mates shoot, there are alternate endings to the ride. Will you get a hero's welcome in Times Square or a loser's send-off?

Because you're actually in a video game, it makes sense that video game rules apply—the more you play, the better you get. Can you spell addictive? Come early if you want to ride more than once.

The Simpsons

The basic premise is that you and the Simpson family are inside Krusty the Clown's vision of an amusement park and evil Sideshow Bob is, as usual, up to no good. You sit in a vehicle and watch the action on a giant screen—but since the vehicle in question is a motion simulator that pitches, leans, and rolls and the special effects on the screen are at times overwhelming, this is a wilder experience than it sounds like. The show is funny, hitting pretty hard on both Disney and SeaWorld, but also fairly gross; at one point you get put into Maggie's mouth as if you were a pacifier.

The Scare Factor

The first moments of the Simpsons ride are by far the most jolting, and it takes a minute or two to get used to the sensations of motion-simulation technology. If you feel yourself getting queasy, look away from the screen, either at something within your car or at the other cars riding alongside you. In terms of the story line, what's there to say? Any kid who is used to the television series knows what to expect: it's a little sinister, a little screwy, more than a little tasteless, and pretty darn funny.

Hollywood Rip, Ride, and Rockit

Hollywood Rip, Ride, and Rockit begins with a straight shot into the sky, sailing 17 stories up at speeds of up to 65 mph. The action never stops as you zoom over to the CityWalk lagoon and back, with six near-miss moments and a record-breaking loop.

The technology is pretty nifty, too. You get to choose your own music for the ride: LED boards in the queue area

Insider's Secret

They've been having technical problems with Hollywood Rip, Ride, and Rockit far more frequently than was expected, even considering the complexity of the ride. There's a chance it might be off-line when you visit or that the format may be revamped.

The Scare Factor

With a height requirement of 51 inches, the Hollywood Rip, Ride, and Rockit is off-limits to many kids, and too intense for most kids under 8, even if they're tall enough to ride. The coaster is really designed for the preteen and teen set.

display song choices or you can just let the coaster's digital sound system choose for you.

Disaster!

The "musion" technology of the preshow, which transforms two-dimensional images into what appear to be three-dimensional images, is quite effective, creating a hologram of actor Christopher Walken interacting with a person on stage. Audience volunteers are pulled into the preshow action, which is a lot of fun. The ride itself puts you in the middle of a San Francisco subway car, where you become victims of an earthquake, complete with fires, broken water mains, and near misses with falling debris. During the ride your experiences are taped—because you're allegedly extras in a disaster movie—and played back to you in the form of a tongue-in-cheek preview.

The Scare Factor

Disaster! is dramatic, but most kids aren't too frightened. The noise level may unnerve toddlers. And be aware that the show has a few adult innuendos that sail right over the heads of younger children but might be inappropriate for preteens.

Twister: Ride It Out

After a taped intro based on the film, you're led into the main show area. There, a five-story-high tornado is created right before your eyes. Along with accompanying fires and explosions, it swirls through the building while you watch from one of two platforms. You'll feel the wind, the rain, and the rumbles; and yes, the flying cow from the movie comes along for the ride.

The Scare Factor

Twister is extremely loud—at 110 decibels, that's twice the volume of a rock concert. Some families routinely bring earplugs to theme parks, but if you don't have them, try placing your hands over your kids' ears. The experience is too frightening for small children, but most kids 6 and up will be fine.

Terminator 2: 3-D

Universal's most high-tech action show combines 3-D effects, live action, and movie clips. The best special effect is the way the actors seem to emerge from the screen and then later run back "into"

The Scare Factor

Although not as violent as the film series, Terminator 2: 3-D has some startling effects that may be too much for kids under 7. Again, it is extremely loud.

the movie. The show is fast and dramatic, just like the film series it's based on, and the ending is explosive.

Because of the size of the theater, Terminator 2: 3-D is relatively easy to get into and is best saved for the afternoon.

E.T. Adventure

This charming ride begins with a brief preshow featuring Steven Spielberg and E.T. Next you move on to the queue area, which winds through the deep, dark woods—it even smells and sounds like a forest. (As a rule, Universal does a bang-up job of setting the mood in queue areas; E.T. is designed to make you feel small and childlike.)

After handing "passports" to the attendant, children under 40 inches tall and the elderly, heavy, pregnant, or other-

Helpful Hint

All the attractions for very young children are in the same area of Universal. If you have preschoolers, hang an immediate right on Rodeo Drive after you enter the park and follow the signs to E.T. Adventure.

wise unsteady are loaded into flying gondolas. Others ride bicycles, and the lead bike in each group has E.T. in the front basket. You rise up and fly over the forest in an effective simulation of the escape scene in *E.T.* the movie. After narrowly missing being captured by the police, you manage to return E.T. to his home planet, a magical place populated by dozens of cuddly aliens.

As you sail past E.T. for the final time, he bids you farewell by name. Magic? Not quite. When you give your name to the attendant before you enter the queue area, it's computer coded onto your plastic passport. As you give up the

Insider's Secret

With all the excitement next door at Islands of Adventure, where the opening of the Wizarding World of Harry Potter has drawn a tremendous amount of media attention, this can be a great time to visit Universal Studios. If you have purchased a two-park ticket, it makes sense to begin your day bright and early at Islands of Adventure (IOA). Thanks to the arrival of Harry and friends, it's busy all day, but mornings are still more tolerable than afternoons, when park attendance swells to the max. Exit IOA around lunchtime, stop for a bite in one of the relatively uncrowded restaurants in CityWalk, then tour Universal Studios in the afternoon.

passport and join your group of bicycles, the cards are fed into the computer, which enables E.T. to say, "Good-bye, Jordan. Good-bye, Leigh. Good-bye, Kim . . ." and so on, as your family flies past.

The Scare Factor

Although the movie clips and general gore level are too intense for preschoolers, most kids 8 and over can stomach the Universal Horror Make-Up Show. Better than adults, frankly. The show has a parental-advisory rating because of the blood and a couple of risqué jokes.

Universal Horror Make-Up Show

This show opens with a bang—or, more specifically, the startling effect of a man running on stage with a knife protruding from his chest. Everything that follows is fast-paced and funny, but a good deal edgier than anything you'd see at Disney. The actors illustrate special horror effects on stage including "cutting" off the arm of an (adult) audience volunteer, and you'll also see clips from *The Mummy, The Fly,* and *An American Werewolf in London,* which has an astounding man-to-beast transformation scene.

Animal Planet Live!

This is an appealing show for all age groups, but younger kids will be especially drawn to the animal stars. Kid volunteers from the audience join the fast-paced and funny performance. Showtimes are printed on your map; because of the large size of the theater, this is a great choice for the most crowded times of the afternoon.

Fievel's Playland

Fievel's Playland is cleverly designed and filled with Wild West–style props, including a harmonica slide that plays notes as kids go down it; a giant talking Tiger the cat; canteens to squirt; cowboy hats to bounce in; spiderwebs to climb; and a separate ball pit and slide area for toddlers.

The centerpiece of the playground is a 200-foot water ride in which kids and parents are loaded into two-person rafts and swept through a "sewer." The ride is zippier than it looks, will get you soaking wet, and is so addictive that most kids clamor to get back on again immediately. The water ride loads slowly, so by afternoon the waits are prohibitive. If you come in the morning, it's possible to ride several times with minimal waits, but by afternoon one ride is all you can reasonably expect. Note that the water ride is closed on cold days.

Fievel's Playland often opens an hour or two after the general park opening. If you ride the big-deal rides and then show up at the playground at the opening time indicated on your map, you'll be able to try the water ride without much of a wait.

A Day in the Park with Barney

Designed to appeal to Universal's youngest guests, A Day in the Park with Barney is actually an enclosed parklike setting with pop-art-style, colorful flowers, and trees. Barney appears several times a day in a song-and-dance show, and there's also an interactive indoor play area for toddlers. This play area is far cooler and calmer than Fievel's next door, and the nearby shop and food stand are never crowded.

"The highlight of my 2-year-old daughter's day was the Barney show," a mother of two from Illinois wrote to us. "The kids sit so close to him and his friends, and the setting is beautiful. I loved watching my little girl sing along during the 'I Love You' song at the end."

Helpful Hint

The Barney preshow is a little uncomfortable—a standing venue with parents having to lift kids up if they have a prayer of seeing the stage. But once you get inside, the area is much more family-friendly and designed to let little kids romp and dance along with the music.

Woody Woodpecker's Nuthouse Coaster

The Nuthouse Coaster is zippier than you'd guess, and kids must be 36 inches tall to ride. Watch it make a couple of runs before you line up with your 4-year-old.

Curious George Goes to Town

Perhaps a better name for this attraction would have been "Curious George Goes to the Car Wash." This large interactive play area is a simulated city that includes climbing areas, ball pits, and lots of chances to get very, very wet. There are fountains in the center and water cannons up above; many parents let their kids wear bathing suits under their clothing so they can strip down and really get into the spirit of the place. If you're up for a maximum splash, a clanging bell over the Fire Department indicates when a big wave of water is under way. The impact is pretty impressive, and this may be the highlight of the park for young kids, but parents of preschoolers and toddlers, beware: the wave hits with enough force to knock small children off their feet.

It's a great way to cool off in summer, so save it for the warmest part of the afternoon. In chilly weather the water is shut off, and Curious George Goes to Town becomes a dry play area.

Beetlejuice's Graveyard Revue

This rock-and-rap show starring Dracula, the Wolfman, Frankenstein's monster, and his bride is primarily aimed at preteens and teens. Beetlejuice is the host, and he offsets the ghoulishness with plenty of goofy humor. Younger kids won't be too frightened of the monsters themselves, but the extremely high volume of the music coupled with pyrotechnics might upset preschoolers. The parental advisory is largely due to some suggestive jokes and the convincing costuming of the characters. The show plays several times in the afternoon, so getting in isn't hard; arrive about 15 minutes before showtime for good seats.

Lucy, A Tribute

Fans of *I Love Lucy* should take a few minutes to walk through this exhibit, which houses memorabilia from the famous TV show, including scale models of the Tropicana and the Ricardos' apartment; clothes and jewelry worn on the show; personal pictures and letters from Lucy and Desi's home life; and the numerous Emmys that Lucille Ball won through the years.

The "California Here We Come Game" is a treat for hardcore trivia buffs. By answering questions about episodes of *I*

Money-Saving Tip

Try not to let the kids stop to shop in the morning; not only should you keep moving between rides while Universal is relatively uncrowded, but each ride empties out through a shop that sells souvenirs related to that attraction. In other words, the shops encourage the ultimate in impulse buying, but hold off purchases until late in the day when you've seen it all.

Love Lucy, game participants get to travel with the Mertzes and Ricardos on their first trip to California. They lost me somewhere in the desert, but perhaps you'll do better.

Insider's Secret

Universal can really throw a party. The park is festively decorated for Christmas, and a special parade runs for the weeks around Mardi Gras.

But the best holiday celebration of the year is Halloween. Halloween Horror Nights are a time-honored tradition at Universal and very popular with Orlando locals. All the movie bad guys are out in full force with plenty of special stage shows and "interactive experiences." Teenagers will love this ultimate spook house, and kids under 7 definitely won't. If you have kids ages 7 to 11, just make sure to stay close to them. Separate tickets are required for this party and should be purchased in advance. Visit www.universalorlando.com for details.

Insider's Secret

Check your entertainment schedule and, if time permits, stop to watch some of Universal's street entertainers that play around the park throughout the day. The Blues Brothers, featuring Jake and Elroy, play in the New York section and offer one of the liveliest shows in the park.

Tips for Your Last Hour at Universal Studios

⊚ Crowds thin at night, so it's a good time to revisit favorite attractions or drop by anything you missed earlier in the day.

⊚ If you want to have dinner at CityWalk, leave Universal about an hour before the official closing time to avoid the rush of exiting guests. For more on CityWalk, Universal's dining and entertainment district, see Chapter 15.

⊚ A new nightime show called Universal's Cinematic Spectacular—100 Years of Movie Memories plays at 9 pm on select nights. Brand-new and narrated by none other than Morgan Freeman, the show draws large crowds, especially during the on-season. Catch a seat around the Universal Studio lagoon at least 30 minutes before showtime.

CHAPTER
15
Islands of Adventure

Islands of Adventure

Jurassic Park River Adventure 10

Harry Potter and the Forbidden Journey 14

Flight of the Hippogriff 13

Dragon Challenge 12

Camp Jurassic 9

THE WIZARDING WORLD OF HARRY POTTER

Pteranodon Flyers 8

Discovery Center 11

JURASSIC PARK

Dudley Do-Right's Ripsaw Falls 5

The Mystic Fountain 16 15 **The Eighth Voyage of Sindba**

Popeye & Bluto's Bilge-Rat Barges 6

TOON LAGOON

Me Ship, the Olive 7

THE LOST CONTINENT

Poseidon's Fury: Escape from the Lost City 17

MARVEL SUPER HERO ISLAND

SEUSS LANDING

Amazing Adventures of Spider-Man 4

High in the Sky Seuss Trolley 18

If I Ran the Zoo 19

Dr. Doom's Fearfall 3

PORT OF ENTRY

Caro-Seuss-el 20

Incredible Hulk Coaster 1 ◆ **Lockers**

One Fish, Two Fish, Red Fish, Blue Fish 21

Storm Force Accelatron 2

22 **The Cat in the Hat**

◆ **Lockers**

KEY

👥 *Restrooms*

First Aid ◆

I slands of Adventure (IOA) is all about rides: full sensory-immersion 3-D experiences, state-of-the-art coasters, watery descents that'll leave you dripping, and kiddie rides so cleverly designed that even the most cynical adults totally get into the spirit. And, during the last two years it's been all about the Wizarding World of Harry Potter, an island so popular that it's allowed Universal to significantly raise the ticket prices and still draw unprecedented crowds.

For information on tickets and multiday passes, see Chapter 14 and note the financial advantages of buying online. Check for any price changes by calling 407/363–8000 or visiting www.universalorlando.com.

Money-Saving Tip

Are you a member of AAA? If so, you'll get a 10% price break on food and shopping throughout Islands of Adventure and Universal Studios. This can be quite a boon, especially in posh restaurants.

Getting Around Islands of Adventure

The layout of Islands of Adventure is reminiscent of a big lollipop, and you enter through the stick—the Port of Entry, which has shops, restaurants, and service areas. Port of Entry ends at the lagoon, and around the water are clustered the six islands of the theme park: Marvel Super Hero Island, Toon Lagoon, Jurassic Park, the Wizarding World of Harry Potter, the Lost Continent, and Seuss Landing.

Because of IOA's essentially circular design, it's an easy park to tour. The sidewalks naturally lead you from one attraction to the next, with no crossroads or choices, and bridges connect each of the islands. The moods of the separate lands are quite distinct. As you walk into the mysterious and mythic Lost Continent, for example, you're greeted by the gentle tinkling of wind chimes; and to enter Jurassic Park you walk through an enormous stone gate flanked by torches. Below your feet you'll see fossil prints in the sidewalk; and if you listen closely, you'll hear the rumbles and calls of dinos in the bushes.

We advise an early-morning lap of the park to ride the big-deal attractions; an afternoon lap to check out the shows, play areas, water rides, and minor attractions; then a final circle in early evening to ride anything you missed—or revisit favorites. Sounds like a lot of walking, but in this user-friendly theme park touring is a snap.

How Scary Is "Scary"? As Dr. Seuss Would Say, "Very!"

Ten of the 12 major attractions at Islands of Adventure have height restrictions—your first clue that this park is loaded with physically wild rides. Measure your kids before you leave home; there's no point in promising your kindergarten-age muggle a ride on Harry Potter and the Forbidden Journey if he's less than 48 inches tall. Here are the specific height restrictions:

The Amazing Adventures of Spider-Man	40 inches
Dr. Doom's Fearfall	52 inches
Dudley Do-Right's Ripsaw Falls	44 inches
Dragon Challenge	54 inches
Flight of the Hippogriff	36 inches
Harry Potter and the Forbidden Journey	48 inches
Jurassic Park River Adventure	42 inches
The Incredible Hulk Coaster	54 inches
Popeye & Bluto's Bilge-Rat Barges	42 inches
Pteranodon Flyers	36 inches

In addition, a couple of the shows are atmospherically scary; Poseidon's Fury and the Eighth Voyage of Sindbad have frightened some preschoolers.

The bottom line? Read the ride descriptions carefully before you board. If the ride is outside (and many IOA attractions are), watch it make a couple of cycles before you decide. And if someone in your family panics while in line, inform the attendant you'll need to do a Baby Swap (or husband swap, as the case may be).

The Islands of Adventure Don't-Miss List for Kids 2 to 6

Camp Jurassic

Caro-Seuss-el

The Cat in the Hat

Flight of the Hippogriff

If I Ran the Zoo

Me Ship, the Olive

One Fish, Two Fish, Red Fish, Blue Fish

Popeye & Bluto's Bilge-Rat Barges (for older kids)

The Islands of Adventure Don't-Miss List for Kids 7 to 11

The Amazing Adventures of Spider-Man

Camp Jurassic

The Cat in the Hat

Dragon Challenge (older kids)

Dudley Do-Right's Ripsaw Falls

Harry Potter and the Forbidden Journey

The Incredible Hulk Coaster (older kids)

Jurassic Park River Adventure

Popeye & Bluto's Bilge-Rat Barges

Poseidon's Fury

The Islands of Adventure Don't-Miss List for Kids 12 and up

The Amazing Adventures of Spider-Man

Dr. Doom's Fearfall

Dragon Challenge

Dudley Do-Right's Ripsaw Falls

Harry Potter and the Forbidden Journey

The Incredible Hulk Coaster

Jurassic Park River Adventure

Popeye & Bluto's Bilge-Rat Barges

Poseidon's Fury

Tips for Your First Hour at Islands of Adventure

- Arrive 30 minutes before the stated opening time, which is generally 9 am. Get tickets and maps, and take care of any business, such as locker or stroller rental.

- Sometimes Port of Entry is open before the rest of the park. If so, browse the shops or have a quick breakfast at Croissant Moon Bakery.

- The tip board will tell you which rides are running. During the on-season, most rides will open immediately; on less-crowded days the rides may come online section by section. Either way, Marvel Super Hero Island and Seuss Landing, the two islands adjoining Port of Entry, will be open, and generally the Wizarding World of Harry Potter as well.

Time-Saving Tip

Express Passes (formerly Express PLUS Passes) are the way to go on crowded days, letting you into every express line in the park on an unlimited basis. Guests of on-site hotels get this perk without having to pay for the pass—just show your resort ID. For off-site guests, Express Passes are for sale at ticket kiosks, Guest Services (aka Guest Relations), and booths around the park. They cost as much as $89 depending upon the time of year you're visiting. They're cheapest in the off-season, obviously. But, then again, in the off-season you probably don't need one.

One major caveat. The ride you most need an Express Pass for is Harry Potter and the Forbidden Journey, and at this writing, it's not included in the Express Pass program.

Quick Guide to

Attraction	Location	Height Requirement
Amazing Adventures of Spider-Man	Super Hero Island	40 inches
Camp Jurassic	Jurassic Park	None
Caro-Seuss-el	Seuss Landing	None
The Cat in the Hat	Seuss Landing	None
Discovery Center	Jurassic Park	None
Dr. Doom's Fearfall	Super Hero Island	52 inches
Dragon Challenge	Harry Potter	54 inches
Dudley Do-Right's Ripsaw Falls	Toon Lagoon	44 inches
The Eighth Voyage of Sindbad	Lost Continent	None
Flight of the Hippogriff	Harry Potter	36 inches
Harry Potter and the Forbidden Journey	Harry Potter	48 inches
High in the Sky Seuss Trolley	Seuss Landing	34 inches
If I Ran the Zoo	Seuss Landing	None
Incredible Hulk Coaster	Super Hero Island	54 inches
Me Ship, the Olive	Toon Lagoon	None
One Fish, Two Fish Red Fish, Blue Fish	Seuss Landing	None
Popeye & Bluto's Bilge-Rat Barges	Toon Lagoon	42 inches
Poseidon's Fury	Lost Continent	None

Scare Factor
0 = Unlikely to scare any child of any age.
! = Has dark or loud elements; might rattle some toddlers.
!! = A couple of gotcha! moments; should be fine for school-age kids.
!!! = You need to be pretty big and pretty brave to handle this ride.

Islands of Adventure Attractions

Speed of Line	Duration of Ride/Show	Scare Factor	Age Range
Moderate	15 min.	!!	7 and up
n/a	n/a	0	All
Slow	3 min.	0	All
Moderate	6 min.	0	All
n/a	n/a	0	All
Slow	2 min.	!!	7 and up
Moderate	7 min.	!!!	7 and up
Moderate	8 min.	!!	7 and up
n/a	25 min.	!!	8 and up
Slow	8 min.	!	All
Slow	60 min.	!!!	7 and up
Slow	8 min.	0	All
n/a	n/a	0	All
Moderate	4 min.	!!!	8 and up
n/a	n/a	0	All
Slow	4 min.	0	All
Moderate	12 min.	!	4 and up
n/a	20 min.	!!	7 and up

(continued)

Quick Guide to

Attraction	Location	Height Requirement
Pteranodon Flyers	Jurassic Park	36 inches
River Adventure	Jurassic Park	42 inches
Storm Force Accelatron	Super Hero Island	None

Scare Factor
0 = Unlikely to scare any child of any age.
! = Has dark or loud elements; might rattle some toddlers.
!! = A couple of gotcha! moments; should be fine for school-age kids.
!!! = You need to be pretty big and pretty brave to handle this ride.

@ If you're staying at a Universal Orlando resort and thus entitled to visit the Wizarding World of Harry Potter an hour before the theme park opens to non-guests, then by all means take advantage of this huge perk and head there first. Ride Harry Potter and the Forbidden Journey immediately, and then visit the shops and smaller attractions.

@ Harry Potter is hot, hot, hot. If that section is open, go there first.

 Helpful Hint
Rides are most likely to be closed for maintenance in winter. Check www.universalorlando.com to see if any attractions are scheduled for refurbishment during your visit.

Islands of Adventure Attractions

Speed of Line	Duration of Ride/Show	Scare Factor	Age Range
Slow	80 sec.	!	4 and up
Slow	5 min.	!!	7 and up
Slow	3 min.	!!	All

@ If not, and if your kids are old enough to enjoy intense rides, veer left to Marvel Super Hero Island. Ride the Incredible Hulk Coaster, Spider-Man, and Dr. Doom's Fearfall in that order. Perhaps because most guests stay off-site and must rise, eat, drive, park, and undertake the substantial trek from the parking garage, Islands of Adventure is relatively empty in the morning (at least the islands that don't involve Harry Potter), and grows more crowded in the afternoon.

@ If your kids are younger, veer right to Seuss Landing and start with One Fish, Two Fish and the Cat in the Hat.

Port of Entry

As the name implies, Port of Entry is where you enter Islands of Adventure. It's a visually charming area, meant to resemble an exotic Middle Eastern seaport, and it's a great place for a group snapshot.

Many of the park services are in Port of Entry: locker rentals ($8–10), Guest Services, film-developing stands, the Lost and Found, and an ATM are all here. You can rent a stroller ($15, $25 for a double) or a wheelchair ($12, $50 for an ECV).

In addition, there are shops and restaurants. The Universal Studios Islands of Adventure Trading Company is a store that's almost as big as its name, and, because it has merchandise from all five islands, it's a good place for wrap-up shopping on your way out of the park.

Confisco Grille, the only full-service restaurant in Port of Entry, offers pasta, fish, and steak as well as lighter fare such as salads and sandwiches. It serves character meals during the on-season. Adjacent to the Confisco is the Backwater Bar, which serves half-price drinks during the 3 to 6 pm happy hour.

Fast-food choices include the Croissant Moon Bakery, which offers bagels, pastries, and a variety of coffees—it's a great place for a quick breakfast as you enter the park. Later in the day sandwiches and desserts are added to the menu. The Arctic Express offers funnel cakes and ice cream, while the Cinnabon next door offers the same gooey treats you find in malls and airports. Some IOA restaurants close in the off-season. But Universal does a good job of estimating crowd flow, so there are always enough places open to serve everyone in the park.

Pause for a second as you near the end of Port of Entry. There's a great view of the Jurassic Park Visitor Center across the water. To your left is the tip board, which gives you information on the opening sequence of the rides, approximate wait times, and upcoming showtimes.

Marvel Super Hero Island

This is the island where superheroes fight bad guys, and you test your mettle on three high-thrill attractions. Most people are so busy dashing to the rides that they don't take the time to appreciate how well this section visually duplicates a comic-book world. Signs are intentionally generic as in "Store," "Arcade," or "Café"; and colors are chosen to give everything a flat grainy appearance.

The Amazing Adventures of Spider-Man

Spider-Man combines actual movement on a track, motion simulation, and 3-D effects. Unlike most 3-D shows, where you're sitting still and the action comes toward you, in Spider-Man you're moving from scene to scene through a comic-book story. It feels as if everything is really happening, especially the 400-foot simulated drop at the end, yet the actual ride movement is very mild. In other words, young kids or people who freak out on coasters can enjoy the ride.

The concept is that the Sinister Syndicate, made up of comic-book villains, has taken over New York City and stolen the Statue of Liberty. (Wonder why the bad guys never nab Boston or Omaha?) The plucky young photojournalist Peter Parker, alias Spider-Man, is nowhere to be found, and the city is in a panic. James Jonah Jameson, the bombastic newspaper editor, is "so desperate for the story that I might have to send a bunch of tourists out in the ScoopMobile." That's your cue.

Insider's Secret

Spider-Man has recently been revamped, with re-animation and even higher definition. You can even see the stitching on Spidey's gloves, and the villains are closer and more real than ever.

As soon as you're loaded in you'll be stunned by the quality of the recently revamped effects, which make you feel as if Spider-Man is on the hood of your car and that bricks are flying toward your face. The ending of the ride, in which you're "thrown" off the top of a New York skyscraper and caught in Spider-Man's net, is the biggest thrill of all.

The Scare Factor

Spider-Man has a 40-inch height requirement, which means quite a few preschoolers qualify to ride.

The actual ride movement has plenty of spins and bumps, but the infamous "drop" at the end is totally simulated, making it far more fun than scary. The real issue is the villains. The Sinister Syndicate throws everything it has at you, and the characters often appear very abruptly. If the in-your-face bad guys are too much for your kids, tell them to shut their eyes.

Also consider what this mother of two from California wrote to us: "Spider-Man is a wonderful ride and my husband's favorite. The first time we rode it with our kids (ages 9 and 11), the younger one was terrified by the fact that the bad guys land on the hood of the car and it really feels like they're reaching out for you. But once she got off the ride and walked around a while, she wanted to try it again."

The first time you ride Spider-Man, skip the Express and single-rider lines, and enter through the main entrance. The reason is that the walk-through to the ride is basically the preshow that tells you who you're fighting and why. Without it, you'll probably be wondering "Why are all these pieces of the Statue of Liberty lying around?"

Money-Saving Tip

As you exit Spider-Man, you'll notice how Universal Orlando cleverly encourages souvenir shopping. While you're still excited about the ride, you exit through a shop full of Spider-Man merchandise. Remember this rule: No souvenir shopping until the afternoon, when you've tried out lots of rides and know what you really want.

But once you've braved the experience once and know that a happy ending is guaranteed, Spider-Man is an attraction that holds up through return trips. Pay attention to detail. For example, when Hobgoblin throws his fiery pumpkins at you, Spider-Man snares the first one in his web, but the second one goes awry and crashes through the wall and into the next scene.

The Incredible Hulk Coaster

This isn't your mother's roller coaster, on which you slowly crank up a hill getting ready for your first plunge. The Incredible Hulk Coaster is big, green, and mean—just like David Banner after he played around once too often with those gamma rays.

The Scare Factor

The 54-inch height requirement eliminates many young kids, and Hulk is a pretty heart-thumping experience—probably too intense for any child under 10. Watch it make a few laps before you decide to ride.

There's a separate line for those who want to sit in the front row, which has the best views, but the longest wait. The movement is slightly wilder in the back of the car. Note the word "slightly." Hulk is plenty intense no matter where you ride.

Time-Saving Tip

Long lines? Even without an Express Pass you can still cut down on your wait by using the single-rider line. After you've gone through an attraction like Spider-Man or Hulk once as a family, older kids might want to ride again on their own. If so, the single-rider line moves much faster than the general-admission line.

Those lockers at the Hulk entrance are there for a reason, and they're free to use. Store everything you can because seven big flips can send car keys and sunglasses sailing.

The ride opens with a "cannon" shot from a 150-foot tube, zooming from 0 to 40 mph during the first two seconds of motion, then immediately flipping over to give riders the sensation of going weightless. You'll make seven different inversions during the course of your ride, and twice disappear into a subterranean trench. Although the ride is wild, it's smooth, with very few jerky movements, and many coaster warriors swear that despite its awesome appearance, Hulk is the most user-friendly coaster in the park.

Time-Saving Tip

On a tight touring schedule? Spider-Man and Hulk are must-sees, but you can skip Storm Force and Dr. Doom.

Dr. Doom's Fearfall

Dr. Victor von Doom is trying to defeat the Fantastic Four by sucking all the fear out of innocent citizens like you and using this collective fear to take over the world. (OK, so logic isn't the strong point of these rides.) The point is that you're strapped into outdoor seats and shot 180 feet into the air. There's a bit

The Scare Factor

The height requirement is 52 inches for Dr. Doom's Fearfall, and whether your child should ride boils down to one question: How does he feel about heights? Most riders, including kids, think this ride is over too quickly to get truly scary. As they say, "The waiting is the hardest part."

of a yo-yo effect—you're raised and lowered several times—but the first five seconds of the ride are by far the scariest. Most riders report that once you're launched, you're fine.

Storm Force Accelatron

This simple spinning ride—the cups spin individually and the discs that they're mounted on also move—is a cranked-up version of the Mad Tea Party at Disney World. It's a good way to entertain younger siblings while older kids tackle the nearby Hulk.

The Scare Factor

Storm Force Accelatron isn't scary, but the double spinning action makes some riders queasy.

Toon Lagoon

Like Marvel Super Hero Island, Toon Lagoon is also devoted to comic-strip characters, but these are the stars of the Sunday funnies—such as Beetle Bailey, Betty Boop, Dagwood, and the kids of the Family Circus. Young kids have no idea who any of these characters are, but the true focus of the island isn't the toon, it's the lagoon; the attractions here are designed to splash you silly.

Dudley Do-Right's Ripsaw Falls

This log flume ride, in which you're helping Dudley and Horse save the perpetually pitiful Nell from Snidely Whiplash, culminates in a breathtaking 75-foot drop. The ride facade is so enormous that it serves as a park icon, and hardly anyone can walk by without stopping to gawk. The actual fall is even more dramatic than it looks; there's an explo-

Insider's Secret

Dudley Do-Right's facade spoofs Mount Rushmore, but also keep your eye out for a clever jab at Disney's Pirates of the Caribbean just before you disembark.

The Scare Factor

Kids ages 7 and up name Dudley Do-Right as one of their favorite rides. The last drop is a definite squealer, so anyone with a fear of heights should think twice before getting in line. The height requirement is 44 inches.

sion of light when the log enters the TNT shack at the bottom of the flume, followed by a second descent, in which you drop an additional 15 feet below the water level.

Needless to say, a descent of this magnitude isn't accomplished without a lot of splash. The water not only flies back in your face, but also sloshes into the log, puddling around your hips and feet. You'll enjoy the ride a lot more when you're ready to get wet—in other words, in the hottest part of the afternoon.

Popeye & Bluto's Bilge-Rat Barges

If Dudley Do-Right is all about splashing, Popeye is about getting drenched straight through to your underwear. Parties of eight are loaded into circular rafts and sent on a wild and winding water journey. If through some miracle you manage to avoid the waves, the boat wash at the end of the ride spares no one. To add insult to injury, you're squirted with water guns by the kids aboard the nearby play area, Me Ship, the Olive.

For this reason, riding Popeye requires a bit of planning. Families in the know wear lightweight soccer-style shorts, don ponchos or plastic bags, or perhaps even bring a whole change of clothes. (If you were planning on buying a souvenir T-shirt anyway, hold off until after you ride when fresh dry clothes are bound to feel great.) Leave cameras and valuables inside the nearby lockers and stow everything else that you can in the central pouch, including shoes and socks.

The Scare Factor
Popeye & Bluto's Bilge-Rat Barges is one of the best big-deal rides for young kids, and parents with kids as young as age 5 report that they loved it. The height requirement is 42 inches. "Our 6-year-old daughter freaked out when she first saw Dudley Do-Right," wrote one father, "and that big drop does look pretty intimidating, even to an adult. But after she'd gone on the Popeye boat ride—three times—she was totally over her fear and willing to go on Dudley Do-Right."

Although there are some sizable dips and drops along the way, the fact that the whole family rides together in a circular raft somewhat dilutes the intensity, making this ride a good choice for kids who are not quite up to Dudley Do-Right's megadrop but still want to try a water ride. And because the rafts hold a fair number of people and load quickly, Popeye never seems to have the daunting lines that are standard at Dudley. All in all, it's a good choice for the afternoon.

Insider's Secret
The three major water rides—Dudley Do-Right and Popeye in Toon Lagoon, and the River Adventure in Jurassic Park—are fairly close together. Ride them all in a row, and you'll only have to dry off once.

Me Ship, the Olive
This is a compact play area designed like a ship, with slides, climbing webs, and buttons that make tooting and beeping noises. Swee' Pea's Playpen is a separate play area for toddlers.

By far the most enjoyable feature of Me Ship, the Olive, is the water guns that allow you to take aim at the occupants of Popeye & Bluto's Bilge-Rat Barges below. If you have a child too young to ride Popeye, take him aboard the Olive while you wait for the rest of the family to ride; he can seek revenge on his siblings as they pass. But watch out—the squirt guns can squirt back!

Insider's Secret

Toon Lagoon is full of great photo ops. You can pose beneath the giant word bubbles, so that it appears you're saying or thinking such phrases as "It must be Sunday—we're in color!" and "I have the feeling people can read my thoughts!" The fountain on Comic Strip Lane is the hangout place for every cartoon dog you can think of and another fun place for a group snapshot.

Jurassic Park

As you walk through the high stone entryway with its torches, note the distant rumbling of unseen beasts, and look down at the fossilized leaves and footprints in the sidewalk before you. The Canadian pines around Dudley Do-Right's Ripsaw Falls have given way to lush tropical vegetation, and the merry beat of Toon Lagoon slows to an ominous jungle rhythm. Is there any doubt you've entered Jurassic Park?

River Adventure

The River Adventure starts out with a mild cruise through the habitats of gentle vegetarian dinosaurs. Hmm, do you think we'll stay on course? If you don't know the answer to that, you have to go back to Theme Park 101.

Sure enough, a playful dino bangs your boat, sending you drifting into a restricted zone, and once you're inside the dangerous containment area, your boat is pulled up a long ramp past vicious little raptors that leap around spitting at you. When the T-Rex at the top decides you'll make a good snack, you escape via an 85-foot plunge—and that's one long, fast, steep descent.

The Scare Factor

Eighty-five feet may sound like a T-Rex-size drop, especially in contrast to the 75-foot drop next door at Dudley, but because you're loaded into much larger boats, the River Adventure fall doesn't feel that intense. Most families report that they found this plunge less frightening than the one at Dudley Do-Right. There's some atmospheric scariness, however, in the form of some very real-looking dinos. It's key to let nervous youngsters know what to expect in advance—that is, you'll get pushed in with the raptors. If it's any consolation, this part of the ride is very short—less than two minutes from the beginning of the climb to the final plunge. Our surveys indicate that most kids 7 and up love the ride.

Camp Jurassic

Of the three play areas in Islands of Adventure, this is the best one for kids ages 6 to 10. The setting is a group of posteruption volcanoes, with caves for hiding, and a multilevel, fairly rough terrain perfect for jumping, climbing, and exploring. There are slides, plenty of netting, and some take-no-prisoners water cannons. Because the Camp Jurassic play area is bigger and more spread out than Me Ship, the Olive in Toon Lagoon and If I Ran the Zoo in Seuss Landing, it's easy for kids to get lost. Unless you're sure they can find their way back to one of the benches where Mom and Dad sit waiting, you may need to go with them.

Pteranodon Flyers

This aerial ride, in which children dangle beneath the wide wings of a gentle flying dinosaur, is the first thing you see when you enter Jurassic Park. Ergo, most kids insist on making a bee-line there. It's indeed a pleasant 80-second flight around lushly landscaped Camp Jurassic, offering you great views of Islands of Adventure. The catch is that only three birds, each holding two riders, are on the track at a time. That adds up to lines that stretch all the way back to the Cretaceous period, even on days when the park isn't crowded. On busy days you can wait more than an hour, and there's no Express line.

The Scare Factor

Pteranodon Flyers is fine for anyone who doesn't have a fear of heights, although there's a bit more swing to the Pteranodons than you'd guess.

In an effort to cut down on the line, Islands of Adventure has limited the ride to kids 36 to 56 inches tall, allowing one adult to ride with each child. In fact, the en-

Insider's Secret

Pteranodon Flyers generally opens around 10 am. The tip board will give you exact times. If your kids are determined to ride, be at the entrance to Camp Jurassic as close to opening time as possible. Once Camp Jurassic is open, the line at Pteranodon Flyers can jump to a 20-minute wait within seconds. And this attraction is not included in the Express Pass.

trance signs almost try to talk you out of riding, telling you that there are height requirements on both sides of the ruler and the ride lasts only 80 seconds. People flock to it anyway. Try to talk the kids out of riding unless you're there on a quiet day when the wait is less than 20 minutes.

Discovery Center

The Discovery Center is like a small, very hip museum. Little kids can make dinosaur sounds while the older ones X-ray eggs and guess which species is inside. The Dino DNA sequencing profile lets you superimpose your face onto a dinosaur, or you can test your scientific knowledge against two other contestants in a raucous game show called You Bet Jurassic.

The biggest kick is when a raptor hatches from an egg, a wonderful little treat in which an authentic-looking animatronics baby pecks his way through the shell. The kids in the crowd get to name it. Being in the Discovery Center for a birth is a bit of a hit-or-miss proposition, but a honking noise alerts you that one of the eggs is getting ready to crack.

The center is cool and relatively uncrowded, making it a good place to drop by in the afternoon, when everyone's energy is flagging.

The Lost Continent

The Lost Continent is probably the most thematically complex island in the park, encompassing three distinct sections. You begin in Merlinwood, which is based on the stories of Camelot and echoes medieval England with thatch-roof houses and Celtic music. Within a few steps, the music and the mood change to indicate you're now in the Arabic section, home to the Eighth Voyage of Sindbad, and a jumble of tented, Middle Eastern shops in the marketplace known as Sindbad Village. There are fortune-tellers, and you can get your hair wrapped, your face painted, or your arm temporarily tattooed.

The last section of the Lost Continent is based on Atlantis. Here you can find the amazing-looking theater where Poseidon's Fury plays, and IOA's most elegant restaurant, Mythos.

The Eighth Voyage of Sindbad

This stunt show usually plays four to six times daily in the early afternoon and evening. (Showtimes are listed on your map.) The 25-minute show has everything you'd expect—fights, falls, drops, daring escapes, and comedy in the form of an inept sidekick whose pratfalls are a lot more dangerous than they look. The theater is large, so you shouldn't have any trouble being seated as long as you show up 15 minutes before showtime. Sindbad is a good choice for afternoon, when you'll welcome the chance to sit down and rest for a while.

Helpful Hint

Feeling queasy from too many coasters? A first-aid station where you can sit and recover is among the shops of Sindbad Village.

The Scare Factor

Sindbad is another loud performance with lots of pyrotechnics, including strobe lights and fog effects. In fact, there's so much fire on stage that those in the first three rows of the audience will feel the heat on their skin. If your kids are easily frightened and sensitive to loud noises, sit farther back.

The Mystic Fountain

As you enter the theater where Sindbad plays, pause for a minute at the fountain in the courtyard. At various times throughout the day—including the periods just before and after a show—the mysterious spirit trapped within the Fountain of Knowledge will talk to you. The result is pretty funny, as the spirit loves riddles, jokes, and questions, and will gently tease any kids willing to step forward and enter the game. Encourage the kids to ask a question and be prepared for lots of punk attitude, as well as an occasional blast of water.

Poseidon's Fury: Escape from the Lost City

This 20-minute walk-through show takes place in one of the most impressive buildings in the whole theme park, a crumbling castle from the lost underwater city ruled by the water god Poseidon. The story line is established in the long, dark (and somewhat scary-for-kids) queue area, where we learn that we're on an archaeological dig at the ancient temple of Poseidon. But there's trouble the power keeps flickering on and off, a professor is missing, and the sleep of an evil priest has been disturbed. He wants to find a powerful trident, and it's up to you, as the new archaeological team, to find the trident and restore it to its rightful owner, Poseidon.

You stand during the whole presentation of Poseidon's Fury, so young kids in the back won't see much (this may be a

The Scare Factor

Poseidon's Fury is a walk-through show, not a ride, but the special effects are intense and the noise level is very high in places. Once you enter the castle, you're literally a captive audience; there are a couple of exit points along the way if children become frightened, but for most of the show you're in a series of darkened rooms. If your children are nervous, stand near the back, especially in the final room where the battle reaches its peak; viewers in the front will feel the fire-and-water effects more intensely than those in the rear.

blessing—see the Scare Factor). If you want a good view of the action, be sure to be among the first in your tour group to exit every room so that you can be in the front row in the next room.

You move from room to room and there are some great special effects along the way. At one point you walk through a swirling tunnel of water. The final scene is a battle between fire and water, with plenty of splashing and pyrotechnics.

Helpful Hint

Needing a little adult time? A glass of wine? A civilized menu? Decadent chocolate desserts? Just across from Poseidon's Fury is Mythos, a great place for a leisurely meal.

The Wizarding World of Harry Potter

The Wizarding World of Harry Potter debuted in June 2010 as one of the most hotly anticipated theme-park attractions ever. It's actually home to three rides. The Dragon Challenge is a spiffed-up revamp of the megacoaster Dueling Dragons, while the Flight of the Hippogriff is a new and improved version of the Flying Unicorn. The big news is the centerpiece attraction, Harry Potter and the Forbidden Journey.

Hogsmeade Village, the dining and shopping section of the Wizarding World, offers great photo ops and fun experiences—such as the chance to mail a postcard home from the official Hogsmeade Post Office and some mystical wand-shopping at Ollivander's Experience. The shops offer replicas of almost everything mentioned in the books, including some rather alarmingly named candies at Honeydukes. Street entertainment includes the Frog Choir, a group of Hogwarts students accompanied by their large, croaking, and quite comical frogs, and the Triwizard Spirit Rally, a processional designed to rev up the already-revved-up crowd.

Guests are so enamored of the wand, jellybean, and robe shopping that Hogsmeade Village can become extremely crowded. Don't imagine you can browse the shops whenever you're ready to drop some cash. There are lines to get into the shops and sometimes even lines to get out, especially at Ollivander's, where the wand-choosing ceremony takes a little time. Young wizards don't like to be rushed.

The restaurant Three Broomsticks, which is a terrific setting in its own right, could probably serve anything and still be packed. The menu includes tasty BBQ, shepherd's pie, and fish-and-chips as well as the über-popular Butterbeer and pumpkin juice. The nonalcoholic Butterbeer is extremely sweet, almost like melted butterscotch, and geared towards the palates of kids. The pumpkin juice tastes a lot like cider and is quite good. Both are also available at kiosks outside the restaurant.

Hogsmeade Village was designed to emulate the narrow winding streets, nooks, and alleys of the *Harry Potter* film series, and the fact that they've done a good job also means that traffic bottlenecks are the norm all day long. It's best to embrace the fact that you'll be moving slowly, and use the time to savor all the wonderful details of this magical and painstakingly re-created world.

Harry Potter and the Forbidden Journey

This attraction, which lies deep within Hogwarts Castle, is the heart and soul of the Wizarding World. The queue is wonderful—which is good news, considering you might be in it for quite a while. You'll meet the four founders of Hogwarts, in the form of framed portraits that come to life and converse with each other. Dumbledore greets you in his office, you pass the famed Sorting Hat, and ultimately wind up in the Defense Against the Dark Arts classroom. Harry, Ron, and Hermione—

played by the movie actors, naturally—persuade you that going off with them to a Quidditch match is far more fun than staying behind for a boring history lecture. One wave of Hermione's wand, and your bench becomes capable of flight.

Your first clue to the intensity of the attraction is that your enchanted school bench comes equipped with harness restraints. Indeed, Harry Potter and the Forbidden Journey is a big-deal ride in both a physical sense, with lots of pitching and jerking action, and a psychological sense, as various villains from the books show up and try to divert your flight. The spider section is especially scary for kids, and let's just say that the Whomping Willow ain't kidding around. When Harry shows up to rescue you and you do finally make it to the Quidditch match, you experience the real feel of flight. And the ride ends on a happy note, with all the students of Hogwarts cheering your victory.

This is a 360-degree wraparound experience, combining live action, robotic technology, and filmmaking tricks that make you feel as if you're actually flying from scene to scene. Make no mistake—Harry Potter and the Forbidden Journey is Island of Adventure's signature ride, representing their highest

The Scare Factor

The 48-inch height requirement on Harry Potter and the Forbidden Journey means that many kids ages 5 to 8 will be able to ride. That said, there are reasons why this journey is forbidden. Older kids love it, and young fans of the book will probably be determined to ride. Just prepare everyone: the bench sometimes feels as if it's flipping over backward, and much of the journey is dark and scary, with dragons and spiders coming from all angles. Note, too, that the attraction has an exit for those who want to go through the queue and see the characters but who aren't up to taking on the actual ride.

technology to date. The entire experience, including the inter-active queue, takes close to an hour. Note that this ride has a minimum height requirement (48 inches) *and* maximum height and weight limits (6'3"; 250 pounds).

The Flight of the Hippogriff

This is a fun little coaster for the younger set, and zippier than you'd guess with some sharp dips and turns. Young Harry Potter fans who aren't up to the Dragon Challenge will enjoy the ride, which is a good "first coaster" expe-rience. The really cool part is that you zoom around a perfect replica of Hagrid's Hut.

The Scare Factor

The Flight of the Hip-pogriff is fast enough to elicit a few squeals, but most kids love it.

Dragon Challenge

This double roller coaster is one of the wildest rides in the park, running at speeds of up to 60 mph. Two suspension-style coast-ers (that is, they hang beneath the track for maximum side-to-side swinging action) operate at once, coming within inches of each other at certain points. For the ultimate thrill seekers, rid-ers in the outside seats are most aware of how close these close calls really are and riders in the front seats get the best view of the impending danger.

The Scare Factor

Dragon Challenge is a very intense coaster with a height requirement of 54 inches. Coaster warriors love it, but it's too much for most kids under 10. The swinging action of the cars make it a rougher ride than the Hulk, for example, and it's not a good choice for anyone prone to motion sickness. Watch it make a few runs before you decide.

Seuss Landing

You'll find nothing but pastel colors and curved lines—even the trees are bent!—on this dreamlike island, where everything looks like it popped out of a Dr. Seuss book. Almost everyone stops in their tracks at the sight of the amazing Caro-Seuss-el and the bright flying beasties of One Fish, Two Fish. But take your time strolling through—some of the best visual treats aren't so obvious.

One Fish, Two Fish, Red Fish, Blue Fish

One Fish, Two Fish is a circular thrill ride designed for young kids. Each fish has a joystick that controls the height of his flight, and throughout the ride you're given instructions such as "Red Fish fly high." If you opt to follow the instructions, that is, go "with the book," you stay dry. But if you disobey and go "against the book," one of the "bad fish" will spit on you. The idea is that this teaches kids to follow directions—I suspect it really shows them how much fun it can be to rebel—but either way it's a terrific ride, and in the finale everyone aboard gets a spritz.

One Fish, Two Fish can draw long lines in the afternoon. Come in the morning if you can.

The Scare Factor

One Fish, Two Fish is OK for any age. The joystick lets you keep it low for kids who dislike heights. Everyone flies high at the end of the ride for a few seconds, but by that time nervous kids have been aboard long enough to get used to the idea. The two-fish cars are big enough to let family members ride together.

The Cat in the Hat

This is a kiddie ride that's not just for the kiddies. A surprising number of kids from age 7 to 15 ranked Cat in the Hat as one of their favorites.

The Scare Factor

Expect some bumping and a few fast, tight spins of the car. Cat in the Hat is designed to appeal to any age, however, and most kids love it.

You board adorable couch-style cars to ride through 18 scenes taken straight from the well-loved book. The basic plot: Mom leaves, and the Cat in the Hat shows up with those well-known literary rowdies, Thing 1 and Thing 2. All sorts of mayhem results, sometimes enough to send your couch spinning wildly, and through it all the poor goldfish frantically tries to maintain order. The Cat in the Hat is like Spider-Man for the younger set. A lot goes on in a short time frame, and if you ride a second time you'll notice even more clever details. The effects are so funny that any rider, no matter what the age, will exit with a grin on her face.

Helpful Hint

Preschoolers will enjoy the Cat in the Hat ride, as well as the other Seuss Landing attractions, much more if they're familiar with the Dr. Seuss books. Read them on the trip to Orlando.

Caro-Seuss-el

The 54 mounts of this ultimate merry-go-round are all lifted directly from the stories of Dr. Seuss. While the up-and-down and round-and-round motion is familiar to any kid who has ever been on a carousel, the real kick is that you can make the beasties blink, flick their tails, and turn their heads. Snapping the kids aboard the colorful Caro-Seuss-el is one of the best photo ops in the whole park.

High in the Sky Seuss Trolley

Once purely decorative, the little cars that circle Seuss Landing were eventually put into motion and are now part of a slow, gentle trolley ride overlooking the attractions and at one point going through the Circus McGurkus Café. The 34-inch height restriction is more due to the construction of the cars than the intensity of the ride; shorter kids might be tempted to stand up just to be able to see out.

In terms of drawing long lines, the Trolley is a bit like Pteranodon Flyers: There are few cars and they move slowly, so board only if you have time to kill or the kids absolutely insist.

If I Ran the Zoo

IOA's third interactive play area was designed with preschoolers in mind, although older kids enjoy it, too. You can jump, climb, and squirt, as well as play tic-tac-toe with a Gak. Trap your friends in a cage of water or wait for the scraggle-foot Mulligatawny to sneeze—there's a silly surprise around every corner. A small water area gives younger kids a chance to cool off and splash around on a hot day.

The emphasis on the big-deal rides makes many families automatically assume that Islands of Adventure is only for older kids. But the three play areas, and the attention to detail in all of Seuss Landing, show that Islands of Adventure has plenty to offer younger siblings as well.

Afternoon Resting Places

Families who'll be staying in the park all day need to build in afternoon rest stops to give everyone a chance to regroup. You basically have three options:

- *Restaurants.* Consider making lunch your big meal of the day. A sit-down meal, either at Confisco Grille, Mythos, or CityWalk is a chance to get off your feet and relax.

- *Shows.* The Eighth Voyage of Sindbad will give you a chance to sit down in a theater for a while. The Jurassic Park Discovery Center, although a museum-style attraction, is a quiet, calm, and cool place to catch your breath.

- *Play areas.* Sometimes kids just need to burn off their pent-up energy. If you suspect they need to climb, run, and play for a half hour, head for one of the three play areas.

Meeting the Characters

The times and places for character meetings are well marked on your map.

The superheroes, including Spider-Man, appear in Marvel Super Hero Island; cartoon characters show up in Toon Lagoon; and the Seuss characters can be found, logically, in Seuss Landing. If you want to be guaranteed autographs and pictures without the elbow of some stranger from Michigan in each shot, make reservations for the character lunch at Confisco Grille.

Sometimes kids are overwhelmed by the characters, especially the Masked Marvels who show up on Marvel Super Hero Island, and the villains, such as Snidely Whiplash in Toon Lagoon and that nasty green Grinch in Seuss Landing. If your child appears nervous, don't push her forward; let her watch other kids pose for pictures for a while and she may loosen up. Asking for an autograph is a great way to break the ice.

CityWalk

CityWalk is the dining, shopping, and entertainment complex that links Universal Studios with Islands of Adventure. A fun destination in its own right, CityWalk also provides more dining options than what's in the parks. If you'd like a break from touring, exit the park and head for lunch at CityWalk.

Dining during the dinner hour can sometimes be problematic, since crowds from both Universal Studios and Islands of Adventure exit through CityWalk, creating bottlenecks. Reservations help. If you're staying on-site, make CityWalk dining reservations through Guest Services at your hotel. If you're staying off-site, you can make reservations at a well-marked booth as you enter CityWalk from the parking deck in the morning. CityWalk has shows and concerts every night, including a Blue Man Group production.

Good choices for family dining include:

@ *Bubba Gump Shrimp Co.* Shrimp . . . shrimp . . . and more shrimp in a casual, family-friendly environment. (Other types of seafood are on the menu as well, along with steaks and sandwiches.)

Money-Saving Tip

You can shop and dine at CityWalk without buying a ticket or paying a cover charge until around 8 pm, when the club-hopping starts. And, once it does, if you want to visit several CityWalk clubs on a parents' night out, you can buy a one-price, all-clubs Party Pass for about $12 in the off-season, $20 in the on-season. The cover charge for one club is usually around $7. Note: during the off-season, specials abound. You can frequently visit CityWalk for free with a multiday Universal Orlando theme-park ticket.

- *Hard Rock Cafe.* The Hard Rock—and this is the world's largest, by the way—is munchie central, with indulgent snacks like potato skins, nachos, and the signature Pig Sandwich.

- *Jimmy Buffett's Margaritaville.* The menu focuses on southern Florida and Caribbean foods, but you can also find cheeseburgers in Paradise. The Volcano Bar erupts margaritas regularly and entertainment consists of Buffett concerts on big-screen TVs and sometimes live music on the pleasant porch.

- *NASCAR Sports Grille.* Expect good ol' boy cuisine such as ribs, steaks, and fried chicken. Race fans will enjoy the memorabilia scattered around the restaurant, the servers dressed like a pit crew, and the rumble of race broadcasts on overhead TVs.

- *NBA City.* It's a basketball-theme restaurant that serves Shaq-size servings of steak, pasta, and sandwiches, as well as hearty appetizers such as buffalo wings and quesadillas. Basketball games, both current and classic, play on giant screens throughout the sports bar and restaurant.

- *Pastamore.* This Italian restaurant doesn't offer much entertainment, but the food is good and the lack of glitz makes it the easiest to slip into when CityWalk is crowded.

Some CityWalk restaurants and attractions are more suitable for adults:

- *Blue Man Group.* The group plays in its own Sharp Aquos Theater next to Universal Studios. The 90-minute shows feature rock music, heavy percussion, audience participation, and lots of zany gimmicks, such as hurling food from the stage into the audience. The three Blue Men—who remain mute and eerily robotic with their shiny blue grease-paint faces—anchor the show, which is popular with older kids. Prices start at $64 for adults, $25 for kids 3–9. Check showtimes and order tickets in advance at www.universalorlando.com or by calling 407/363–8000.

◉ *Bob Marley's.* Modeled after Marley's home in Kingston, Jamaica, this restaurant serves island-influenced dishes like jerk chicken, plantains, and tropical fruit salads. The outdoor patio is the perfect spot for casual eating and drinking, especially at night, when live reggae bands play.

◉ *Emeril's.* The most upscale and expensive option at City-Walk, Emeril's offers amazing food, such as crabmeat-crusted tournedos of beef and citrus-glaze duck. The restaurant is never stuffy or overly formal and is, in fact, the perfect spot for a parents' night out. It never hurts to make reservations before you leave home, so call 407/224–2424 to get your name on the list.

◉ *The Groove.* The most high-energy dance club at City-Walk, the Groove hosts a variety of theme parties, including hip-hop, trance, retro, progressive, Top 40, and alcohol-free teen-oriented nights.

◉ *Hard Rock Live.* A 2,500-seat auditorium adjacent to the Hard Rock Cafe, Hard Rock Live has a "state of the future" sound system and offers an impressive roster of musical acts. The price varies by act; to check out who's playing while you're in town, visit www.universalorlando.com.

◉ *Latin Quarter.* Some of the best food in CityWalk is served at Latin Quarter; examples of dinners include pork loin marinated in orange and cilantro, and broiled red snapper on yellow rice. Musicians play salsa and merengue music, while professional dancers and vacationing wannabes dance far into the night.

◉ *Pat O'Brien's.* This New Orleans import has a casual dining menu but is really known for its huge fruit drinks—

especially the Hurricane, so named because it's rumored to knock you level in two minutes flat.

@ *Red Coconut Lounge.* Another enormous lounge and nightclub with dancing and drinks, this time in a more tropical setting.

@ *Rising Star.* This 440-seat club offers karaoke with a live band and backup singers. Snack food like sliders, wings, and onions rings are available, along with cocktails with cute names like Liquid Courage to help nervous singers get into the mood.

CHAPTER

16

SeaWorld
and
Discovery
Cove

SeaWorld

SeaWorld is a low-stress experience, and much less frenzied than the other Orlando parks. Easily toured in six or seven hours, it's laid out so that the crowds pretty much flow from one scheduled animal show to another, working in the smaller attractions along the way. SeaWorld is so beautifully landscaped that you often can't see one stadium from the other, and the sense of space is a welcome change after a week spent at Disney. But the openness also means that children up to age 5 will benefit from a stroller. Strollers are $15, $20 for a double. You can also rent wheelchairs for $12 and ECVs for $50.

SeaWorld admission is $82 for adults and $74 for children ages 3 to 9, excluding tax, but if you buy your tickets online the price drops about $10. Parking is $14, with preferred parking at $20. Call 800/SEA–WORLD (800/732–9675) or visit www. seaworldorlando.com for more information.

If you're headed to the other SeaWorld parks, combo tickets are available. Two-park tickets for SeaWorld and Aquatica are $125 for adults and $117 for kids, a fairly significant savings and, once again, if you buy online expect a $10 price break. Prices for

Discovery Cove vary seasonally but begin at $199 if you're willing to forego the dolphin swim. If you want to swim with the dolphins, prices range from $286 to $307. For updated info on all ticket combinations and prices, visit www.seaworld.com.

Shows

For years SeaWorld's claim to fame has been its animal shows, especially those that feature the dolphins, the sea lions, and the park icon, Shamu. These three classics are periodically updated to feature new technological advances, but most of this is window-dressing. It's hard to improve upon the grandeur

Insider's Secret

Be forewarned that if you opt to sit in the "splash zone"—the first 10 rows of the stadium—Shamu's good-bye wave will leave you drenched straight through to your underwear. Kids enjoy the blast of saltwater, at least on a summer day, but if you're touring off-season or catching a nighttime show, it's wiser to sit farther back and laugh at the unwary tourists down by the tank.

Kids also love the acrobatic show, which plays several times a day in its own theater, and Pets Ahoy!, a show starring a talented cast of dogs, cats, and other animals rescued from animal welfare leagues. You can come up front and meet the animal stars after the show. During busy seasons, such as summer and Christmas, SeaWorld often offers extra shows with kid appeal, such as the Elmo and Abby Treasure Hunt, featuring stars from *Sesame Street*.

A new attraction, TurtleTrek, is devoted to increasing awareness of environmentally vulnerable sea turtles and takes place in a 360-degree domed theater, where a 3-D animated film will make you feel as if you're completely submerged in the underwater world of the turtles.

and charm of the animals themselves. See them if you do nothing else.

The dolphin show, the sea lion show, and the Shamu show all take place in enormous open-air theaters, so touring Sea-World is as simple as consulting your map for showtimes and being at the theater about 30 minutes early, 40 in the on-season. SeaWorld does a good job of keeping tabs on crowding and providing accurate estimates on how early you need to be there.

Rides

There are only three mainliner attraction rides, but they pack quite a punch. Plus, since the shows are the main attraction, the lines for the rides are shorter than at Disney and Universal. A mother of three from Michigan visited SeaWorld in the off-season and reported, "After all the time we spent waiting in line for rides at Disney and Universal, we were stunned to find that two of the rides at SeaWorld had practically no waits at all. The kids loved Kraken and were able to ride it several times with no wait."

Journey to Atlantis
SeaWorld's version of Splash Mountain, Journey to Atlantis takes you on a sometimes-gentle, sometimes-not water-flume ride through the lost city of Atlantis, then drops you down a steep incline to a great big splash below. If you have a rain poncho, bring it. This one's a soaker.

The Scare Factor

The Journey to Atlantis height requirement is 42 inches. Kids 7 and up should be okay.

You start by boarding Greek fishing boats and are promptly lured by sirens into the depths of the lost city. The tiny boats twist, dodge, and dive through the water. For the first drop, the tracks come out of the front of the building, but the sirens pull you back for the second, unseen, 60-foot, S-shaped drop. The story line is weak and somewhat confusing compared with Splash Mountain, but the two drops near the end of the ride are totally thrilling.

Kraken

Kraken reaches speeds of 65 mph, with seven loops and three different points where it plunges underground into misty tunnels. We're talking major intensity. When I first read about Kraken, I suspected the name referred to the sounds your back and neck made as you rode. Not so. The motion of the ride is surprisingly smooth and the name actually refers to the great underwater dragon-monster of ancient Norse mythology.

The Scare Factor
The height requirement for Kraken is 54 inches. Kids under 8 should not ride.

Manta

Manta is both beautiful and powerful, much like the creature it's named for. Riders fly face down in a horizontal "superman" position, hanging beneath the wingspan of the manta. With a track that's over 3,000 feet, a variety of swooping dips and turns, and speeds of up to 60 mph, it's quickly become a park icon.

The Scare Factor
Manta's height requirement is 54 inches. It's definitely too much for kids under 8.

Kiddie Rides at Shamu's Happy Harbor

SeaWorld also has some very simple kiddie rides inside Shamu's Happy Harbor, a play area across from Shamu Stadium. They include:

- Sea Carousel, a fish- and dolphin-theme merry-go-round
- Jazzy Jellies, swirling jellyfish that rise into the air

- Ocean Commotion, a spinning boat ride

- Swishy Fishies, a gentle teacup ride

- Flying Fiddler, a chair ride that rises and gently drops, a kiddie version of Dr. Doom at Islands of Adventure

- Shamu Express, a small coaster

Money-Saving Tip

In line with Disney's Fastpass and Universal's Express Pass, SeaWorld has the Quick Queue option to get you to the front of the line at its rides. But unless you're traveling on an especially busy day, you won't need it. SeaWorld has a limited number of rides, and they're rarely overwhelmingly crowded.

Standing Exhibits

SeaWorld is also known for its fascinating standing exhibits, such as the Penguin Encounter, where you can observe the tuxedoed charmers both above and below the ice floe, and witness their startling transformation from awkward walkers to sleek swimmers. Check your map, which is also your entertainment schedule, for feeding times, when the trainers slip about on the iceberg with buckets of fish and the penguins waddle determinedly behind them.

If your kids are too cool to like cute, try the Terrors of the Deep exhibit, where you'll encounter sharks, moray eels, and barracudas up close.

Insider's Secret

At the dolphin, stingray, and sea-lion exhibits you can buy fish and feed the animals. This is exciting for the kids and the ultimate photo op.

The California sea lions live at Pacific Point Preserve, and in the Key West section you can find the endangered manatee, as well as dolphins, stingrays, sea turtles, and other species indigenous to the Florida Keys. There are underwater viewing tanks where you can observe many of the animals from a different perspective. These exhibits don't have special showtimes and can be visited at your leisure as you circle the park.

Wild Arctic is dedicated to polar bears. You can opt to ascend to the top of the exhibit either via a simulated helicopter ride or by walking. (Kids must be 42 inches tall to take the simulator ride.) The ride is a total snooze in comparison to the Disney and Universal simulator rides so you may as well save yourself the time and just walk to the top of the exhibit. The fun part is seeing the bears anyway, especially watching them from the underwater tanks.

Coming Soon

Antartica: Empire of the Penguin is slated to open in late 2013. Details on the attraction are few at this writing, but SeaWorld does bill this new attraction as "the coldest in SeaWorld history." All we can really assume is that those lovable penguins are about to get a new and far more elaborate home. Stay tuned!

Preschoolers and Toddlers

Small children at SeaWorld welcome the numerous chances to get close to the animals, so save plenty of time for the standing exhibits, where you can feed a sea lion or reach over to touch a dolphin or stingray. At theme parks it's easy to get caught up in dashing from show to show but, especially with preschoolers, it's essential to slow down and savor the small moments of animal interaction.

Helpful Hint

Appropriately, the crowd at SeaWorld moves in waves. The shows are timed so that you can move around the park in a circular fashion, taking in one show after another.

This also means, however, that if you want to visit standing exhibits, feed the animals, or play in Shamu's Happy Harbor, some periods are far more crowded than others. For example, Shamu's Happy Harbor is virtually empty while the nearby Shamu show is going on, but the minute the show is over a flood of people head for the playground.

The solution? If you have young kids and would like to be able to play in the Harbor or interact with the animals in a calm unrushed manner, make note of when the shows are in session and visit the play area or standing exhibits then.

Another kick for kids is Shamu's Happy Harbor, a play area that's not only happy but huge, with an elaborate web of climbing nets, a ship with water-firing muskets, a splashy climb-through fountain area, ball pits to sink into, and padded pyramids to climb. After a few hours spent in shows or exhibits, drop by and let the kids just play for a while. You can usually hop right onto any of the six kiddie rides. "Shamu's Happy Harbor is just that—happy," said one dad from Pennsylvania. "We have three kids under 6, and we just parked the strollers and let them play for awhile. They loved getting wet and splashing around and there was absolutely no wait for the kiddie rides."

A separate play area for smaller kids ensures that they don't get tangled up in the webs, whacked by an older kid on a tire swing, or, worst of all, lost. Because several of the play areas involve water, some parents let kids wear their bathing suits under their shorts and totally cool off. There's a midway and arcade next door where older kids can hang out while the younger ones play.

The Baby Care and Lost Child Center, which has a shady porch and rockers, is also in Shamu's Happy Harbor—convenient, since this is the part of the park where you're most likely to lose track of your child.

SeaWorld Adventure Camps

SeaWorld hosts educational camps for all age groups. Preschoolers (with a parent along) can participate in morning camps that explore how the animals are fed or how they play hide-and-seek in their environments. Grade-school-level children have lots of choices; there are weeklong camps that study dolphins, manatees, sharks, and other SeaWorld residents. Teenagers can participate in weeklong resident camps where they go behind the scenes of the park and assist the trainers in caring for the animals. Most of the day camps take place in summer, although some programs are offered periodically throughout the year. Prices begin at $210 per child/adult pair for preschool camps, $280 per child for grade-school offerings.

Another neat option is the Family Sleepover. Held in summer and on major holidays, this behind-the-scenes party culminates in participants grabbing a sleeping bag and bedding down in the midst of one of SeaWorld's exhibits. (At present you're sleeping with the fishes, so to speak, in the manta exhibit.) Prices begin at $78 per person; if you'd like to include admission to SeaWorld for the day following the sleepover, the price rises to $103.

For information on all your options, call 800/406–2244 or visit www.seaworld.org.

Behind-the-Scenes Tours

It's easy to get an insider's look at SeaWorld thanks to tours where you see the animals up close and observe how trainers care for them.

The most elaborate is the dolphin tour ($50 adults, $30 children), which allows you to meet a trainer during your backstage visit and interact with a dolphin family. The penguin tour ($40 adults, $20 children), sea lion tour ($40 adults, $20 children), and Behind the Scenes tour ($30 adults, $10 children) are also family-friendly and offer chances to interact with the animals. For younger kids, consider the Family Fun tour ($75 adults, $55 children). There's less information, but you do get to feed the sea lions and dolphins, pat a penguin, get reserved seating for the Shamu show, have a light lunch, and hobnob with the Shamu character.

These tours make great fodder for school projects. You can reserve the tours in advance at www.seaworldorlando.com. If you haven't made reservations, it's often possible to book a tour on the same day you're visiting. The tour booth, on the left as you enter the park, is easy to spot.

Discovery Cove

Discovery Cove offers you a chance to actually have up-close encounters with dolphins and other sea life. You get to swim and play with bottlenose dolphins and snorkel through clouds of fish in a coral-reef lagoon. Or you can just enjoy the tropical island ambience of beach chairs, hammocks, swaying palm trees, cooing birds—and hardly any people.

That's right. The most unusual thing about Discovery Cove is what it doesn't have. Crowds. This is a reservations-only park that admits a mere 1,000 people per day. With such a low number of guests, you truly have the personal attention of the staff, which includes expert trainers (many of them drafted from SeaWorld, Discovery Cove's sister park).

You check in at a concierge desk (!), and from there a guide takes you on a walking tour of the park, explaining all the activities. A swim in the dolphin lagoon is the undeniable highlight of the day, but reserved for guests 6 or older. The trainers teach you about dolphin behaviors and then lead you out into the water where you play with the dolphin and learn how to communicate basic com-

Helpful Hint
Bring beach shoes. Discovery Cove's pools are quite rocky.

mands. Once you and the animal get used to each other, you can end the session by grasping his dorsal fin and going on a wild ride across the bay.

"Expensive, yes," says a father from Baltimore. "But not out of line when you consider the price of similar dolphin swims in the Caribbean. And at Discovery Cove the trainers spend a lot of time with the guests talking about the animals. I'm very glad my sons had the chance to experience this."

The saltwater coral lagoon offers a variety of experiences, including the chance to snorkel among tropical fish. Since the water is calm, clear, and warm, and there are thousands of fish, this is a great first snorkeling experience for young kids. In the ray lagoon, you can play with gentle stingrays, some as big as four feet in diameter, whose barbs have been removed, or you can swim alongside barracuda and sharks kept behind Plexiglas.

Discovery Cove has added the Grand Reef, which offers multiple areas for exploration. You can swim or wade among exotic fish and rays or cross a bridge to walk over a shark lagoon.

A freshwater tropical river meanders its way through the park. As you float along you pass through several different settings, including a tropical fishing village, an underwater cave, and an immense aviary that houses 300 birds from all over the world.

The newest section, the Freshwater Oasis, is shallower, almost a watery walking trail, and takes you through habitats of the marmoset monkeys and Asian otters, two of the most playful animal species on earth. There are Adirondack chairs spaced out along the way if you'd like to wade out of the stream and relax with a drink beneath the shady rainforest canopy.

Insider's Tip

Discovery Cove has recently added a new experience. The SeaVenture is an underwater walking tour that allows guests ages 10 and older to get up close and personal with schools of fish and velvety rays. Because each guest wears a diving helmet, certain medical requirements do apply. Check www.discoverycove.com for details.

So what do you pay for this bliss? Depending upon the season, prices range from $286 to $307 per person if you opt for the dolphin swim. The price is $199 without the dolphin swim. (Special rates for Florida and Georgia residents can also drop the price to $199.) Since kids under 6 aren't allowed to participate in the dolphin program, the price is automatically $199 for children 3 to 5. Children under 3 are free. For details and reservations (remember, they're a must), call 877/434–7268 (877/4–DISCOVERY) or visit www.discoverycove.com.

When you've explored to your heart's content, there's no better way to end the day than by snoozing in your hammock on a white-sand beach. Discovery Cove is all-inclusive, meaning breakfast and lunch are provided, as well as wine and beer for the adults throughout the day. Swim vests, wet suits, snorkels, sunscreen, beach umbrellas, lounge chairs, lockers, and beach towels are also included in the price.

Aquatica

Aquatica, SeaWorld's 60-acre water park, is positioned as a competitor to Disney's Typhoon Lagoon and Blizzard Beach. It's outfitted with all the slides and wave pools you'd expect from an Orlando water park and plenty of special SeaWorld touches as well.

Aquatica draws large crowds, and after a certain capacity is reached, the park closes to ensure the safety of its guests. To avoid being shut out, come first thing in the morning or—if you're visiting in the summer with its extended evening hours—arrive in late afternoon, when people are beginning to drift out.

Aquatica admission is $48 for adults and $42 for children 3 to 9, excluding tax. The price drops to $42 for everyone if you buy in advance online. The two-park combo tickets ($120 adult, $112 child) are a good deal if you're also planning to visit SeaWorld. Visit www.aquaticabyseaworld.com for more details.

Attractions include:

- *Dolphin Plunge.* In the park's signature ride you zip 300 feet down a narrow tube into a lagoon holding two Commerson's dolphins. The plunge lives up to the hype—the dolphins, not so much. The bottom part of the tube is see-through, which means, theoretically, you can see the dolphins as you pass, but you move through in seconds, and there's water splashing your eyes the whole time. In other words, most people are zipping by so fast that they see zip. There are only two slides going on this ride, so expect to wait about an hour at peak times. Riders must be 48 inches tall.

- *Taumata Racer.* In the aquatic equivalent of a bobsled run, you climb into one of eight lanes and start your descent down 300 feet of slides, which includes a 360-degree turn at the top. The thrill as you crest the top of the slide is palpable (be sure to hold on tightly to your blue mat) and the eight lanes mean that the line for this slide moves more quickly than Dolphin Plunge's. Riders must be 42 inches tall, and kids below 48 inches must wear a life vest.

@ *Roa's Rapids.* A flowing current is the highlight of this attraction that takes you along rapids and occasional waterfalls. Roa's is a lot of bang for the buck: There's no line (though the waters can get crowded with visitors at times), and, after strapping on your life jacket you'll wade into the rapids via a wide entrance lane (and you exit the same way). You can hold on to your child as you bob around, and you're free to circle the rapids as many times as you wish. "Soooo much fun," wrote a teen from Ohio. "The current really challenges you, and we were pooped by the time we got out."

@ *Loggerhead Lane.* In contrast to Roa's Rapids, this is indeed a lazy river. A high point is that the lane leads to a 10,000-gallon grotto filled with thousands of colorful fish and a view of the Commerson's dolphins. There's next to no pull, so you might have to paddle a bit, especially if you want to choose the turn with the fish grotto.

@ *Tassie Twister.* This zippy little tube ride empties you into a large circular bowl, where you make a few wild revolutions before slipping down another tube, which leads you back into the Loggerhead Lane lazy river. (The resemblance to a toilet is impossible to overlook.) Fun and wild without being too scary, this is a good test to see if kids are up to handling the bigger flumes.

@ *Walkabout Waters.* Here, in one of the world's largest interactive water-play areas, a colorful 60-foot fortress provides 15,000 square feet of family slides, pools, water cannons, and two large buckets that periodically dump water on frolickers below. "A great option for families with preschoolers," said one mother. "Nothing scary at all and once my kids warmed up on the family slides, which let us all go together, they felt brave enough to do a few things in the general park."

Insider's Secret

From an animal standpoint, the Dolphin Plunge, prominently featured in Aquatica ads, is a bit of a letdown. "The website plays it up like you swim with dolphins," wrote one mother from Georgia. "The reality is that the clear tube that runs through the dolphin tank is only for a couple of seconds at the end of the ride—blink, and you miss it totally. Fortunately, the rest of the park was great."

◎ *Omaka Rocka.* Picture a waterslide with both high-speed tubes and half-pipe funnels that are designed to emulate the movements of skateboards and snowboards. The flumes help you pick up speed so that by the time you enter the funnels and begin the side-to-side action, the sensation is close to sheer weightlessness. The splashdown is massive. Older kids and teens love this one, which has a height requirement of 48 inches and a weight limit of 250 pounds.

◎ *Wahalla Wave and Hoo Roo Run.* These family raft rides are side-by-side. Wahalla Wave is a winding descent from a six-story-high mountain, while Hoo Roo Run is more of a straight shot down with a couple of bumps along the way. Both are a lot of fun, and since riding together dilutes the intensity, they're another chance to break nervous kids in. "My twin 8-year-old sons weren't so keen at first," said a mom from London. "But all riding together made it a family adventure, and they got off with the giggles. Only trouble was, they liked it so well we had to do both slides again, and I almost never got them to move on and see more of the park." Riders must be 42 inches tall and kids under 48 inches must wear a life vest.

ⓔ *Whanau Way.* You climb into tubes and have a choice of four descents, each winding with periods of darkness and a couple of steep drops along the way. You can also choose between one- and two-person tubes. Whanau Way is one of the most popular attractions in the park, but because there are four points of descent, the line moves fairly rapidly.

ⓔ *Kate's Kookaburra Cove.* This play area has fountains and an array of small slides. Tucked away behind the cabanas that surround Big Surf Shores, Kate's never seems to be quite as crowded as Walkabout Waters. Note: Kids must be no taller than 48 inches to play.

ⓔ *Big Surf Shores and Cutback Cove.* Twin side-by-side lagoons provide different waves for different tastes. Since the pools are independent, one can generate crashing waves with five-foot swells while the other might provide gently rolling surf that laps the shore. A plus for parents is that it's easy to move from one pool to the other, and the park's white-sand beach faces the pools, providing a good base of operations if you're spending a lot of time in this area.

Index

Notes

Notes

Notes

Notes

Notes

Notes

Notes

Notes

Write to Us

We love to hear from families about their trips to Walt Disney World, Universal Orlando, and SeaWorld. Stories and feedback from families like yours help shape this book. If you'd like to share your travel experiences with us, please take a few minutes to respond to any or all of the questions below. We might quote your responses in the next edition. You can either fill out this survey online at www.fodors.com/disneysurvey, email us at kwwiley@fodors.com or write to me at Fodor's, 1745 Broadway, New York, NY 10019. Thanks for your time!

— Kim and Leigh

1. When did you last visit Walt Disney World and/or Universal Orlando? How long did you stay?

   _____

   _____

2. What are the ages of your children?

   _____

   _____

3. Did your family travel alone or with friends and extended family? How many people were in your party?

   _____

   _____

4. Where did you stay? Were you pleased with the hotel? Did you feel it offered a fair level of services and amenities for the price?

   _____

   _____

5. Which park did your family most enjoy? (For questions 6–12, if there's a split of opinion among family members, please put the age of the respondent beside the choice.)

   _____

   _____

6. What was your family's favorite attraction in the Magic Kingdom?

   _____

   _____

7. What was your family's favorite attraction at Epcot?

_____

_____

8. What was your family's favorite attraction at Disney's Hollywood Studios?

_____

_____

9. What was your family's favorite attraction at the Animal Kingdom?

_____

_____

10. Did you visit Universal Orlando? If so, what was your family's favorite attraction at Universal Studios? At Islands of Adventure?

_____

_____

11. Did you visit SeaWorld or Discovery Cove? If so, what was your family's favorite attraction?

_____

_____

12. Were there any attractions that proved to be too frightening or too intense for your child? If so, please describe the situation.

_____

_____

13. Did you take part in any character meals? If so, did you enjoy it?

_____

_____

_____

14. Did you purchase a dining plan? If so, did you think it offered good value?

_____

_____

15. Besides character meals, did you have any other memorable dining experiences?

_____

_____

_____

16. Did you visit either of the Walt Disney World water parks? If so, which one and how did you like it?

_____

_____

17. Did you visit Downtown Disney or CityWalk? If so, which shops, restaurants, and attractions were your favorites?

_____

_____

18. Do you have a "never again" story—something about traveling around Walt Disney World or Universal Orlando that you learned the hard way?

_____

_____

_____

_____

19. Do you have a "best of all" story or experience that stands out as the highlight of your trip?

_____

_____

_____

_____

20. What advice would you give to other families traveling to Walt Disney World or Universal Orlando?

_____

_____

_____

_____